"Structural linguistics has generally ruled the day from Ferdinand de Saussure's famous *Course in General Linguistics* (1916) through various versions, including its American types, particularly in the work of Leonard Bloomfield, until our own times. Saussure's most-recognized critics include the enormously influential Noam Chomsky, as well as Jan Koster, who chided the earlier work as failing to recognize the full range of natural language, but did not put into question its secular fundamentals, which owe much to Immanuel Kant and his progeny. An unjustly ignored figure in this history is Kenneth L. Pike, a Christian, long associated with the approach of tagmemics, which faults structuralism for separating language from the person and his history. In this brilliant and lucid account, Pierce Hibbs invites us to rediscover Pike's contributions, adding to it a robust defense of the implications of his views for a Reformed and biblical faith. He boldly finds the ultimate source of all language in the divine Trinity. Fresh and compelling, it is required reading for anyone wishing to navigate the challenging field of linguistics and make Christian sense of it."
—**William Edgar**, Professor of Apologetics, Westminster Theological Seminary, Philadelphia

"The last century has witnessed a major preoccupation with language among philosophers. Theologians, too, have often tried to understand the language of God—his Word. Often these studies have endorsed relativism of various kinds—the view that true communication is really not possible. Reformed theologians have resisted these relativistic theories. But more helpfully, some Reformed thinkers over the last century have developed a positive understanding of language, based on Scripture. This began with Vern Poythress's theological appropriation of the tagmemic system of Christian linguist Kenneth Pike. Pike's system emphasizes threefold distinctions: particle, wave, field; contrast, variation, distribution. Poythress finds in these triads reflections of the Trinity. Hibbs has written an excellent popular book about this development. The present volume contains the research

I0808010

behind that book and sets it forth in a rigorous, technical, but very clear way. I have profited much from his formulations. This book will sharpen and encourage our thinking about the Trinity, the Word of God, and the centrality of language in a Christian understanding of the world."
—**John M. Frame**, Professor of Systematic Theology and Philosophy Emeritus, Reformed Theological Seminary, Orlando

"Having mastered the linguistic philosophy of Kenneth Pike, mined the Trinitarian theology of Cornelius Van Til, and meditated on the creative thought of his mentor, Vern Poythress, Pierce Hibbs in this work peers into the interlocking mysteries of language and the Trinity. How fitting that he stands on the shoulders of this triad of scholars—Pike, Van Til, and Poythress—to offer his own stimulating perspective on these subjects. In brief, Hibbs argues that Pike paints a picture of language that analogically reflects the triune God, who upholds all things by the word of his power. The writing is crisp and clean, the content is full, and the case is made. Read, reflect, and rejoice!"
—**Carlton Wynne**, Assistant Professor of Systematic Theology and Apologetics, Westminster Theological Seminary

The Trinity, Language, and Human Behavior

Reformed Academic Dissertations

A Series

Series Editor
John J. Hughes

The Trinity, Language, and Human Behavior

A Reformed Exposition of the Language Theory of Kenneth L. Pike

Pierce Taylor Hibbs

P&R
PUBLISHING
P.O. BOX 817 • PHILLIPSBURG • NEW JERSEY 08865-0817

The Trinity, Language, and Human Behavior: A Reformed Exposition of the Language Theory of Kenneth L. Pike. Pierce Taylor Hibbs, Th.M., MAR, B.A. Submitted to Westminster Theological Seminary, May 2017, in partial fulfillment for the award of a Th.M. degree in Systematic Theology. Supervisors: Lane G. Tipton and Vern S. Poythress. Examiner and committee chair: Carlton Wynne.

Printed in the United States of America

ISBN: 978-1-62995-408-0 (pbk)

For Christina,
who sacrificed so much so that I could finish this;
for my dad,
whom I wish was with me now;
and for Vern Poythress,
who first introduced me to the brilliance of Pike's theory
and whose friendship and support have been a Godsend

Contents

Series Introduction

P&R Publishing has a long and distinguished history of publishing carefully selected, high-value theological books in the Reformed tradition. Many theological books begin as dissertations, but many dissertations are worthy of publication in their own right. Realizing this, P&R has launched the Reformed Academic Dissertation (RAD) program to publish top-tier dissertations (Ph.D., Th.D., D.Min., and Th.M.) that advance biblical and theological scholarship by making distinctive contributions in the areas of theology, ethics, biblical studies, apologetics, and counseling.

Dissertations in the RAD series are *curated*, which means that they are carefully selected, on the basis of strong recommendations by the authors' supervisors and examiners and by our internal readers, to be part of our collection. Each selected dissertation will provide clear, fresh, and engaging insights about significant theological issues.

A number of theological institutions have partnered with us to recommend dissertations that they believe worthy of publication in the RAD series. Not only does this provide increased visibility for participating institutions, it also makes outstanding dissertations available to a broad range of readers, while helping to introduce promising authors to the publishing world.

We look forward to seeing the RAD program grow into a large collection of curated dissertations that will help to advance Reformed scholarship and learning.

John J. Hughes
Series Editor

Foreword

I am excited to see this book bring together two figures that up to now have usually not been considered together—the linguist and Bible translator Kenneth L. Pike and the Reformed apologist and theologian Cornelius Van Til. Kenneth Pike was a devoted Christian and a brilliant linguist. He offered a genuinely Christian and Trinitarian approach to language. But secular linguistic theory was moving in other directions as his theory blossomed and grew, and within his lifetime his work seldom received the attention that it deserved within the broader academic community. To some extent, analogous things might be said of Cornelius Van Til. During his lifetime he was appreciated by his students, but received a good deal of misunderstanding, rejection, and neglect from the broader community in philosophy, theology, and apologetics. In my opinion, both of these men were too radical, too penetrating, too innovative in a good sense to be immediately embraced. They were swimming against the tide.

These two men were not just contrarian. Primarily they were following in the path of loyalty to God and to their Savior Jesus Christ. They both in their ways appreciated the centrality of the Trinity and the centrality of the personal character of God. For Van Til, the centrality of God led to the centrality of human beings made in the image of God, and the centrality of human loyalty either to God or to man as a substitute god. That orientation of mankind toward loyalty or disloyalty made all the difference in apologetics. For Pike, the centrality of God led to the centrality of language—particularly the language of the Bible—and the centrality of human beings as language users. For both thinkers, God, the true God of the Bible, was absolutely central. But in addition, human beings as full persons were indispensable to their fields of study. Van Til had human commitments of the heart squarely at the heart of his apologetics. Pike had human interaction with God and man squarely at the heart of his theory of language.

Both Pike and Van Til were deeply affected by the Trinitarian character of God. For Van Til, the centrality of God meant centrality of the true God, who is one God in three persons. Apologetics should not defend a bare monotheism, not further defined, but should defend the God who is, the God who is Trinitarian. For Pike, the centrality of persons led to triads of perspectives reflecting the Trinity. For Pike, language was not a bare abstract, but the gift of God. And that God, as the Trinitarian God, reflected his Trinitarian nature in the very structure of language. The affinities between Van Til and Pike are fascinating. Now we have before us a book that expounds those affinities. We are blessed by its insights.

The fruits arising from these affinities may be many. Among them I would suggest two for further attention.

First, the secular world is spinning out sophisticated but reductionistic, inadequate views of language. If we are Christians, we need something more robust than mere rejection, mere reaction. And we need to exercise more critical discernment than we show if we merely follow the latest philosophical or literary fads, with small attempts at identifying problems and adjusting to them. We need to ask positively about how language fits into a Christian worldview. Van Til supplies the Christian worldview directly, while Pike supplies the robust, anti-reductionistic view of language within that worldview.

Second, because language is central to human living, a number of secular visionaries are exploring how to find our way in human living through sustained exploration of the nature of language. In the minds of these visionaries, everything is "interpretation." We can profit from a Christian analogue to such exploration of language. And Hibbs's book gives us a beginning and a foundation, by expounding the significance of Kenneth L. Pike to the larger world—not only the linguistic world, but the world of theology and human life.

Vern S. Poythress
Professor of New Testament Interpretation
Westminster Theological Seminary

Acknowledgements

I would like to thank my wife, first and foremost, for her help with this project. She has written none of it, and she has written all of it. Advanced study, I am reminded now more than ever, is a family affair. Thank you, Christina, for doing this with me.

I would also like to thank Dr. Poythress, who first directed me to the work of Kenneth Pike. We have had many illuminating discussions on Pike's approach to language and life, and I am sure that I would not understand the extent, applicability, and impact of Pike's work were it not for his help. He has succeeded, to his joy I'm sure, in making me a full-fledged Pikean. His friendship and guidance have been a great blessing to me.

I am also grateful for Leslie Altena's guidance and support throughout this project and for her relentless enthusiasm and passion as a language teacher. By simply working with her, I have learned more about language than I can express.

Abbreviations

Bib Sac	*Bibliotheca Sacra*
CVD	Contrast, Variation, Distribution
FMD	Feature, Manifestation, Distribution
GPR	Grammar, Phonology, Reference
IJST	*International Journal of Systematic Theology*
JSNT	*Journal for the Study of the New Testament*
LC	Kenneth L. Pike, *Linguistic Concepts: An Introduction to Tagmemics*. Lincoln, NE: University of Nebraska, 1982.
LRUT	Kenneth L. Pike, *Language in Relation to a Unified Theory of the Structure of Human Behavior*, 2nd ed. Paris: Mouton, 1967.
PWF	Particle, Wave, Field
WTJ	*Westminster Theological Journal*

1

Introduction

What does language have to do with the Reformed doctrine of the Trinity? What do a Connecticut-born linguist and a Dutch Reformed apologist have in common? These two questions lie at the base of this project. Answers to each question should be clear by the end, but it will help at the outset to provide an apology for the union of language theory and Trinitarian theology, for such an apology raises a pivotal theological point: language theory and theology proper are inextricably intertwined.[1]

Language Studies and the Trinity

Recent academia and Reformed theology have witnessed an insurgence of interest in language studies and the Trinity, respectively.[2] Why is this the case? Certainly, many reasons could be offered

[1] Another way of putting this is to say that "language reflects God in his Trinitarian character. We can appreciate language more deeply, and use it more wisely, if we come to know God and understand the relation of God to the language we use." Vern S. Poythress, *In the Beginning Was the Word: Language—A God-Centered Approach* (Wheaton, IL: Crossway, 2009), 9.

[2] With regards to linguistics, consider a selection of titles from the last decade: *The Language of Symbolism: Biblical Theology, Semantics, and Exegesis* (2006), *The Unfolding of Language: An Evolutionary Tour of Man's Greatest Invention* (2006), *How Language Works* (2007), *The Language Instinct: How the Mind Creates Language* (2007), *The Oxford Handbook of Philosophy of Language*

based on the secular and Christian book markets, but I propose one that is more theological than market-driven: language and the Trinity go hand in hand because the Trinity is a communicative being, and language is an image-bearing capacity of communicative creatures bound in covenantal relationship with that being.[3] Theologically

---

(2008), *In the Beginning Was the Word: Language—A God-Centered Approach* (2009), *Speaking of God: Theology, Language, and Truth* (2009), *The Truth (and Untruth) of Language: Heidegger, Ricoeur, and Derrida on Disclosure and Displacement* (2010), *The Incarnation of the Word: The Theology of Language of Augustine of Hippo* (2011), *Through the Language Glass: Why the World Looks Different in Other Languages* (2011), *Language, Cognition, and Human Nature: Selected Articles* (2013), *The Cambridge Handbook of Linguistic Anthropology* (2014), *The Language Hoax: Why the World Looks the Same in Any Language* (2014), *The Language Myth: Why Language Is Not an Instinct* (2014), *The Routledge Handbook of Language and Culture* (2014), *The Oxford Handbook of Linguistic Analysis* (2015), *The Oxford Handbook of the Word* (2015), and *When the Word Becomes Flesh: Language and Human Nature* (2015). With regards to the doctrine of the Trinity in the broader Reformed tradition, a list of selected titles is just as lengthy, even if we begin in 2010: *The Deep Things of God: How the Trinity Changes Everything* (2010), *Trinity and Election in Contemporary Theology* (2011), *Delighting in the Trinity: An Introduction to the Christian Faith* (2012), *The Trinity and the Vindication of Christian Paradox: An Interpretation and Refinement of the Theological Apologetic of Cornelius Van Til* (2014), *Paul and the Trinity: Persons, Relations, and the Pauline Letters* (2015), *Traces of the Trinity: Signs of God in Creation and Human Experience* (2015), and *One God in Three Persons* (2015). Publication trends are not arbitrary; they reflect the interests of the day. Clearly, in our day the interest lies in language and the Trinity. These are perhaps perennial topics of interest, as they should be, but that does not discount the importance of studying the relations between them.

[3] "The fact that the eternal Son of the Father is called Word or *Logos*, seems to mean, among other things, that there is—and has been from all eternity—talk, sharing and communication in the innermost life of God. The true God is not silent; He talks." Douglas Kelly, *Systematic Theology: Grounded in Holy Scripture and Understood in Light of the Church*, vol. 1, *The God Who Is: The Holy Trinity* (Ross-shire, Scotland: Mentor, 2008), 487. "Language is wonderful and mysterious. It is so because it is a gift of God to us. It reflects and reveals him. . . . According to the Bible, God himself can speak, and does speak. We are made like him, and that is why we can speak. When we use language, we rely on resources and powers that find their origin in God." Poythress, *In the Beginning Was the Word*, 9.

speaking, it would be curious to witness a rising interest in language *without* concurrently witnessing a rising interest in theology proper. To study God is to delve into the communion he holds with himself and with us via linguistic revelation; to study language is to wade into the mystery of interpersonal communication that has its source in the Trinity.[4] In this regard, scholars who study one and completely ignore the other tend to walk with a limp.[5]

That both content areas are drawing attention simultaneously in our day means the time is ripe to continue the discussion of the centrality of language to all of life, not because language is a biological faculty that sets the human race apart, but because language is a divine behavior rooted in God himself and thus reflects his character in its depth and complexity. And included in "all of life" is

[4] "The New Testament indicates that the persons of the Trinity speak to one another. . . . Not only is God a member of a language community that includes human beings, but the persons of the Trinity function as members of a language community among themselves. Language does not have as its sole purpose human-human communication, or even divine-human communication, but also divine-divine communication." Ibid., 18.

[5] This is not to say that one cannot focus on either language studies or theology proper. Such a focus would be what Poythress calls an "emphasizing reductionism," which is unavoidable. "Exclusive reductionisms" are the problematic sort because they insist on "the exclusive correctness of one's own form of emphasizing reductionism." See Vern S. Poythress, *Philosophy, Science, and the Sovereignty of God* (Phillipsburg, NJ: P&R Publishing, 1976), 48–49. In this case, I am arguing against exclusive reductionisms that ignore language studies or theology proper *even when the opportunity for acknowledgement presents itself.* For example, in theology proper, we might discuss language theory, or at least mention it, when referring to the immanent Trinity and the interpersonal relations of the Father, Son, and Spirit. God communicates—he "speaks"—with himself, so why not reflect on the nature of language at this point? For details on speech as an essential attribute of God, see John M. Frame, *Systematic Theology: An Introduction to Christian Belief* (Phillipsburg, NJ: P&R Publishing, 2013), 522–23. In language studies, when we search for either the root of our communicative faculty or the purposive nature of linguistic behavior, it would seem apropos to reflect on the Trinity as a communicative being or at least to reference God's utterly purposive and effective speech (Isa. 55:10–11).

our doctrine of God himself. But what, exactly, is the connection between our understanding of language and theology proper?

Language Theory and Theology Proper

I noted that language theory and theology proper are "inextricably intertwined." What do I mean by this? Language and the Trinity are clearly related, as suggested above, but there is more to this connection than a vague relation.

It seems to me that language theory and theology proper have their roots woven together in the soil of revelation, both general and special. Our communicative capacity and our knowledge of God are bound together because the world itself is linguistic, since it has been spoken into being, and because God's special revelation has been delivered in language, in words.[6] Jonathan Edwards wrote long ago, "As the system of nature, and the system of revelation, are both divine works, so both are in different senses a divine word. Both are the voice of God to intelligent creatures, a manifestation and declaration of himself to mankind."[7] We might clarify this by saying that nature is not itself verbal communication of the creator, but rather a spoken channel through which we receive divine revelation, and in

[6] I set this out in more detail in "World through Word: Towards a Linguistic Ontology," *WTJ* 79, no. 2 (Fall 2017): 345–64. Along these lines, Bavinck writes that "the world itself rests on revelation; revelation is the presupposition, the foundation, the secret of all that exists in all its forms." Herman Bavinck, *The Philosophy of Revelation* (Grand Rapids, MI: Wm. B. Eerdmans, 1953), 27. Perhaps even more relevant is Poythress's claim that "If indeed God spoke to create the world, then the world from its beginning, and down to its roots, is structured by God's language. Language is not an alien imposition on the world but the very key to its being and its meaning. And if God governs the world even today through his word, then language, God's language, is also the deepest key to history and to the development of events." Poythress, *In the Beginning Was the Word*, 24.

[7] Jonathan Edwards, "The 'Miscellanies': Number 1340," in *Christian Apologetics Past and Present*, vol. 2, *From 1500*, ed. William Edgar and K. Scott Oliphint (Wheaton, IL: Crossway, 2011), 237.

that sense, it "speaks" of God. Special revelation, however, is unique as the *verbal* communication of God. Nevertheless, both general and special revelation are linguistic in the sense that the former is spoken into being and upheld by the Word of God's power (Heb. 1:3) and the latter is God's actual communication to creatures within the arena of general revelation. Thus, we can say that we know God by way of inherently linguistic revelation (in nature and in Scripture), which is simply a restatement of Cornelius Van Til's *revelational epistemology.*[8]

This revelation is itself reflective of the Trinity. Consider the question that Ralph Smith poses and answers:

> Why should God reveal himself? Because He is a triune God for whom the eternal fellowship and mutual communication of Father, Son, and Spirit is essential. It is not possible to imagine the Christian God not communicating because communication is an aspect of His covenantal life as God. Why would God reveal Himself in words? Because there is

[8] "The creation of God is a revelation of God. God revealed himself in nature and God also revealed himself in the mind of man. Thus it is impossible for the mind of man to function except in an atmosphere of revelation. And every thought of man when it functioned normally in this atmosphere of revelation would express the truth as laid in the creation by God. We may therefore call a Christian epistemology a *revelational epistemology*." Cornelius Van Til, *In Defense of the Faith*, vol. 2, *A Survey of Christian Epistemology* (Phillipsburg, NJ: Presbyterian and Reformed, 1969), 1. Note that "Christian philosophy is a way of restating what God has authoritatively revealed about Himself, the world, man, etc.—the Christian worldview—and thus the way in which we know anything at all is first and foremost a matter of revelation." Greg L. Bahnsen, *Van Til's Apologetic: Readings and Analysis* (Phillipsburg, NJ: P&R Publishing, 1998), 164. See also John M. Frame, *Cornelius Van Til: An Analysis of His Thought* (Phillipsburg, NJ: P&R Publishing, 1995), 115–19. For an introduction to revelational epistemology in more plain language, see G. K. Beale and W. Andrew Hoffecker, "Biblical Epistemology: Revelation," in *Building a Christian World View*, ed. W. Andrew Hoffecker and Gary Scott Smith, vol. 1, *God, Man, and Knowledge* (Phillipsburg, NJ: Presbyterian and Reformed, 1986), 193–216.

> something about human language that is so perfectly analogous to the communication of the Persons of the Trinity that the Second Person may be called the Word of God. Human language is an analogue of one of the modes, perhaps the most important, of divine communication. For God to have given us verbal revelation, then, is what we would have expected.[9]

Our knowledge rests upon the revelation of this triune God and is only valid when received in covenantal submission to him, specifically in submission to Christ's LORDSHIP. Thus, "no sinner knows anything truly except he knows Christ, and no one knows Christ unless the Holy Ghost, the Spirit sent by the Father and the Son, regenerates him."[10] This is especially the case with language itself, which is part of revelation and gloriously reflects the Trinity. So, Van Til is not exaggerating when he writes that "no human can utter a single syllable, whether in negation or affirmation, unless it were for God's existence."[11] Apart from the Trinity, language itself would be vacuous.

[9] Ralph A. Smith, *Trinity and Reality: An Introduction to the Christian Faith* (Moscow, ID: Canon Press, 2004), 72. On revelation as Trinitarian, see Kelly, *The God Who Is: The Holy Trinity*, 261; John M. Frame, *The Doctrine of the Word of God* (Phillipsburg, NJ: P&R Publishing, 2010), 48; Robert Letham, *The Holy Trinity: In Scripture, History, Theology, and Worship* (Phillipsburg, NJ: P&R Publishing, 2004), 359–60. Letham also notes on page 411 that "the God who has made himself known for our salvation has revealed himself to be triune," and "only by the gracious action of the Trinity, breaking into our darkness and death and arousing us to new life, can we ever know him." This Trinitarian revelation, we must remember, is not merely creative; it is also redemptive, and "the foundations of creation and redemption are the same. The Logos who became flesh is the same by whom all things were made. The first-born from the dead is also the first-born of every creature. The Son, whom the Father made heir of all things, is the same by whom he also made the worlds." Bavinck, *The Philosophy of Revelation*, 27–28. On the link between the Trinity and redemptive revelation, see B. B. Warfield, *Biblical and Theological Studies*, ed. Samuel G. Craig (Philadelphia: Presbyterian and Reformed, 1968), 55–56.

[10] Van Til, *A Survey of Christian Epistemology*, 5.

[11] Ibid., 11. See also Pierce Taylor Hibbs, "Imaging Communion: An

Because of the intrinsically linguistic nature of reality, which was spoken into being by the self-communicating, tripersonal God, we come to know what we know by language—either by God's creational language made manifest in the world around us (and within us) or by God's direct verbal address to his people in history.[12] All knowledge of who God is and what he is like (theology proper) is, in this broader sense, linguistically mediated.[13]

Thus, language theory and theology proper are bound up with one another because both are Trinitarian; both are mysteriously incomprehensible and yet vital to our everyday existence.[14]

Argument for God's Existence Based on Speech," *WTJ* 77, no. 1 (Spring 2015): 35–51.

[12] "External and objective revelation demands an internal revelation in the subject." Herman Bavinck, *Reformed Dogmatics*, vol. 1, *Prolegomena*, ed. John Bolt, trans. John Vriend (Grand Rapids, MI: Baker Academic, 2003), 348. Also see Frame, *Doctrine of the Word of God*, 37–39.

[13] Van Til offered a schematic for the various means of revelation. We can receive revelation *about* nature, man, and God; we also receive revelation *from* nature, man, and God. But in every case, we cannot pull ourselves away from the fact that all such revelation is linguistic: nature and man were spoken into being; man is a communicative creature; and God is the self-communing Trinity. Though it is important to remember that, to us, general revelation is nonverbal in the sense that God speaks *through* it but not *in* it (whereas *in* Scripture we have the very speech of God to us), we can still say that language, in some sense, pervades every particle of reality. Cornelius Van Til, *Introduction to Systematic Theology: Prolegomena and the Doctrines of Revelation, Scripture, and God*, ed. William Edgar, 2nd ed. (Phillipsburg, NJ: P&R Publishing, 2007), 121–22. See also Cornelius Van Til, *The Defense of the Faith*, ed. K. Scott Oliphint, 4th ed. (Phillipsburg, NJ: P&R Publishing, 2008), 75–83. On the inescapable nature of revelation, see ibid., 174–78. On the necessity of God's revelation for our knowledge, see Louis Berkhof, *Systematic Theology*, new ed. (Grand Rapids, MI: William B. Eerdmans, 1996), 34–35.

[14] We will deal with this periodically when discussing God's incomprehensibility. For now, note that "we see in God himself the logical origin for the words in language. Words do not come out of nowhere. Out of his bounty, his goodness, God has supplied human beings with all the words in each particular language. He has not given words in isolation, but words that are tied to and related to one another in their meanings, their sounds, and their ability to form constructions that communicate rich truths. And it is not a gift that is

All of this means that language is profoundly Trinitarian, and the Trinity is profoundly linguistic! What we think of one has repercussions for what we think of the other. If we consider language a mere vehicle of thought, what does that say about our understanding of God?[15] Perhaps it says that we may be tempted to see God as a vehicle for blessings or as an instrument for advancement. If we

---

unrelated to the Giver. The gift reflects the Giver in mysterious ways. Words, with their ability to describe, reflect God who describes himself, as is hinted at in his self-description, 'I am who I am.' God describes himself to himself in the communication and communion of the persons of the Trinity, in unity and diversity. And then that unity in diversity is reflected in the unity (contrastive-identificational features), diversity (variation), and interconnectedness (distribution) that exist in any one single word." Poythress, *In the Beginning Was the Word*, 279. Also consider Oliphint's words on theology proper, particularly the relation between God's simplicity and his triunity: "Surely there is mystery in God's simplicity; perhaps nothing is more complex than God's simplicity! There is mystery, in other words, in God's triunity. These biblical truths, which we must affirm, go together. And yet, even as we affirm them, we have no laws of thinking or experience that show us exactly *how* these aspects of God's character actually cohere. They do cohere; there is no darkness or mystery in God. But we cannot see exactly *how*—not in this life, nor in the next." K. Scott Oliphint, "Simplicity, Triunity, and the Incomprehensibility of God," in *One God in Three Persons: Unity of Essence, Distinction of Persons, Implications for Life*, ed. Bruce A. Ware and John Starke (Wheaton, IL: Crossway, 2015), 229.

15 In terms of the medium of writing, this would be akin to the *surrogational model*, in which "what a sign signifies is explained in terms of its being a surrogate or substitute for something else." Roy Harris, *Signs of Writing* (New York: Routledge, 1995), 50. We might think here of Plato's *Cratylus* and other logocentric models of signification. Logocentrism, in brief, "stands for the harmonious alliance between reality, thought, and language." Kevin J. Vanhoozer, *Is There a Meaning in This Text? The Bible, the Reader, and the Morality of Literary Knowledge* (Grand Rapids, MI: Zondervan, 1998), 60. There is certainly truth to the surrogational approach, and I am not opposed to our thinking that, in some ways, written words are "surrogates" of thoughts, but they are much more than that. I believe words are also instruments for communion, which highlights not just *what they are* but *what they do*, in a more Trinitarian sense. Temporal words foster communion because the eternal Word has intimate communion with the Father and Spirit.

think of God as an impersonal monad or absolute, what does that say about our understanding of language?[16] Perhaps we may fail to see language as a means of fostering communion, and so we use words out of a sense of selfish ambition rather than out of a love for communal peace in the body of Christ. Of course, these are generalities, but that does not mean there is no truth to them. The point is that our understanding of language, which might be thought of as peripheral to our theology, is actually at the center of it. That is why it is so critical to be conscious of our approach to language.

An Apology

Now that we know a bit about the relationship between language theory and theology proper, we should clarify why this project is an appropriate setting to investigate that relationship further. To start, we might ask, why is it so important to add this particular study to the queue of theological books and monographs dealing with the nature and structure of language, or with the doctrine of the Trinity? To say that language and the Trinity are topics of current interest is one thing, but why does the theoretical convergence of a Connecticut-born linguist (Kenneth Pike) and a Dutch Reformed apologist (Cornelius Van Til) warrant our attention?

My simple answer to the question may seem presumptuous, but I do not think it is an exaggeration. Given what we know

[16] This would follow in the footsteps of Plato's rather nebulous "unifying principle" of *the Good*, which "gives being to the objects of knowledge and so is, as it were, the unifying and all-comprehensive Principle of the essential order, while itself excelling even essential being in dignity and power .... The Idea of the Good gives being to the Forms or essences of the intellectual order, while science and the wide ocean of intellectual beauty is a stage on the ascent to the essentially beautiful. Plato is clearly working towards the conception of the Absolute, the absolutely Perfect and exemplary Pattern of all things, the ultimate ontological Principle." Frederick Copleston, *Greece and Rome: From the Pre-Soctratics to Plotinus*, A History of Philosophy 1 (New York: Image Books, 1946), 176.

about language as an image-bearing gift of God, and given what the Reformed tradition holds about the centrality of the Trinity, the joint study of these two thinkers seems to offer a unique and biblical exposition of the nature of language. If language is an image-bearing gift of God, then it should be appreciated for its divinely-endowed potency and depth. If the Trinity is the centerpiece of Reformed theology, then we should have a distinctly Trinitarian approach to language that accounts for the depth and incomprehensibility of the Godhead. This is where the language theory of Kenneth Pike and the theology of Cornelius Van Til merge. At the intersection of their thought, we find a truly Reformed and Trinitarian understanding of language—an understanding that is faithful to the biblical witness and calls upon linguists and theologians alike to bow in awe before the God who spoke the world into being and upholds it by the word of his power (Heb. 1:3). I am not suggesting that this is the only way to view language, but it is certainly an important one that deserves our attention. The Reformed tradition needs to see just how insightful and methodologically felicitous Kenneth Pike's approach to language was, especially in conjunction with key Van Tillian teachings. However, as we will see, Kenneth Pike extends this even further, for if language is a phase of human behavior, then we can easily extend what we have learned about language to the rest of life, hence the title: *The Trinity, Language, and Human Behavior.*[17]

The Outline of What Follows

In the pages that follow, we first focus our attention on the language theory of Kenneth Pike. Next, we expose the Trinitarian structure of Pike's approach and then note key areas of overlap between his thought and that of Cornelius Van Til. We will conclude with

[17] On the benefits of expanding a perspective to include all of reality, see Vern S. Poythress, *Symphonic Theology: The Validity of Multiple Perspectives in Theology* (Phillipsburg, NJ: P&R Publishing, 1987), 24–28.

some reflections on Pike's language theory as it relates to metaphysics and epistemology. Throughout the project, I will reinforce the thesis that *Kenneth Pike's language theory offers us a picture of language that faithfully represents the incomprehensible, Triune God of Scripture.*

2

The Language Theory of Kenneth L. Pike

We begin with a general exposition of Pike's language theory. Though he often critiqued himself for being lazy, Kenneth Pike produced an imposing amount of work, and, over the course of some forty years, developed an extensive theory of language and human behavior.[1] In a 1956 article, he revealed that he had been working on a theory of the structure of human behavior for several years.[2] This theory later came to fruition in his magnum opus, *Language in Relation to a Unified Theory of the Structure of Human Behavior* (hereafter *LRUT*). This work was Pike's first attempt at a full exposition of his theory, quite revolutionary in its approach to language and human behavior, and strongly inspired by his former teacher, Edward Sapir, to whom the volume was dedicated.[3] While I will draw on this seminal work to explain Pike's theory, it was not until the early 80s that Pike's theory was concisely set forth a second time in *Linguistic Concepts: An Introduction to Tagmemics*

[1] In a two-part article, I have developed an overview of Pike's language theory in its relation to personalism and the Trinity in *WTJ* (Fall 2015 and Spring 2016): "Where Person Meets Word."

[2] Kenneth L. Pike, "Towards a Theory of the Structure of Human Behavior (1956)," in *Kenneth L. Pike: Selected Writings to Commemorate the 60th Birthday of Kenneth Lee Pike*, ed. Ruth Brend (Paris: Mouton, 1972), 106.

[3] Pierce Taylor Hibbs, "Where Person Meets Word Part 1: Personalism in the Language Theory of Kenneth L. Pike," *WTJ* 77, no. 2 (Fall 2015): 370n46.

(hereafter *LC*). In this later work, we find a clear and simple outline of Pike's theory in its most mature form, and so I will mainly be following that outline in this chapter, with slight modifications. I will focus on bare exposition, offering further explanation and examples for elements of Pike's theory that are more complex or which might be more foreign to us today. My aim here is to give a bird's eye view of the breadth of Pike's theory—as it developed over forty years—so that, in the following chapter, we can explore its Trinitarian structure.

I. Etic and Emic Viewpoints

II. Observer Perspectives
   A. Particle Perspective
   B. Wave Perspective
   C. Field Perspective

III. Linguistic Units
   A. Contrast and Identification
   B. Variation
   C. Distribution

IV. Hierarchy
   A. Grammar
   B. Phonology
   C. Reference

V. Context
   A. Form-Meaning Composites
   B. Sharing as Prerequisite to Change
   C. Universe of Discourse

However, before we get to Pike's theory itself, we need to broach the ancient subject of what language is, not for all linguists but for Pike himself.[4] This will help us to understand something of the breadth of his language theory.

What Is Language?

The question of what language *is* has baffled minds and filled pages for centuries. It is an ancient question deserving our attention not simply because it is fascinating but because, theologically, language gets at the heart of what it means to be made in God's image, what it is to be human.

As with every concept, definitions for language vary in their scope. While the narrow definitions have the advantage of focusing our attention, they may blind us to features or components of the thing in question. Broader definitions, though they may seem unwieldy and impractical to specialists, have the advantage of relating the concept in question to the complex and multifaceted network of human experience. Thus, Pike's former teacher, Edward Sapir, wrote of language,

> while [language] may be looked upon as a symbolic system which reports or refers to or otherwise substitutes for direct experience, it does not as a matter of actual behavior stand apart from or run parallel to direct experience but completely interpenetrates with it. . . . For the normal person every experience, real or potential, is saturated with verbalism. This explains why so many lovers of nature, for instance, do not feel that they are truly in touch with it until they have mastered the names of a great many flowers and trees, as though the primary world of reality were a verbal one and as though one could not get close to nature

[4] There is a staggering number of answers to this question, since it has been the fascination of philosophers for centuries. An overview of some of the popular definitions of language can be found in A. P. Martinich and David Sosa, eds., *The Philosophy of Language*, 6th ed. (New York: Oxford, 2013), 651–738.

> unless one first mastered the terminology which somehow magically expresses it. It is this constant interplay between language and experience which removes language from the cold status of such purely and simply symbolic systems as mathematical symbolism or flag signaling. This interpenetration is not only an intimate associative fact; it is also a contextual one. It is important to realize that language may not only refer to experience or even mold, interpret, and discover experience, but that it also substitutes for it in the sense that in those sequences of interpersonal behavior which form the greater part of our daily lives speech and action supplement each other and do each other's work in a web of unbroken pattern. If one says to me, 'Lend me a dollar,' I may hand over the money without a word or I may give it with an accompanying 'Here it is' or I may say 'I haven't got it' or 'I'll give it to you tomorrow.' Each of these responses is structurally equivalent, if one thinks of the larger behavior pattern. It is clear that if language is in its analyzed form a symbolic system of reference, it is far from being merely that if we consider the psychological part that it plays in continuous behavior.[5]

Pike would adopt this approach in his own definition of language as a "phase" of human behavior. In *LRUT*, he writes,

> Language is behavior, i.e., a phase of human activity which must not be treated in essence as structurally divorced from the structure of nonverbal human activity. The activity of man constitutes a structural whole, in such a way that it cannot be subdivided into neat 'parts' or 'levels' or 'compartments' with language in a behavioral compartment insulated

[5] Edward Sapir, *Selected Writings in Language, Culture, and Personality* (1963; repr., London: Forgotten Books, 2012), 11–12.

> in character, content, and organization from other behavior. Verbal and nonverbal activity is a unified whole, and theory and methodology should be organized or created to treat it as such.[6]

This is important to grasp at the outset because it has momentous implications for metaphysics and epistemology. Language is structurally related to how we think, especially in terms of our perception (epistemology), and to who we are as communicative beings (metaphysics).[7] If this is the case, then our understanding of language significantly shapes our entire worldview. More will be said about this in the conclusion for this book. For now, it is critical that we keep in mind Pike's broader definition of language because it explains why he begins his theory where he does: not with language as a verbal system or set of structural rules, but with *people*.[8] To discuss language adequately, one must begin with persons, and persons always have a position in and perspective on the world.

[6] Pike, *LRUT*, 26. See also Viola G. Waterhouse, *The History and Development of Tagmemics* (The Hague: Mouton, 1974), 15. Elsewhere Pike offers other definitions of language that comport with this. "Language is not merely a set of unrelated sounds, clauses, rules, and meanings; it is a total coherent system of these integrating with each other, and with behavior, context, universe of discourse, and observer perspective." Pike, *LC*, 44. "Language is a part of behavior. It is not isolated from nonverbal action, but is integrated with it, and takes its meaning from social settings, intents, and reactions." Ibid., 72–73.

[7] Note the connection Pike makes between language and epistemology ("thinking processes") in the following quotation: "Of incalculable importance to the analyst of international and personal misunderstandings is the appreciation of the fact that not only sounds, grammar, games and overt activity can contain similar etic inventories of events arranged in different emic systems, but that thinking processes also may be similarly different in so far as these processes utilize words whose meanings are subject to a comparable kind of structuring, and in so far as basic epistemological attitudes, emotional outlook and moral character is also structured." Pike, *LRUT*, 51.

[8] Hence the statement at the end of *LC*: "Personal interaction is given priority over identification of things or abstractions. It is *persons* who perceive, imagine, and sense relations." Pike, *LC*, 136.

Emic and Etic Viewpoints

For Pike, the perspectives or viewpoints people have can be treated at two levels: *emic* and *etic*, and *particle/wave/field* (hereafter PWF).[9] The emic and etic distinction, coined by Pike himself, was drawn from the ending morphemes of the words *phonemic* and *phonetic*.[10] These are essentially two different ways of viewing the same data or experience.[11] I find it

[9] I distinguish "viewpoints" from "perspectives" here arbitrarily, just to distinguish the etic-emic concept from PWF.

[10] This discussion is taken directly from Hibbs, "Where Person Meets Word: Part 1," 371–74, used with permission.

[11] Here, again, Pike incorporates the teaching of Edward Sapir, with whom he worked closely in the late 1930s, conversing with him about linguistics into the late hours of the night. Sapir wrote, "It is impossible to say what an individual is doing unless we have tacitly accepted the essentially arbitrary modes of interpretation that social tradition is constantly suggesting to us from the very moment of our birth. Let anyone who doubts this try the experiment of making a painstaking report of the actions of a group of natives engaged in some form of activity, say religious, to which he has not the cultural key. If he is a skillful writer, he may succeed in giving a picturesque account of what he sees and hears, or thinks he sees and hears, but the chances of his being able to give a relation of what happens in terms that would be intelligible and acceptable to the natives themselves are practically nil. He will be guilty of all manner of distortion. His emphasis will be constantly askew. He will find interesting what the natives take for granted as a casual kind of behavior worthy of no particular comment, and he will utterly fail to observe the crucial turning points in the course of action that give formal significance to the whole in the minds of those who do possess the key to its understanding. This patterning or formal analysis of behavior is to a surprising degree dependent on the mode of apprehension which has been established by the tradition of the group. Forms and significances which seem obvious to an outsider will be denied outright by those who carry out the patterns; outlines and implications that are perfectly clear to these may be absent to the eye of the onlooker. It is the failure to understand the necessity of grasping the native patterning which is responsible for so much unimaginative and misconceiving description of procedures that we have not been brought up with. It becomes actually possible to interpret as base what is inspired by the noblest and event holiest of motives, and to see altruism or beauty where nothing of the kind is either felt or intended." Sapir,

helpful to substitute the word *insider* for emic and *outsider* for etic.[12]

A simple example will serve to illustrate: consider an extraterrestrial who is watching people drive in and out of a gas station. Some people, he notices, get out of their metal boxes, remove a square piece of plastic from their pockets, and then insert it into a machine next to them before quickly pulling it back out. Then they push lightly on the machine, remove a hose from it, attach the hose to their metal box, and wait a few minutes. Finally, they put the hose back in its place and push lightly on the machine once more. But at this point, the alien is puzzled: after lightly pushing on the machine, some people take a small piece of paper from it, but others do not. All the alien can confirm is that this phenomenon happens, but he cannot attach meaning to it from the perspective of these people. Why do they not all take a slip of paper from the machine? Is the machine withholding? Is it judging them based on their parking skill? Does it depend on the color of the car they drive?

Imagine the same scenario from the perspective of a person filling his car up with gas. When he sees the man next to him push a button after fueling and not receive a slip of paper, the action is instantly meaningful. He knows that the man simply does not want a receipt for the transaction. He can draw a number of conclusions about this action that the alien cannot: perhaps the man hates clutter; perhaps he wishes to help the environment by saving paper; perhaps he is in a rush and would rather not wait for a receipt to print out.

Selected Writings, 546–47. For Sapir's understanding of what Pike would later call the *emic-etic* distinction, see ibid., 556.

[12] Pike, *LRUT*, 37. Waterhouse defines the contrast between emic and etic as follows: "The etic view has to do with universals, with typology, with observation from outside a system, as well as with the nature of initial field data, and with variant forms of an emic unit. The emic view is concerned with the contrastive, patterned system of a specific language or culture or universe of discourse, with the way a participant in a system sees that system, as well as with distinctions between contrastive units." *The History and Development of Tagmemics*, 6.

And, what's more, while the person has an instant understanding of the potential meaningfulness of the action, he may be unaware of all of the things that the alien observed because his rote execution blinds him to certain details. The alien considers how strange it is for a piece of plastic to go in and out of a machine and then cause that machine to respond. He wants to know how this works. The person, on the other hand, probably could not care less. He has thoughtlessly removed and inserted his card into the slot at the gas pump countless times. He does not think about how the magnetic strip in his card is read by the machine, or how his pin number is related to the magnetic strip, etc. So, both the alien and the person at the gas pump notice certain things about the same event; each perspective yields unique and useful results; each has its advantages and limitations. The alien would not survive socially in the man's culture. The man would not survive in his own culture if he thought of every single activity he performed with meticulous scrutiny. The alien's view and man's view are complementary.

The emic and etic viewpoints are thus foundational in our interpretation of experience. Every person is always either an insider (emic) or an outsider (etic) who may wish to become an insider and thus better understand the behaviors of those around him.

When applied more narrowly to units of language (morphemes, words, phrases, clauses, paragraphs, etc.), the emic-etic distinction manifests itself in the context of human *responses* to language. For Pike, linguistic "units are different etically when instrumental measurements can show them to be so. Units are different emically only when they elicit different responses from people acting within the system."[13] Consider the words "hey" and "hello." Etically, these words are different—they have different spellings and different pronunciations. Emically, they are the same in the sense that each is a common greeting often used to open a conversation. A person's *response* to either one would likely be indistinguishable. So, there can

[13] Pike, *LRUT*, 38.

be etic difference with emic sameness. Conversely, there can be emic difference with etic sameness. A non-native English speaker might hear the verb "draw" in two sentences.

> *He drew a map so that he would understand how to get there.*
> *He drew his conclusion after careful study.*

Here the spelling and pronunciation of "drew" is identical in each sentence. Yet, if the non-native English speaker assumes that this etic identity is equal to emic sameness, significant misinterpretation results. The same might happen in conversations when homophonous words occur. "He said 'no'" is very different semantically from "He said 'know.'" The meaning of the utterance would be deduced from context and from the participant response. If the listener had just asked the question, "Did he say 'yes' or 'no'?" then we would *know* which word was meant.

Now, when discussing language, Pike would often focus on the emic, since that is the perspective of native speakers who exchange meaningful discourse with one another.[14] Yet, based on the discussion above about language as a phase of human behavior, we can predict that he would not restrict emic units of language to verbal elements. They include non-verbal elements as well (actions, environments). Pike referred to the context of each emic unit as its "distribution." For him,

> Every emic unit of language behavior must be studied in reference to its distribution—distribution in reference to verbal behavior, and distribution in reference to nonverbal cultural behavior. Within the study of the distribution of language units in nonverbal contexts is included the consideration of the nonverbal responses of individuals to speech addressed to

[14] Note, however, that *both* perspectives are helpful and necessary. They complement one another. Ibid., 40–41.

> them. Just as the verbal replies of a speaker help one determine meanings of elements of communication, so the nonverbal ones do likewise. To attempt to analyze or describe language without reference to its function in eliciting responses—verbal and nonverbal—is to ignore one of the crucial kinds of evidence which is essential if the emic structure of language is to be determined, whether one is dealing with the larger units of that structure, such as the sentence, or smaller ones, such as some of the emic units of the sound system.[15]

This, once again, has important implications for our understanding of language because it seems to break down the walls partitioning language from other areas of study. Yet, even within language, this is a staggering conclusion. Demanding that verbal analysis account for nonverbal behavior seems to remove any sense of compartmentalization—the sort that we might expect in advanced studies within a discipline. Pike's students seemed to notice this. I was once told of a story about Pike delivering a guest lecture at a university. When he explained some aspects of his language theory and the inclusion of nonverbal behavior in the study of language, one of the students asked, "But if this is true, then where do you stop the analysis?" Another student quickly replied, "That's just it—it doesn't stop! It goes all the way back to God!"[16] I mention this anecdote to point out that distinguishing between etic and emic viewpoints does little to narrow the field of analysis. Even when studying language from an emic perspective, Pike's theory allows for (and even invites) jaw-dropping complexity and depth. We will discuss the theological implications of this in a later chapter.

The etic and emic viewpoints are foundational for Pike because they reflect the vantage point from which language is always studied

[15] Ibid., 39–40.

[16] This anecdote was given to me by Vern Poythress. This is not a verbatim rendering, but it captures the main idea.

(in fact, from which reality is always perceived). There is always an observer or a participant when it comes to our study of language, and this observer is drawing on etic and emic approaches to reality. This is basic to our understanding of human communication, for it applies not just to languages but to individual persons. For Pike, "each person to some extent constitutes a separate sub-culture, with his own emic organization. For a common emic structure, a common experience is prerequisite, both verbal and nonverbal, in a unified whole. Since this never occurs for any two people, there are always problems of understanding."[17]

Of course, emic and etic perspectives highlight not only communicative problems but also communicative solutions and strengths. Each person's emic understanding is stretched when he encounters an etic (i.e., new or foreign) situation. That encounter can become a learning experience by which his emic understanding is added to or further developed. Whether positively or negatively, however, the emic-etic distinction brings out our social grouping into insider and outsider communities. These groupings must be accounted for in any study of language, and in any study of human behavior in general. They separate the foreign from the familiar in our experience, and they account for the nature of our responses to others.

Observer Perspectives: Particle, Wave, and Field (PWF)

The emic and etic viewpoints functioned conjointly with what Pike referred to as observer perspectives: *particle*, *wave*, and *field* (PWF).[18] Viola Waterhouse defines these concisely in discussing the structure of language, but she substitutes "static," "dynamic," and "functional" for PWF respectively, which Pike himself did in the late 1950s. "Structure may . . . be viewed from three complementary perspectives: static, dynamic, and functional. In the STATIC view,

[17] Pike, *LRUT*, 51.

[18] This is one of the significant developments in Pike's theory. In *LRUT*, the

structure is composed of discrete particles. In the DYNAMIC view, structure is made up of waves, with nuclei and margins. In the FUNCTIONAL view, structure is seen as patterned system, or field."[19] Later, Pike expands on his definitions:

> Each of the three views of language contributes an insight into its structure. The particle view leads one to study carefully the psycholinguistic data which support segmentation of sequences into chunks of behavior, and the identification of variants as members of units. The wave view accounts better for the physical data of continuous articulatory movements or sound waves. The field view leaves room for a theory of classes and systems of phonemes, morphemes, and tagmemes. Sequence of units is easiest treated under a particle view; smearing of unit borders under a wave view; structure of system, or universe of discourse, under a field view.[20]

Yet, as we might predict, his description of these perspectives would be expressed most accessibly in *LC*. As we turn there, we should give each of these perspectives distinct treatment.

PWF perspectives were not discussed until the twelfth chapter (out of seventeen), and there only received limited treatment. In *LC*, they occupy the third, fourth, and fifth chapters, thus taking a more prominent place in his thought. In *LRUT*, Pike gave the weight of his attention to the feature, manifestation, and distribution modes (later contrast, variation, and distribution), and meant for the PWF perspectives to supplement them. In *LC*, however, he adds that the PWF perspectives focus on the *observer*, while contrast, variation, and distribution (CVD) focus on linguistic units themselves. See Pike, *LC*, 41. Pike describes the particle view as "static," the wave as "dynamic," and the field as "functional." Pike, *LRUT*, 511. For use of these perspectives in language theory within a Christian context, see Poythress, *In the Beginning Was the Word*, 50–59. For examples of the use of these perspectives in nonverbal behavior and philosophy, see Vern S. Poythress, *Redeeming Philosophy: A God-Centered Approach to the Big Questions* (Wheaton, IL: Crossway, 2014), 143–44.

[19] Waterhouse, *The History and Development of Tagmemics*, 6.

[20] Pike, *LRUT*, 513.

Particle

In *LC*, Pike has perhaps the most succinct definition of the particle perspective.

> Human nature experiences the world—sometimes—as made up of *particles*, that is, as "things." Houses, trees, and people seem to be obvious physical objects. But often an experience or concept which obviously is not an object is also talked about *as if* it were one. . . . Our mental computers seem to be able to operate only if the whole world is processed into bits, each of which can when appropriate be treated as a particle.[21]

The particle perspective treats units of language and human behavior as if they had discrete borders. Language, in other words, "may be viewed as if it were STATIC—permanent bricks juxtaposed in a permanent structure, or as separate 'frames' in a moving-picture film."[22] This perspective, for Pike, seems to have largely governed the study of language in the twentieth century for various reasons, one of which being that it appeals to common sense. In his earliest published discussion of PWF, he notes,

> This particle view reflects a commonsense attitude: Language is made up of words, with sharp boundaries between them. A language, for some people, would appear to be ideally comprised of a dictionary. Once one has the dictionary of a language one seems to have under control the heart of the language, if one thinks this way. This view appears to be very common in some areas of our culture.
>
> A more sophisticated particle view aims at an analysis

[21] Pike, *LC*, 19.

[22] Kenneth L. Pike, "Language as Particle, Wave, and Field," in *Selected Writings to Commemorate the 60th Birthday of Kenneth Lee Pike*, ed. Ruth M. Brend (The Hague, Paris: Mouton, 1972), 129.

> of great simplicity. It attempts to reduce high-level language structures to combinations of a few small units in more and more restricted groupings. The unit chosen is the sound—the PHONEME—or a component of a phoneme. If one has a list of the sounds and the possible restrictions on the combination of these sounds, one is assumed to know the structure of the language. This view—though I have oversimplified it—has had high prestige in the United States in the past few years.[23]

As an example, consider the sentence "He wrote a book." This sentence contains four words: a pronoun, a verb, an article, and a noun. The sound of each word in the sentence can be distinctly pronounced, and the sentence as a whole, from this perspective, is the syntactical product of putting the words in this particular order. We might say that the sentence is composed with linguistic bricks, one set next to another.

This applies to nonverbal human behavior as well. The physical action of writing a book can be viewed as a separate chunk of activity, with relatively clear starting and ending points. As a chunk of human activity, the writing of a book can be compared and contrasted with other similar units: building a house, planting a garden, preparing a Sunday school lesson, etc.

Whether in verbal or nonverbal behavior, the particle perspective seems requisite for us if we are to function in reality. For Pike, "Our mental computers seem to be able to operate only if the whole world is processed into bits, each of which can when appropriate be treated as a particle, punched into our mental IBM cards."[24] We will revisit this notion of stability when we treat Pike's theory theologically, in the following chapter.

Lastly, with reference to time, the particle view would be

[23] Ibid., 130.
[24] Pike, *LC*, 19.

synchronic, focusing on a unit at a single moment, rather than looking at how that unit might be expressed or developed over an extended period of time (diachronically).[25]

Wave

If we were to read the previous example sentence and give equal attention to each unit, it would sound choppy and fragmented: "He—wrote—a—book." Spoken naturally, this sentence might sound more like, "Ee roaddabuk." The neat borders between the units are smeared together. This is where the wave perspective comes into play: it focuses on the fluid transitions between sound sequences or between lexical and syntactical units or even between segments of human behavior, recognizing margins and nuclei. If we accent both "wrote" and "book," the sentence more explicitly represents this wave-like structure. "Wrote" and "book" would each be a nucleus (highpoint) of a wave, and the other words would be marginal.

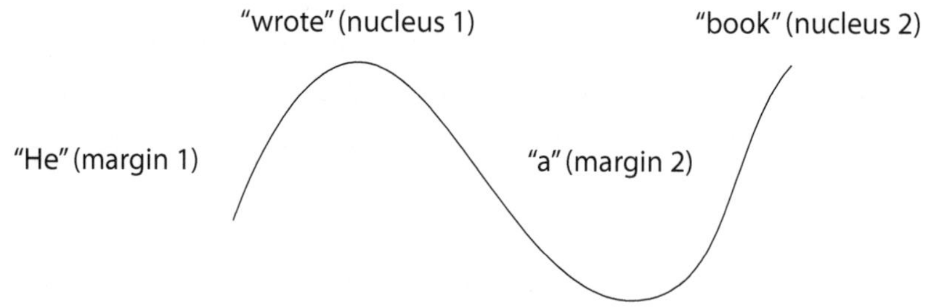

Fig. 2. 1. Example of a Wave Structure

For Pike,

> The clearest or steadiest part of a sound during slow pronunciation can be called the *nucleus* of a *wave*. The borders, or transitions, from one sound to another can be called the

[25] Pike, "Language as Particle, Wave, and Field," 140.

> *margins*. In wave types which interest us we often look for their nuclei and margins. If our attention is almost exclusively on the nucleus, however, we may be thinking in terms of particles. When our attention is on the whole flowing movement from margin to nucleus to margin, we are thinking in terms of the unit as a wave.[26]

While this applies to sentences such as the one in figure 2.1, it is important to note that the wave perspective, as with each of the other perspectives, applies to smaller and larger units of discourse as well, including events. A conversation or paragraph can be viewed as a wave, as can an afternoon or a lecture. Within language, Pike also mentions grammatical, phonological, and referential waves. We will discuss the phonological, grammatical, and referential hierarchies later in this chapter, but it is helpful to see how each of these hierarchies might be manifested under the wave perspective.

Grammar Waves. In terms of grammar, we can perceive in a particular unit

> a central, crucial, nuclear part of a construction which may or may not be preceded or followed by less important elements which in some way modify it. When such a wave is made up of just one word, the nucleus may be called a *stem*, and the margin a *prefix* or a *suffix* as in *inactive* or *singing*. A two-word phrase, smaller than a clause, may also have its head and modifier, as in *my* (margin) *alligator* (nucleus). When two clauses are in a sentence, one may be independent, nuclear, and the other dependent, as in *The doctor treated the boy* (nucleus) *after he broke his leg on a skate board* (margin). Similarly, a question-answer relation gives a higher level of nucleus-margin: *Will you come? Perhaps.*[27]

[26] Pike, *LC*, 26.
[27] Ibid., 27.

Grammatical waves draw our attention to central elements in a language unit (nuclei), which can aid in the interpretation of and response to that unit. We recognize this even in casual conversation. When I am asked, "Where's your brother?" I can respond in several ways, each of which is based on an independent clause, such as, "He's in the front yard." We choose almost instinctively to shorten our response to questions like this, and we do so by selecting the nuclear element in context. Notice how strange it would be if I were to reply to the above question with a marginal element of the example response: "He," or "the," or "is." None of these responses provides the essential information that the speaker is looking for. But if I say, "front yard," the speaker immediately recognizes this as an answer to the question. That is, in part, because I have given the speaker the nucleus of my response, which corresponds to the nucleus of his question: "where."

Phonological Waves. A phonological wave "can be as short as a single sound or as large as a lecture. Each may have nucleus and margins."[28] In a word or phrase, the nuclei would be the stressed syllables, and the margins would be the unstressed ones. In the sentence, "He wrote a book," we might stress the single syllable of the verb "wrote" and the single syllable of the noun "book." The marginal, unstressed syllables would be the pronoun "he" and the indefinite article "a."

In a larger segment of speech, such as what contemporary English language teachers refer to as "speech paragraphs," the nucleus might be considered the topic sentence, which is pronounced more slowly and with a higher key as compared to the developing sentences.[29] As with grammatical waves, phonological waves can draw our attention to nuclear and marginal elements so as to help us interpret and respond to the elements that are important

[28] Ibid.

[29] For an example, see Greta Gorsuch et al., *English Communication for International Teaching Assistants*, 2nd ed. (Long Grove, IL: Waveland, 2012), 61–62.

to the speaker. A lecturer would be taken back if a student began asking several questions about a marginal element of the lecture. "That's not what the lecture was about," the professor might say. What he means is, that is not the nuclear element that you should be inquiring about.

Referential/Lexical Waves. We can also have waves in terms of reference: the real-world phenomena and meanings to which language is attached. "A referential wave shows highlighting of reported events, or of argument, or of exposition. Thus a story can be viewed as a wave: a premargin may set the stage; the plot warms up; the climax (nucleus) occurs; the hero gets out of trouble and lives happily ever after (postmargin)."[30]

Perhaps more concrete is a *lexical wave*, which deals with a word's meaning. For Pike,

> a word may comprise a *lexical wave* with a *central meaning* normal to the most frequent or nonspecial set of contexts and a set of marginal meanings which occur when the central meaning is modified by other words in the context. For example, *to run* is basically (in my *intuition*) referring to the action of a man (or creature) in his feet moving rapidly toward or away from some place; but *a run in a stocking*, or *to run the business*, or *to run into trouble*, or *He ran out of words* are marginal. In such instances, we may also sometimes speak of the nuclear meaning as *normal*, and the marginal one as *off-norm*.[31]

In terms of nonverbal behavior, we can even have *perceptual waves*, such as when we view a painting and "focus on the item or figure as nucleus and on the setting as marginal."[32]

[30] Pike, *LC*, 27.
[31] Ibid., 28–29.
[32] Ibid., 29.

Field

Lastly, there is the field perspective. We can examine "sets of relationships which occur when units are linked to one another by their presence in some larger system. A total set of relationships and of units in these relationships we call a field."[33] The field perspective reminds us that

> No item by itself has significance. A unit becomes relevant only in relation to context. Outside such a relationship the item will be necessarily uninterpretable by the observer. A simple circle, for example, may be interpreted by an observer as a numeral, if it is in the context of the number 1,000. On the other hand the circle may be interpreted as a letter of the alphabet in the context of *pop* . . . . The observer interprets data relative to context—within a field. In this sense a datum of sensation "becomes" a "fact" of human significance when seen relative to its distribution in an environment—relative to a field as structured in the perception or imagination of some person.[34]

Just as we can have various kinds of waves, we can have various kinds of fields: there can be fields of relationships in terms of grammar, phonology, and reference (or semantics). The pronoun "He" in the sentence "He wrote a book" is part of a class of personal pronouns that stand in for particular subjects, each of which can occur in a particular grammatical slot. Subject pronouns ("he," "she," "it," "they") can occur in the subject position of an English sentence, whereas object or reflexive pronouns ("him," "himself") cannot. Likewise, the vowel sound that ends the pronoun is understood in reference to a group of vowel sounds in the English language, each of which has a distinct articulation involving the position of the tongue and lips

[33] Ibid., 30.
[34] Ibid.

as well as the vibration of the vocal cords. We understand "he" as having a distinct meaning from "ha" or "huh" or "hoe."[35] Similarly, we understand the meaning of independent clauses with reference to the structure and meaning of dependent clauses. For example, the clause "if he goes to the doctor's on Tuesday" is structurally and semantically different from the clause "he goes to the doctor's on Tuesday." The former is conditional (marked by "if" at the beginning of the clause) while the latter is declarative.

The Nature and Necessity of the Perspectives

Now, each of the observer perspectives views the same data. Pike used an illustration for this, which I have reproduced below. Note how the same material, the same "stuff," is present in each perspective, and in the simultaneous use of all three.

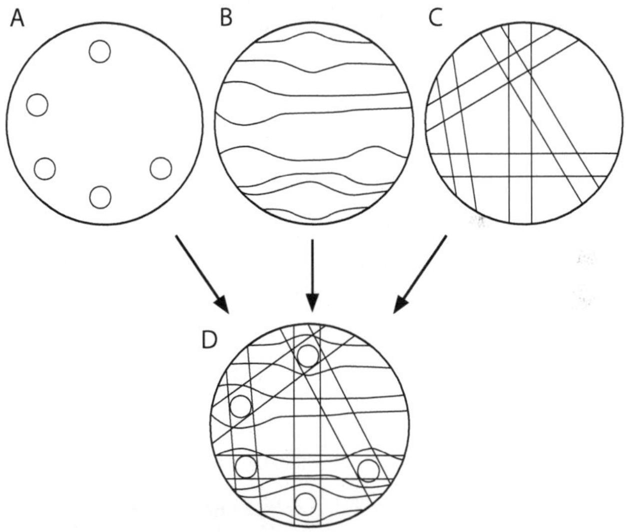

Fig. 2.2. Particle, Wave, and Field Observer Perspectives[36]

[35] Ibid., 31–32.

[36] Reproduced by permission from Kenneth L. Pike, *Linguistic Concepts: An Introduction to Tagmemics* (Lincoln,NE: University of Nebraska Press, 1982),

Each perspective is of the same data. And, for Pike, "each of the three views must be retained, supplementing one another, if we wish to preserve an empirically and theoretically adequate view of language."[37] We might say that each perspective is always present, if not in the foreground, then in the background. While an observer can choose to focus on one of these perspectives at a time, that focus does not eclipse the other two. What's more, if we take another step back psychologically, each of the units viewed by one of these perspectives can be viewed again by another perspective. "Even a wave, when it is viewed as a unit, may itself be treated as a particle, just as the particle, when viewed in its physical smearing aspects, can be viewed as a wave."[38]

A natural question in all of this is, why do we need *these* perspectives? Why is each necessary? Why do we need to *choose* a perspective? The simple answer to the latter question is that humans are finite creatures who must focus. "Human nature requires that people *focus* attention in some direction—on some element or concept or view. The person who tries to watch construction out of the corner of his eye while he drives down the road is likely to end in the ditch. Language reflects this capacity for directing focus."[39] No person can focus on everything simultaneously, giving equal attention to every unit of language or human behavior. We *choose* what we will see, what to place in the foreground and what to leave in the background at a given moment.

As to the former question, why we need these three perspectives (and not others), Pike was content to say that these were the perspectives that adequately accounted for the data of language and human experience. In other words, his selection and use of the PWF perspectives was driven strictly by empirical data.[40] We will, however, in the following chapter suggest a theological reason why Pike discovered and used these particular perspectives throughout his career.

---

fig. 2.2. © 1982 by the University of Nebraska Press.

[37] Pike, "Language as Particle, Wave, and Field," 130.

[38] Pike, *LC*, 27.

[39] Ibid., 26.

[40] Reflecting on the feature, manifestation, and distribution modes (which

Each of the perspectives seems to account for the phenomena of experience satisfactorily, and yet each requires the other two.[41] The particle perspective, we noted before, is necessary for our stability and daily function in the world. If the world were not in some sense understood as static or stable, we would not be able to cope with reality. While there is change all around us, there must be some stability in order for the basic concept of identity to hold. I am still me, even though I have fewer hairs on my head today than I did yesterday. The seminary where I work has many buildings that are, over time, slowly aging and decaying. Yet, when I arrive at work each morning, I do not claim to arrive on a different campus. There is stability amidst the dynamics and development of life, just as there is semantic and structural stability amidst the dynamics and development of language.

Yet, the particle view in and of itself is inadequate. We need the wave perspective as well because we must be able to account for the change we see around us and the change that occurs in language.

> It would seem probable . . . that no variety of a static, particle view of language can provide the most useful conceptual framework for the description of dynamic historical change. Within a wave view of language, change over a period of time or over a geographical area could presumably be described more easily through intermediate, transitional, fusion stages than is provided by the particle view. To allow for this approach, however, one must assume that fusion can take

are tied to the PWF perspectives), he writes, "we use three modes, not two, because we have not been able to handle the data with two alone (and two distort the picture by leading to a system of separable parts additive rather than to a system of overlapping, simultaneously occurring elements). We use three rather than four or more since by a repeated application of the three we seem to be able to take care of the empirical data (and do not wish to add more than are empirically necessary). The choice of three, therefore, has been strictly an empirical one." Pike, *LRUT*, 85.

[41] I develop this in a theological setting in "Do You See How I See? The Trinitarian Roots of Human Perception," *WTJ* 79, no. 1 (Spring 2017): 59–76.

> place not only between particular segments in a sequence, but between systems in time, and that these systems in some sense act as waves with identifiable components.[42]

Pike is here picking up on the "diachronic" nature of the wave perspective. Because there is change, development, and progress both in reality and within units of language, we must be able to account for it somehow, and we do. We account for it, according to Pike, by seeing life and language not only in discrete chunks but also in waves, in movements that build, crest, and settle one upon another. Without the wave perspective, we could not process the units of language or our behavioral experiences coherently.

The field perspective, however, is also vital, for it extends beyond the synchronic particle perspective and the diachronic wave perspective into the systematic, relational nature of language and human behavior. A word, for instance, is never understood simply as a unit or even simply as a wave in motion.

> A word is seen not as part of a sequence alone, but as part of a whole class of words which are not being uttered at that particular time but are parts of the total potential behavioral field. A word is viewed against this larger background; it is viewed in reference to its contrastive relationships with words which are not being uttered at that particular moment. A word is seen as part of a total language system. It exists only as part of that system. Its meanings develop only in contrast to other words in the system. Its function is explicable only against the backdrop of the total language behavioral events of that system.[43]

[42] Pike, "Language as Particle, Wave, and Field," 139. The "systems" Pike is referencing here are the grammatical, phonological, and referential hierarchies, which we will explore in the pages ahead.

[43] Ibid., 140.

The field perspective, in other words, is

> a necessary antidote to an over-segmentation which treats as the only object of study the particular bits and pieces in a particular sequential relation or event. The necessity for this correction derives from the nature of language behavior itself. Language is a vehicle for communication. Yet communication cannot be done with abstract sequences by themselves. Communication requires understanding, and understanding requires a MEMORY reservoir, or pool of common experience, or field, against which particular speech events at a particular moment stand out as figure on ground, and provide the structure which provides the potential for patterned events. Without the total ground, the figure has no meaning, and no perceptual impact.[44]

All of this is to say that we need *all* of the observer perspectives, even though we choose one of them to focus on a particular unit of language or human behavior at a time. The nature of these perspectives as complementary and overlapping, combined with their equal necessity, is critical for Pike. Yet, these perspectives always have some object in view, something on which to focus. And that object is, for Pike, structured in three distinct ways. This leads us to the next tier of his theory.

Linguistic Units with Contrast, Variation, and Distribution (CVD)

Oftentimes when I speak with those who are familiar with Pike's language theory, they say something like, "Oh, yea—Kenneth Pike—particle, wave, and field." What many people do not know is that Pike's theory was built primarily on the triad of contrast,

[44] Ibid.

variation, and distribution (hereafter CVD). His magnum opus was largely dedicated to what he called the feature, manifestation, and distribution modes (hereafter FMD). These modes were perspectival, in a way similar to that of the PWF perspectives. Yet, one of the distinguishing marks between the two triads is that the PWF perspectives give more attention to the *observer* while the FMD modes give more attention to the linguistic or behavioral *unit* under focus. It is worth noting here his initial descriptions of the FMD modes before moving on to consider their more mature form (CVD).

Feature, Manifestation, and Distribution Modes (FMD)

When reading the following descriptions, remember that Pike's theory is meant to address both verbal and nonverbal behavior, so the phrase "emic unit of activity" includes both verbal and nonverbal behaviors.

> The *feature mode* of an emic unit of activity will in general be viewed as composed of simultaneously occurring identificational-contrastive components, with its internal segmentation analyzed with special reference to stimulus-response features (including purpose or lexical meaning, where relevant). Example: the voicing, bilabiality, and occlusion of /b/ contrasted with the voicelessness, alveolarity, and continuant sibilant nature of /s/ . . .
>
> The *manifestation mode* of an emic unit of activity will often be viewed as composed of nonsimultaneously occurring physical variants (or nonsimultaneous components), with its internal segmentation analyzed with special reference to the hierarchy of the mechanisms of its physical production. Phonological example: The /t/ at the beginning of *tatter* is followed by a characteristic puff of breath, whereas the one in the middle, for American English, has a light flip of the tongue. Morphological example: The phonological component of the plural morpheme in *tubs* and in *houses* differs.

> The *distribution mode* of an emic unit of activity will be seen as composed of relational components, including its class membership and its function in a slot of a hierarchically-ordered larger construction (its external distribution), and its internal segmentation (its internal distribution), especially in reference to the hierarchy of mechanisms of its physical production. Example: The sound /b/ is a member of a class of consonants, which occur in the pre-syllabic slot of a syllable. The morpheme *boy* is a member of a class of animate nouns; may occur in subject, object, and other positions in the clause, and internally is made up of a characteristic sequence of sounds comprising a syllable.[45]

This language may be too technical for some readers, but here is what Pike is saying about each mode essentially. The feature mode looks at elements of a linguistic unit in terms of what sets it apart from other units (contrastive) and what serves to identify it no matter where it occurs (identification). An example he often gave was the difference in the initial consonant sound in words such as "zeal" and "seal." The "z" sound has an articulation that contrasts with that of the "s" sound—both are sibilants, but the "z" sound is voiced whereas the "s" is not. This contrast also serves to identify the "z" sound when it occurs in all of its other contexts. We know, for instance, that "zero" and "zephyr" can be identified as beginning with the same sound. Thus, the "z" sound not only contrasts with the "s" sound; it also serves as an identifying marker when the language user does not need to be explicitly aware of that contrast. That is why Pike would use the phrase "contrastive-identificational" features. Though the phrase is not as eloquent as we might like, it does have the advantage of including the elements that Pike had in mind (both *contrast* and *identity*).

The manifestation mode examines the particular physical variant (or occurrence) of the linguistic unit. Variants here involve both

[45] Pike, *LRUT*, 85–86.

shared identity and uniqueness. For example, we might pronounce the word "says" thousands of times. In one sense, every occurrence is the same to us. Yet, each particular pronunciation is also in some sense unique—each is a manifestation (hence the title of this mode) of the same linguistic unit, though that unit may sound slightly different in certain contexts. The sounds surrounding the unit in focus affect our pronunciation of it. "He says," may be pronounced rapidly as "ee-sez." In that pronunciation, there is a particular movement from the vowel sound in "he" to the sibilant "s." In the phrase "Jonathan says," there is another unique movement—this time from the ending consonant "n" to the sibilant.

This mode is perhaps more easily recognized with an example of nonverbal behavior. There are many different ways I can begin eating breakfast when I walk into the kitchen. I can pray and thank God for the food I have, or I can open the refrigerator and scan the shelves for yogurt, or I can sit at the counter and think about what options I have, or I can go directly to the pantry and take out the bread. Each of these actions is a manifestation of the same emic unit of behavior, that of "beginning breakfast." Variants, in this sense, might be thought of as simply *unique occurrences*; they are the particularities that fill our day to day activities.

Lastly, the distribution mode examines the placement of the unit and its internal components with reference to larger systems. The verb "says" fills a particular syntactical slot within a sentence, serving as the action, and it is taken from a class of verbs that could also have filled that particular slot. Internally, "says" is comprised of a pattern of sounds: consonant-vowel-consonant. It also ends with a singular morpheme ("s") that is taken from a group of other potential endings ("ing," indicating the participle or progressive tense, or no "s," indicating the plural). The distribution mode, in other words, looks at units in terms of where they occur (slot), what classes of words they are taken from (class), and what internal components they have, each of those internal components being part of a system or matrix (such as verb endings, consonant-vowel patterns, and so on).

Now, each of these modes has a "smallest unit" with which a person can begin analysis. First, in the feature mode, the smallest unit is an *emic motif.*[46] In terms of nonverbal behavior, we can think of an emic motif as simply an irreducible chunk of human activity. In terms of verbal behavior, an emic motif is a *morpheme*. Second, in the manifestation mode, the smallest unit is called the *acteme*, which is

> characterized by identificational-contrastive components constituted of a physical activity; it is manifested by free or conditioned, simple or complex, fused or clearly-segmented variants; it is distributed not only within the larger units of the manifestation mode of the behavioreme, but is simultaneously distributed within minimum or large units of the feature mode of the behavioreme . . . and it occurs within . . . a structured physical setting.[47]

A *phoneme* is a verbal acteme. Recall that phonemes are merely sounds that lead to different meanings for speakers of the language. The "l" sound leads to a unique meaning in the word "legion" as compared to the "r" sound in "region." A native speaker will thus interpret the two words as different in meaning. Third, in the distribution mode, the smallest unit is called the a *motifemic-slot-class-correlative* (the name needed work), which is "characterized by an emic slot

[46] "An EMIC MOTIF (or motifeme) is a minimum, active, trimodally structured, emic segment or component of human activity, within the hierarchy of the feature mode of a minimum or included behavioreme or hyper-behavioreme." Ibid., 150. A "behavioreme" is simply an emic unit of behavior that has a specified purpose within the system. Pike describes it as "an emic segment or component of purposive human activity." Ibid., 121. A verbal behavioreme Pike called an "uttereme." A hyper-behavioreme is simply a complex behavioreme: a behavioreme that contains within it more than one smaller behavioreme.

[47] Ibid., 291. Notice here that each of the smallest units within each mode can itself be viewed perspectivally with the feature, manifestation, and distribution modes.

correlated with a morpheme class."[48] A *tagmeme* is a verbal motifemic-slot-class-correlative (which is where Pike's theory—*tagmemics*—gets its name).

These minimum units in each mode are then built upon hierarchically to form more complex structures and units of discourse or behavior. For example, in the feature mode, the morpheme would be understood as the lowest level of the hierarchy, and it would be added to at successive levels to form words, phrases, clauses, sentences, paragraphs, etc.

The foreign vocabulary and neologisms here have likely contributed to Pike's initial work (*LRUT*) not being as widely accepted as it might have been. It is perhaps for that reason that Pike later simplified his theory and replaced some of these terms with more accessible ones in his *Linguistic Concepts*. Though the ideas above would remain in the background of his theory, he would eventually abandon the terminology and replace it with a new triad and a simplified set of "sub-terms."

Contrast, Variation, and Distribution (CVD)

The CVD triad would come to replace the FMD modes and would allow Pike to set forth his theory in terms that could be more readily received by the layman. As with his initial exposition of his thought, Pike wanted his theory to apply not just to language but to all of human behavior. So, the introduction of contrast and identification (replacing the feature mode) for a unit would take on the following language.

> Recognition of a unit involves a curious difficulty: We do not know what something is unless we know something about what it is *not*. Recognition is, in part, negative. In part, it deals with the contrast between units, rather than with the identification of isolated units. One does not know what a

[48] Ibid., 194.

> horse is if he cannot tell it from a cow. One does not know Susie James if one cannot tell her from Susie Pennyfeather.
>
> The same components which help us to see that one unit differs from another also help us to *recognize* the unit when it is no longer close to the one which we separated it from. If, for example, we treat *seal* and *zeal* as two different words, with the /s/ and /z/ being two different sounds as components of the two words, then we can use either /s/ or /z/ to recognize words where they do *not* pair up in contrasts—as *zebra* is clearly recognizable even when no **sebra* can be found (with the asterisk before the word meaning that no such instance is known). Features which are contrastive in relation to some contexts are *identificational* in others.[49]

The final line betrays the older terminology (i.e., "features"), but aside from that, the theory is dressed in more casual attire. The number of neologisms is reduced (e.g., "emic motif") to make room for a clear and applicable analytical principle: contrast and identity are critical components of linguistic and behavioral units. We do not always note this contrast and identification, and sometimes the contrastive-identificational features of two linguistic units are considered irrelevant. The difference in meaning between "he studied her face" and "he examined her face" is virtually unnoticeable to many people. When contrast and identity become important, however, is when the distinction between units has semantic or interpretive ramifications within a social setting. Thus, Pike writes, "the human being learns most easily to pick up contrasts between elements which are highly significant to him. If, for example, two similar words are such that one is obscene and the other is not, it is astonishing how much faster he learns to hear the relevant contrast of sound than he does if he has no social problem growing out of error."[50] This same phenomenon

[49] Pike, *LC*, 42.
[50] Ibid., 44.

also applies to units that serve similar semantic functions but differ in their connotations or contextual appropriateness. The hushing sound ("sshhh") and the verb "shut up" express the same broader meaning—telling another person to keep quiet. But someone sitting in a pew at church would likely never turn to his neighbor and tell him to shut up. The contrast between the two expressions demands awareness by the speaker, lest he be misinterpreted as rude and offensive.

As we will see in the pages ahead, contrastive-identificational features can be seen in units within their grammatical, phonological, and referential contexts. The quality of our voice when we are under extreme pressure or stress is noticeably different from its quality when we are relaxed. There may be stuttering, abrupt pauses, rapid articulation, or a general "shakiness" in the former context, each of which can serve as a contrastive-identificational component of a particular word we have spoken within that context. This can have profound effects on the meaning of the utterance. When we here a shaky voice quickly repeating "I'm fine, I'm fine, I'm fine," we do not interpret that to mean that the person is actually "fine." We infer the opposite: that the person is under duress or is extremely nervous. Examples such as this show how important the contrastive-identificational components of a linguistic unit can be.

Variation (replacing the manifestation mode) is likewise more accessibly expressed by Pike in his later work (*LC*). He introduces the notion of variation in reference to the phenomenon of change. "Normal social behavior requires that we be able to recognize identities in spite of change. Unless we can do so, there can be no human society as we know it."[51] In other words, there are "those features of a unit which may change *without causing the loss of recognizability* of the unit. The appropriate observer readily recognizes that certain changes do not affect deeper identities."[52] To put this in terms that might be understood in light of Pike's earlier work, he is saying

[51] Ibid., 52.
[52] Ibid.

that we can have multiple variants (physical manifestations) of the same linguistic unit. To use a previous example, every day I probably utter the word "say," but each time I do so, the variation is ever so slightly different (as would be perceived with advanced recording equipment). Yet, this is never recognized as a set of different verbs by those to whom I speak. No one replies, "What do you mean by 'say'? You pronounced the same word yesterday but with more emphasis on the 's.'" The concept of variation is meant to show that there can be change without the loss of identity. Again, this is true for units of language and human behavior with regards to reference, grammar, and phonology.

Referentially, I enter the same office every day and sit in the same chair, but the office is a slight variation on the version from the previous day: the carpet fibers might be dispersed in new locations or combed in a certain direction because of the vacuum cleaner; the paint on the wall has aged several more hours; dust particles have gathered on the computer keyboard, etc. These environmental changes do not mean that I have entered a new room—at least not in any sense that the average person would understand. This is still the same office, even amidst *minor* environmental variation. If there were *major* environmental variation (e.g., the room had caught on fire and was mostly destroyed), then would I be tempted to say that this is no longer "my office."

Grammatically, there can be *free* or *conditioned* variation. An example of free variation would be the placement of the adverb "yesterday" in the sentence, "Yesterday I went to church." There is no change in meaning if I say, "I went to church yesterday." Because none of the other grammatical units are affected by the change in placement, this is considered free. An example of conditioned variation would be the change in subject in the sentences "He considers it difficult" and "They consider it difficult." The change of pronoun in the subject position conditions the change that must occur in the verb, from singular to plural. One point that is important to note in these examples is that sometimes variation is intentionally different (emic), reflecting a distinct purpose of the language user, while other times variation is unintentionally different (etic).

Phonologically, there can be changes in intonation that are purposive and affect meaning as well as those that are unintentional and should not affect meaning. Typically in English, the intonation rises at the end of a question such as "How have you been?" Yet, if the intonation does not rise at the end of the utterance, that does not necessarily mean a question is not being asked. The grammatical form (placing the helping verb before the subject) and referential meaning supplement the pronunciation—which is always the case in language (there is an interlocking and overlapping relationship for grammar, phonology, and reference). However, intonation can be critical when the intended meaning is sarcastic. The intonation patterns for the sentence, "He's as smart as Einstein" are prime examples. If my intonation goes up on the word "Einstein," I am likely being sarcastic, but if it remains flat, I may be speaking more literally and offering someone a compliment.

In sum, the variation of a linguistic unit (whether referentially, grammatically, or phonologically) shows us that there can be continuing identity or sameness of some kind even in the midst of change.

Lastly, distribution (a term that remained the same in Pike's earlier and later theoretical formulations) brings out the necessity of seeing relationships and systems within language and human behavior.

> Some place must be the point of origin for the coordinates which allow one to identify oneself in a place in the larger world. Something must tell us where we are, beyond reference to our immediate environment. Reference to successively larger patterns of occurrences, to a larger *universe of discourse*, is necessary if one is to know the significance of a person, a thing, or a word. Knowing that I'm behind my nose does not tell me how to find the way to town. I need to be

> oriented in reference to a larger context, to a universe—or to a discourse. The *I* of a discourse (in relation to *you*) suggests that the speaker knows something about his social relations. But unless one goes beyond oneself and his neighbor to a hierarchically ordered outside world, he is in some sense lost within himself.[53]

We find in this statement an awareness of the relational nature of language and reality. Just as persons, places, and events are interconnected in a complex web of purposive human behavior, so the bits and chunks of language—morphemes, phonemes, tagmemes, words, phrases, clauses, paragraphs—are interrelated and are drawn from matrices of structurally similar items. This is important not just for the sake of our understanding of broader relationships within language and human behavior, but even for the foundational notion of identity. The identification of a linguistic unit cannot be known in utter isolation. "Knowledge of identity includes knowledge of relevant distribution."[54]

As with the contrast and variation elements of the CVD triad, this distributional element applies not only to language but to persons.[55] "A person, like a word in grammatical construction, has a place in a particular social structure which in part identifies him by providing for him certain social roles . . . . In turn, he himself comprises part of that larger kinship structure, just as the noun phrase does not exist without words."[56] We will explore the implications of this in the final chapter.

Distribution in the context of language primarily refers to *slots*, *sequences*, and *classes*. "A word or the class of words of which it is a member is in part . . . characterized or identified by the structured *sequences* (*grammatical constructions*, *syntactic units*) of which it is a

[53] Ibid., 60.
[54] Ibid., 62.
[55] This is discussed in greater detail in the final chapter.
[56] Pike, *LC*, 62.

part. That is, a unit is in part defined by the constructions in which it occurs, in addition to the class of items of which it is an appropriate substitute member within such structure sequences."[57] One member of a class of animate nouns, for example ("John," "Ralph," "the dog," "a groundhog"), can fill the slot of the subject position in the sentence "_________ walked across the street."

Distribution, however, not only draws our attention to classes of words that can fill particular slots in a sequence. It also forces us to reject the notion that there are, in any pure sense, "random" occurrences of linguistic units, that is, the occurrence of units without reference to a symmetrical and structured whole.

> Human nature is such that for verbal and nonverbal systems to be operable at all, they must have *some* symmetry about them. Totally random structures are not serviceable in human interaction; a field structure lies at its heart. This does *not* affirm that no exceptions can occur; nor does it affirm that no irregularities will be found. Rather, it affirms that *some* degree of systematization can be found in every functioning structure. It follows that human nature cannot be described accurately, purely in terms of isolated units of sound, purely in terms of classes of such sounds without reference to a system, or in terms of a miscellaneous list of rules for combining them. Nor can mere lists or taxonomies of events, gestures, behavior elements, abstract semantic components, or abstract formal rules of action describe human activity in a way satisfactory to us. Somewhere, to some degree, the distributional relation of a unit to a background system must enter the definition of every unit either as an implicit underlying assumption or as an explicit part of the descriptive mechanism.[58]

[57] Ibid.
[58] Ibid., 65.

Before ending this section, we should note that the CVD triad, which came to replace the FMD modes, is meant to show that *every linguistic unit is "trimodally" structured.* In other words, every unit of language has contrast, variation, and distribution. What's more, the elements of this triad overlap and interlock. Take, for example, the word "studied" in the sentence "He studied early in the morning." In terms of contrast and identity, "studied" is a unique sequence of sounds that expresses a particular action. It is also set apart from other forms of the verb by its final morpheme (which follows the pattern for verbs ending with the letter "y"). However, the word in this particular sentence is also a variant, both of the verb "study" and of the possible class of verbs that could fill this particular slot (e.g., "ran," "ate breakfast," "meditated"). The latter element brings out the distributional mode—the verb is from a class of similar units that fill a slot in this grammatical sequence. All this is to say that, when viewing every linguistic unit, we have various triads that are present simultaneously, including the PWF perspectives for the observer and the trimodal structuring of a unit according to CVD. The final triad that we have yet to explore is that of grammar, phonology, and reference (GPR). We have hinted at this in various places, but now we can give it more specific treatment.

Grammar, Phonology, and Reference (GPR)

The GPR triad is unique in the sense that it foregrounds the hierarchical nature of language and human behavior. This hierarchical nature is presupposed with PWF and CVD, but takes a prominent place when we come to focus more explicitly on grammar, phonology (including pronunciation), and reference (or meaning). Before discussing each element of this triad, note that thus far we have moved from *perspectives* (PWF) to *units* (CVD) to *hierarchical structure* (GPR). This order of exposition is intentionally mirroring that which Pike presented in *LC*. Perhaps one of the reasons why he did this was to save more complex matters for later in the book.

This hierarchical discussion is thus building upon what Pike has introduced at a more fundamental level (i.e., the nature of human observation and of individual linguistic units), but it was bound to come sooner or later, since "the relevant structural inclusion of parts within a whole, with the whole in its turn becoming one part of a still larger whole, is an important component of [his] approach."[59]

Grammar

The grammatical hierarchy, like each of the other hierarchies, is broken up into somewhat discrete *levels*, though sometimes the boundaries between these levels are fuzzy. For Pike, "each major type of level has some *kind of function* in behavior. Its structural arrangement, its form, has simultaneously a general kind of impact on the hearer (which we can call the *meaning* of that level)."[60] Pike suggests several hierarchical levels that have some broad impact in social settings, the latter of which are grammatical. This is illustrated in figure 2.3.[61]

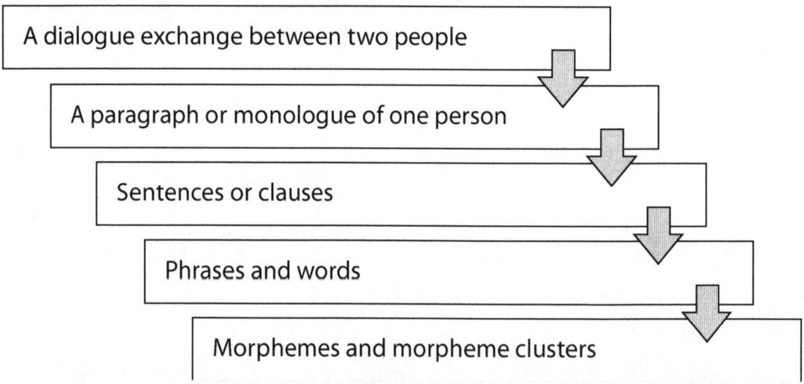

Fig. 2.3. Levels of the Grammatical Hierarchy

[59] Ibid., 70.
[60] Ibid., 72.
[61] This is taken from examples he provides on p. 73 in *LC*.

Pike is quick to point out that the precise emic function of each of the levels is complex and should not be oversimplified. The sentence level, for example, may not merely serve a confined set of behavioral functions. Instead, the person analyzing the language must keep the context in mind and draw conclusions about the function of each unit in the hierarchy as it is related to the larger universe of that particular discourse. Certainly, we may find patterns within language and even across languages, but it would be reductionistic and unhelpful to come up with a discrete list of functions for each level of the grammatical hierarchy and then attempt to fit the actual manifestations of language into the categories we have developed. Structural analysis is meant to serve language, not vice versa.

Still, this would not prevent Pike from developing a somewhat systematic approach for analyzing linguistic units. This is where we encounter the now famous (at least in linguistic circles) notion of *tagmemes*. In simple terms, a tagmeme is a *unit-in-context*. However, there are for Pike four components of that context, as illustrated in figure 2.4.

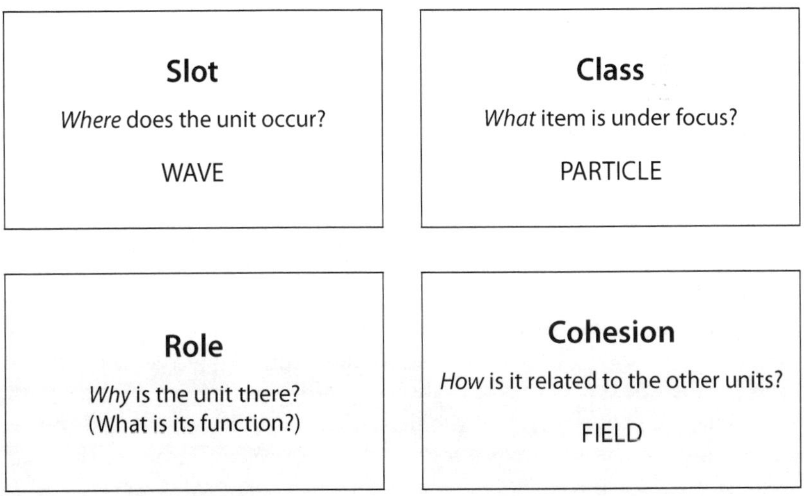

Fig. 2.4. The Tagmeme

Four question words help to solidify the function of each box.[62] The slot is the syntactic location where the unit occurs. The subject of a sentence, for instance, can go in the initial slot of a simple clause: "He wrote a book." The class comprises the group of items (fillers) that appropriately fit the slot. The role box highlights the function of the unit. Here, "He" would be considered subject-as-actor. Cohesion would then draw our attention to the necessary background that might be controlling the item under focus. We can say a bit more about each of these boxes.

With regards to structural slots, "hierarchical grammatical structures are characterized by parts making up wholes, which in turn make up other larger entities. But for a *general* entity to be recognizable as emically the same, with etic variation involving substituted parts, those parts must somehow be seen as occurring within constant structural positions."[63] These constant structural positions are *slots*. Each slot is filled by a class of substitutable items. "At any point in a grammatical structure we can expect to be able to substitute one of various lexical items for another without affecting the *proportion* (the general, not lexically specific, relationship) between the various kinds of chunks of the unit."[64]

[62] Though the issue is too complex to get into here, there is debate within the field of tagmemics as to the necessity of the four boxes. For one example of a revision to the four-box tagmeme, see Vern. S. Poythress, "Hierarchy in Discourse Analytics: A Revision of Tagmemics," *Semiotica* 40, no. 1/2 (1982): 107–37. For my part, it seems that the cohesion box treats linguistic units at a fundamentally larger level than that of slot, class, and role. Notice that the role box does not have a PWF perspective attached to it. If the cohesion of a linguistic unit were treated elsewhere, that would leave us with a three box system (Slot-Class-Role) in which we would naturally pair the field perspective with the role box since role is always determined with regards to a frame of reference. Of course, each of the perspectives (PWF) can be used to view the slot or the class or the role, but Pike attached one of the perspectives more prominently to each box.

[63] Pike, *LC*, 76.

[64] Ibid.

Regarding the role of a particular unit, he writes,

> the *same* class may have a sharply *different* role from one sentence to another. If I say *I smelled a skunk*, the role of the skunk in the act is quite different from that in *The skunk smelled me*. Who is doing what? In the one case it is I who am doing the smelling; in the other it is the skunk. But in the passive form, *I am smelled by skunk*, I am not doing the smelling, even though I am the subject of the clause. It is this kind of fact that forces a long-known difference between form and function in grammatical relations.[65]

Pike adds that there can be etic variability when it comes to the meaning of a certain role. For instance, the actor in one sentence can be voluntary but in another sentence may be involuntary.[66]

Lastly, with regards to cohesion, "something has to tie words together in some kind of coherent whole, or talk and the perception of the world revealed by that talk would be a random madhouse. Talk structures must have their parts in internal *systemic agreement*, often marked as such by particular bits."[67] These bits can include the background frame of reference concerning the number for verbs, nouns, and pronouns (i.e., subject-verb and pronoun-antecedent agreement), or even the selection of a pronoun. "It," for example," would be a more cohesive choice than "him," if we are referencing a stone or some other inanimate object. The use of the present tense in telling a story, for Pike, would be another example of cohesion.[68]

The slot, class, role, and cohesion elements are related to other terminology that has long been "known to linguists: (1) *syntagmatic* relation to a sequence of parts in a larger whole [slot], (2) *paradigmatic* class, of appropriate replaceable parts in a comparable place

[65] Ibid.
[66] Ibid., 77.
[67] Ibid.
[68] Ibid.

[class], (3) *pragmatic* relevance of behavioral function of that kind of chunk [role], (4) *agreement* of items."[69]

The purpose of Pike's tagmeme was to account for the detail that linguists encountered in the field. The complexity of this four-box system, in other words, is meant to accommodate the complexity of detail that analysts find in living language. In addition—and this is crucial for Pike—the tagmeme was introduced and employed by Pike and many others as a tool that, in principle, showed "that *all* units are perceived as relevant *only* in relation to an including context or a set of contexts."[70] This affirmation in itself might be easy to accept. Where Pike's thought truly became radical (in the best possible sense of that word) is when he suggested—in the spirit of Edward Sapir—that tagmemic theory could be expanded to consider human behavior *beyond* language. In other words, language as a whole must fit into its cultural context, amidst a panoply of other human behaviors that are also part of one's emic context.

Phonology

There will be, no doubt, similarities between the grammatical and phonological hierarchies, though Pike would be quick to say that none of the hierarchies is always coterminous with the others in its boundaries for parallel levels.[71] While the grammatical hierarchy builds upon the morpheme at its base, the phonological hierarchy builds upon the phoneme. This is not, however, to be understood as a fundamentally different unit, for while we discuss a unit in terms of its place in the grammatical hierarchy, "at the *same time*, the *same substance*—for example, the same sentence—is arranged differently, into phonological chunks."[72] Yet, the distinct boundaries of elements

[69] Ibid., 79.

[70] Ibid.

[71] For details, see *LRUT*, 565–85. For Pike, the hierarchies each represent and structure the same data. This has obvious Trinitarian connections, as will be made more explicit in the following chapter.

[72] Pike, *LC*, 84.

within each hierarchy is part of the justification for the hierarchies themselves. The expression "I'd" is only one unit phonologically but two units grammatically (representing "I would" or "I had").

The phonological hierarchy, while built upon the phoneme, predominantly focuses on the syllable and the stress group. Figure 2.5 represents the general levels of the phonological hierarchy, mirroring the previous diagram of the grammatical hierarchy.

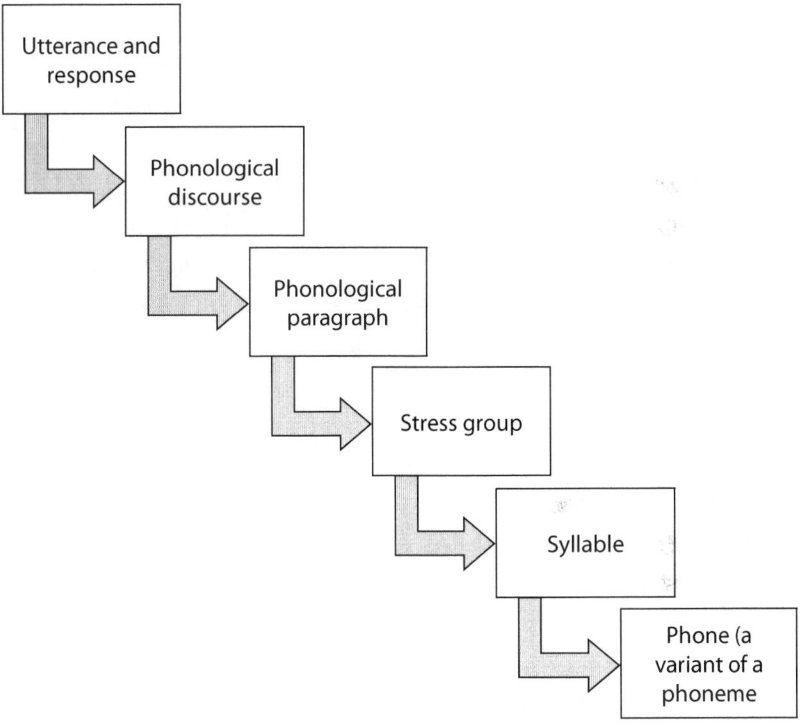

Fig. 2.5. Levels of the Phonological Hierarchy

We should note at this point that each of the hierarchies seemed to pair well with one of the PWF perspectives. The grammatical hierarchy, with its focus on structural units, naturally draws out the particle perspective. The phonological hierarchy, because of the attention given to movements of sound, pairs with the wave perspective.[73] The referential hierarchy, focusing on the linguistic systems in context and the interrelations of real world referents, suits the field perspective. Of course, each of the perspectives can be used with each of the hierarchies, but there is a natural appropriation of a prominent perspective for each one.

Phonemes can thus be seen as waves of sound, and their placement within syllables and words helps us to distinguish them from one another, when such distinctions are emically relevant.[74]

> The articulatory movement toward the nucleus of such a wave of sound, or the movement away from that nucleus, can be important and contrastive. This can be seen, for example, if one merely hums the sounds *m*, *n*, and the sound -*ng* of *song*, without a vowel; they sound much more alike than they seem to us if we speak aloud the words *sum*, *sun*, *sung*—where the glide off from the vowels helps to enhance our perception of the contrast. Similarly, the (usually) longer vowel in *cub* may help us to tell the -*b* from the -*p* of *cup*, where the vowel may be shorter.[75]

This applies also to the elements at higher levels of the phonological hierarchy. A syllable, for instance, is a unit with "a nuclear element

[73] Pike does, however, dedicate a small section of his chapter on the phonological hierarchy to the "field characteristics of phonology seen via intonation" (*LC*, 91), which is quite helpful in reminding us that intonation "contours" (as he called them) often reflect the speaker's attitude. The acoustic patterns and voice quality of a speaker, in other words, are almost always emically relevant (94–95).

[74] Consider, for instance, the dialectically different pronunciation that I hear of the word *roof* in certain suburban areas of Philadelphia: *ruf* (pronounced like *rough*). Here there is an etic difference, but that difference is not emically relevant, since the same noun is meant referentially in both cases. A non-native English speaker, however, may not realize this and consider *roof* and *ruf* to be two different words.

[75] *LC*, 86.

comprising at least a vowel or a syllabic consonant . . . , and sometimes two or more vowels . . . in some languages; and with a post-margin consonant or group of consonants."[76] Likewise, a stress group has an accented syllable or word, and a phonological paragraph has "nuclear theme material" that may be "pronounced slowly, distinctly, loudly, and with relatively high pitch, whereas a marginal element, such as an aside . . . may be more rapid, softer, lower in pitch, and perhaps less distinct."[77]

One of the strengths of Pike's phonological hierarchy—and of Pike's theory in general—is its ability to capture authentic speech sounds in the real world, including dialectical variation. And because the phonological hierarchy interlocks with the grammatical and referential hierarchies, the linguist and the layman can adequately account for more of the data presented to them in authentic situations. For example, my grandmother had a heavy New England accent. When pronouncing the word *more*, she would say what sounded like *moe-ah*. Thus, her pronunciation can be understood phonologically as comprised of two distinguishable speech sounds, and yet I had no problem understanding her because, grammatically, I understood what morpheme she meant in the context (reference).[78] This brings us to the final hierarchy.

Reference

The referential hierarchy focuses on the meanings and behavioral activities referenced by linguistic units, including the social and physical background of those units. It foregrounds our understanding of real-world identity and semantic difference.

The referential hierarchy is clearly distinct from the grammatical and phonological hierarchies, though it interlocks with them.

[76] Ibid., 89.

[77] Ibid.

[78] As another example of the interlocking of hierarchies, Pike suggested that we can have phonological tagmemes (*LC*, 96). There can also be referential tagmemes (*LC*, 101).

For example, in a single paragraph, we may encounter the following words: "God," "He," "the Lord," "God almighty," and "Yahweh." Each of these words is phonologically different, and there are clear grammatical differences between each word: some are single nouns, one is a pronoun, two are noun phrases. However, the *reference* for all of these words is the same. That is to say, there is a common referential unit being manifested here with grammatical and phonological variation. This makes perfect sense because "*Every* manifestation (mention) of a referential unit *must* be in *some* grammatical form; the difference is that the emically same referential item may be in many *different* grammatical forms."[79] Yet, while there is a clear distinction between hierarchies, there are nevertheless paired hierarchical levels. Just as a word (grammatical) and a name (referential) can be viewed on the same level of their respective hierarchies, so can a phrase and the mention of a name as part of a larger group. Before drawing additional connections between the hierarchies, however, it would be helpful to get a sense of what the levels of the referential hierarchy look like as compared to those in the other hierarchies.

A glance at figure 2.6 reveals that the lowest level of the referential hierarchy is not a morpheme or a phoneme but a *contrastive feature*, namely a physical or semantic component of a unit. Following this level is that which contains *names* or *actions*.[80] Perhaps paralleling the level of the sentence on the grammatical hierarchy is the *simple event* in the referential hierarchy—a single actor and action. From there, events can be compounded with other events, leading to more and more complex "event-groups."[81]

[79] Pike, *LC*, 98.

[80] I have added "actions" to "names" here, the latter of which is what occurs in Pike's discussion on pages 97–99 of *LC*. "Names," it seems to me, can certainly cover the labels we have for actions. Pike may well have meant to include actions, but the use of "names" alone might suggests that he has only nouns in mind, which does not seem to be the case.

[81] This is my terminology, not Pike's.

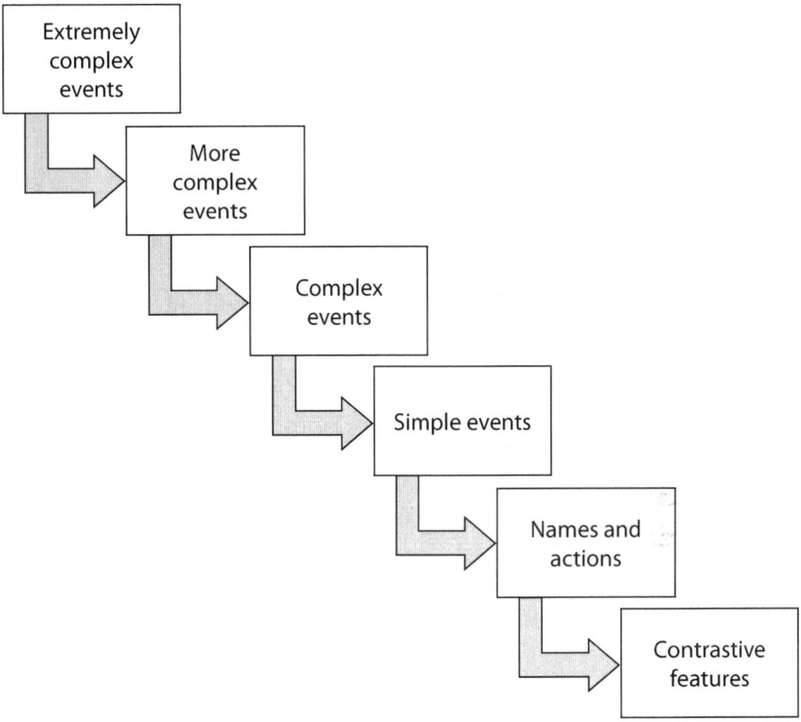

Fig. 2.6. Levels of the Referential Hierarchy

Now, we have examined a tagmeme in the grammatical hierarchy, and Pike noted that there can also be phonological and referential tagmemes. The latter might be helpful to explore given the distinctness of reference as compared to grammar and phonology. Remember that the tagmeme has four boxes: slot, class, role, and cohesion.

> *Purpose* . . . finds its place in the role cell, in the description of the event; and so likewise does the relevance in the description of a member of the cast or of a prop. On the event level it is relevant, for example, that a joke is *intended* when one says *Socrates drank himself to death*. On the level of cast, likewise, it is relevant to know who is the hero—or

> the villain—in a film . . . . That is, the role cell may be filled explicitly by the analyst, or tacitly by the native reader; pure formal analysis without reference to meaning or purpose or relevance cannot provide an analysis which can satisfy those who wish to know sensibly "what happened."
>
> Such roles can be complicated. An event may have a purpose leading to a larger purpose; or motives may be mixed (dual). And a person's role may appear different from the point of view of different observers, each of whom has his own *interpretations* of (or guesses about) the purposes of others. . . .
>
> An event as described may enter a marginal slot in a series of events leading toward the crucial, nuclear event under attention. The item filling that slot of the description is one member of the paraphrase set identifiable by the speaker as (emically) the same from his point of view . . . .
>
> But for the narration of an event to be intelligible to the hearer, there must be a degree of cohesion of *actual expectancies* of the hearer with the expectancies expected *of* him by the speaker, and a degree of coherence—if the hearer thinks that facts are being recounted—with the view of reality as believed in by the hearer.[82]

Pike offered a diagram, which I have simplified in figure 2.7, to summarize the referential tagmeme.

It is very important to note—in light of the broader implications of Pike's theory—that a *person* can also be a tagmeme. Any individual performing an action fits into a slot in a sequence of events, is a particular member of the class of persons that could fill that slot, plays a unique role in the event, and engages coherently with the patterns of behavior and assumptions in a given context. Every person, for Pike,

[82] Pike, *LC*, 100.

Slot

Where the subvent occurred, as nuclear or marginal event to the including event

Class

What happened, emically defined as being one member of a paraphrase set acceptable to the narrator

Role

Why the actor performed the event (or the alleged cause)

Cohesion

How the event coheres with underlying belief systems

Fig. 2.7. The Referential Tagmeme

> lives in *referential space*—in interlocking tacit or implicit frames of reference of *time* sequence, *spatial* array, *physical* relationships, *logical* coherence, *social* structures, *psychological* involvement, *belief* systems about reality, *intersecting events*, and others. No person can bring into words all at one moment the content of each of these in all its detail. Selection must be made if one is to talk at all; the balance must be left unstated at that moment, even though it remains as a strong force controlling much of the talk.[83]

The referential context—the frame of reference—is thus a foundational component of communicative reality.

In ending our discussion of the grammatical, phonological, and referential hierarchies, it is imperative to keep in mind that these hierarchies are not isolated from one another. Rather, "there are . . . three separate structurings of the same substance, but structurings

[83] Ibid., 103.

which may not have the same beginnings and endings or sequential (or other) relationships of all or of some of their parts."[84]

We come now to the final part of our initial outline: the importance of context. This will bring the chapter to a close.

The Importance of Context

It can scarcely be overstated how important context was to Pike throughout his career. Indeed, tagmemics takes its name from the tagmeme, which he defined early on as a *unit-in-context.*

Curiously, he begins the final section of *LC* with a discussion not about context but about observers. This may seem odd, but it makes sense if one is familiar with Pike's theory. *Every* discussion of language and its analysis (along with our analysis of the rest of human behavior) begins with the *person.* This was accounted for in our etic-emic discussion and the PWF perspectives. We are reminded, both at the beginning and the end of Pike's language theory, that *persons* are central to our use and understanding of language. It is perhaps this feature of his theory that helps to distinguish Pike's thought from the panoply of language theories that we find today. Many theories—intentionally or inadvertently—introduce the study of language as a scientific, impersonal enterprise. Pike would never accept this, for it betrays a fundamentally *impersonal* view of reality. I have argued elsewhere that this runs against the grain of his biblical worldview (and, by implication, every biblical Christian's worldview).[85] Thus, he writes,

> One can avoid many problems of the moment and pacify the snarls of a dominant scientific paradigm by agreeing to accept its overpowering postulates. ("Do you want to know a sure

[84] Ibid., 112.

[85] Hibbs, "Where Person Meets Word: Part 1"; "Where Person Meets Word Part 2: The Convergence of Personalism and Scripture in the Language Theory of Kenneth L. Pike," *WTJ* 78, no. 1 (Spring 2016): 117–34.

> way to conciliate a tiger? Let him swallow you.") But if those postulates cancel the possibility of including the observer himself in the situation and among the data observed, and hence of observer flexibility in choice of viewpoint and in the possibility of adopting different viewpoints for different purposes of the moment, one has allowed his scientific freedom to be swallowed up and science itself to become *nothing but* an unattainable abstract ideal in a dreamed-of unreachable reductionism, or else in an abstracting idealism which splits me from you, us from things, and things from human knowledge.[86]

The final part of his book is then broken up into a triad (which we might expect) of elements that, from three different perspectives, cover the same material as that addressed in the previous sections. "This is inevitable in tagmemic theory," he says, "since *each* of its perspectives covers *all* the same data."[87] We will end the present chapter, then, with a summary of Pike's thought on form-meaning composites, sharing as prerequisite to change, and universes of discourse.

Form-Meaning Composites

Again, at the outset of his chapter on the relationship between form and meaning, he openly declares,

> I am rejecting all views of language or life which claim that *abstract* forms comprise basic reality. Here, as over against centuries of work by some scholars, *form* is a term used to refer to concretely structured elements which include a physical component, not idealized disembodied realities, essences, ideas—or even rules or relations. In addition to

[86] Pike, *LC*, 109.
[87] Ibid.

> form, a meaning, relevance, value, significance, deduced cause, result of a deduced cause, or some other *observer-related component* is always demanded in our affirmation of the existence of any unit of rational behavior, of the existence of the observability of any concrete object or event, or of any object or event as deduced by man or imagined by man.[88]

What Pike is getting at here is that form and meaning, as observed by a person in a particular situation, are inextricably bound up with one another. "Each unit of each level of each hierarchy—grammatical, phonological, and referential—has a physical component. In tagmemic theory there is no semantic hierarchy abstracted away from all physical manifestation."[89] This is fairly novel since Pike is accustomed to seeing linguists throughout history treat form and meaning in relative isolation or in abstraction.

The form-meaning units of language manifest themselves in each of the hierarchies. Yet, because each of the hierarchies was simply a distinct structuring of the same "substance," Pike would need a word that referenced this shared substance. He would come to call that substance *lexicon*. While it may be confusing to some, he did not mean by this term what many today understand by it (the particular vocabulary of a given field). Instead, lexicon included "the *particular utterance or part of an utterance under attention* at the moment, provided that it is a unit containing at least one morpheme."[90] He considered this to be "hierarchically extended lexicon." "By hierarchical extension of the lexicon we mean the *particular* language-manifested elements at any level of the hierarchy, whether dictionary entries (*lexicon proper*), or phrases, sentences, discourses, or conversations."[91] Figure 2.8 is a reproduction of the same figure Pike used to show how lexicon related to the three hierarchies. I have supplemented his

[88] Ibid., 111.
[89] Ibid.
[90] Ibid., 112.
[91] Ibid., 112.

original diagram to suggest where the PWF perspectives and CVD components would fit in. In this sense, figure 2.8 is representative of Pike's entire theory, aside from the emic-etic distinction.

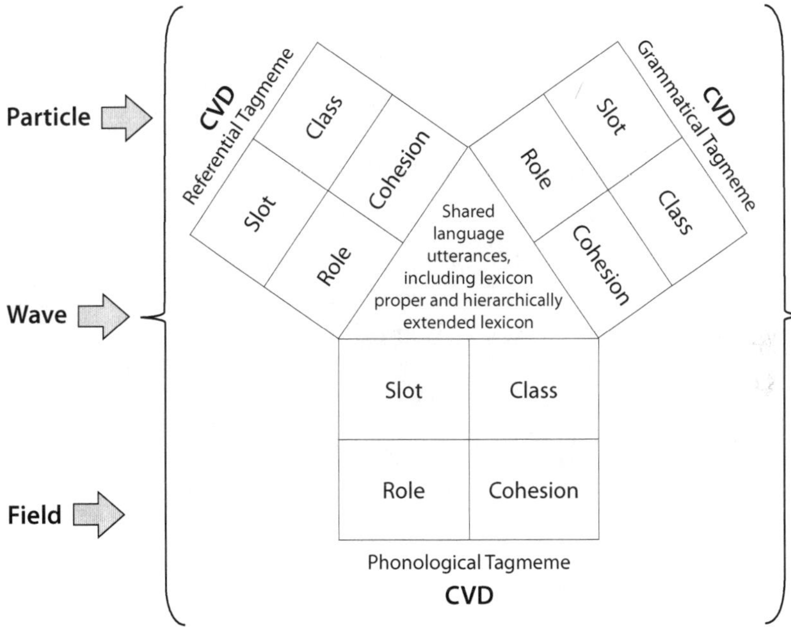

Fig. 2.8. Summary Diagram of Pike's Theory

In his description of the original diagram, he writes, "An emic utterance is a behaviorally meaningful simultaneous combination of three structures which share their momentary lexical manifestation including lexicon, extended hierarchically to embrace the reading of a poem or the presentation of a lecture."[92]

This diagram situates *form-meaning composites* within his theory as a whole, but these units warrant additional treatment.[93] He writes,

[92] Ibid., 113.

[93] The following discussion is taken directly from Hibbs, "Where Person Meets Word: Part 1," 374–77, used with permission.

> I do not treat an abstract semantic component divorced from the concrete body of expression. Meaning is tied to form, so that it exists only where there is form of some kind; it is never postulated either apart from form or apart from an observer who emically structures the concrete or pretended material which he sees, imagines he sees, deduces the presence of, or creates in nightmare or in science fiction.[94]

Each of the types of tagmemes in figure 2.8, in other words, only exists concretely in a participant context of some sort. Why did Pike insist so strongly on our understanding of form and meaning in this way? It seems there were larger issues at play that ran beneath his theoretical treatment of form and meaning.

The relationship between form and meaning stretches all the way back to Plato, who posited ideal forms in abstraction from contextually meaningful particulars with variation.[95] The danger in doing this within linguistics is that it creates an imaginary dualism. Form and meaning are never separated. There are no pure forms—such

[94] Pike, *LC*, 116.

[95] For a discussion of Platonic reductionism and its relation to a Trinitarian view of language modeled on Pike's thought, see Poythress, *In the Beginning Was the Word*, 326–31. The relationship between form and meaning is also embedded in the relationship between the one and the many, between universals and particulars. The debate on the nature of these relationships has weighty theological implications and is at the foundation of one's view of reality. For Christians (and for linguists following Pike's thought), just as form cannot be separated from meaning, and just as the one cannot be separated from the many, so the persons of the Godhead cannot be separated from one another. God is both one and three—neither feature takes precedence over the other. There is in God perfect harmony between unity and diversity. See Cornelius Van Til, *Introduction to Systematic Theology: Prolegomena and the Doctrines of Revelation, Scripture, and God*, 2nd ed., ed. William Edgar (Phillipsburg, NJ: P&R Publishing, 2007), 122.

In explaining the delay in the study of discourse by American linguists, Pike shows that he was aware of the trail of debris left by Plato's thought. It was Plato, after all, "who predicated philosophy on a 'reality' composed of thought-features abstracted from source-particulars, from things-as-directly-known.

things would be meaningless.[96] Certainly, for the sake of analysis we can temporarily talk about form and meaning *as if* they were separate. And Pike would not disagree here.[97] He would, however, protest that emic units of language can never really be treated this way in the world.

> We try very hard to avoid studying form by itself or meaning by itself. We deal with them both together. We can never discuss either of them unless, lurking somewhere in the

---

Above all, the problem [of a delayed study of discourse] may have arisen from separating the things-in-themselves (or abstract features of things, situations, or events) from the reality of *person*—person as observer, person as reality, person as investing every 'thing-in-itself' with an *observer relation* as its discoverer, its watcher, or its deducer." Pike, *Tagmemics, Discourse, and Verbal Art*, Michigan Studies in the Humanities 3 (Ann Arbor, MI: University of Michigan Press, 1981), 3.

[96] Leonard Bloomfield notes that "the study of language can be conducted without special assumptions only so long as we pay no attention to the meaning of what is spoken. This phase of language study is known as *phonetics*." Shortly thereafter he asserts, "since we can recognize the distinctive features of an utterance only when we know the meaning, we cannot identify them on the plane of pure phonetics." *Language* (Chicago: University of Chicago Press, 1984), 75, 77. He also adds that we all operate on the fundamental assumption "that each linguistic form has a constant and specific meaning." *Language*, 145. In practical terms, we never isolate a form from its meaning; nor do we receive a meaning without a form. "The child, for the sake of learning, must learn both meaning and sound. He must learn both the meaning of the word 'dog' and how the word sounds. How will he learn the meaning of a particular word or sentence unless he can identify its distinct sounds that distinguish that word from all the other words and sentences with quite different meanings? The sound has to be there all the time to access meaning. And conversely, the meaning has to be there for the sound to make any difference. . . . Language . . . . is never pure meaning or pure sound. The sound (or a writing system or a sign language) must identify the meanings. And the meanings make the sounds significant." Poythress, *In the Beginning Was the Word*, 263–64.

[97] "For convenience, one may on occasion discuss the form and meaning aspects *as if* they were separate, while taking pains to indicate that such an expedient is a distortion which must be corrected at proper intervals and in the relevant places in the discussion." Pike, *LRUT*, 63.

> background, is the other. Even when a person tries to talk about the isolated forms of words, he knows that they are meaningful—or he knows that somebody knows that they are meaningful—or he is not handling language. Similarly, if a person tries to make a classification of isolated possible meanings, he is likely to end up without helpful results unless somehow these meanings arise from words which are tied into some language system or systems of cultural behavior.[98]

Theoretical dichotomies that dissolve in the context of real human behavior are useless, but the problem runs deeper than practicality.

When we maintain a gap between form and meaning, not only do we distort the nature of language and fail to perceive reality as it is, but we also reduce it or oversimplify it so as to make it essentially *im*personal, for what person could ever value or even acknowledge a meaningless linguistic form? And who could arrive at an understanding of formless meaning? Perhaps this is why Pike was so vigilant in guarding against it. It can be easy to see the world as a kaleidoscope of vapid forms, with nothing more than functional significance in relation to a physical environment. Or, to narrow the plane, it can be easy to treat aspects of language impersonally and reductionistically, such as how Chomsky spoke of grammar theory as "completely formal and non-semantic."[99] The trouble is that reductions of this kind exclude *people* from the process of inquiry, and this inevitably leads

[98] Pike, *LC*, 16–17.

[99] Noam Chomsky, *Syntactic Structures* (The Hague: Mouton, 1957), 93. According to Pike, Chomsky "insists that grammatical structure be identified 'independently of any semantic consideration,' since he affirms that 'those who regard semantics as providing the basis, in some sense, for grammar' have implicit to this view the claim that 'there are semantic absolutes, identifiable in noises independently of the grammatical structure assigned to them.' . . . I affirm the necessity of dealing with form and meaning at the same time, to some degree, and deny the necessity of treating semantic elements as absolutes independent of all lexical and grammatical data." Pike, *LRUT*, 149.

to deception.[100] A theorist who denies his own personal involvement in theorizing is a wizard behind the curtains. Reality cannot be adequately analyzed or interpreted using a methodology that ignores the truth that at all times and places it is *people* who are doing the analyzing and interpreting, and because people are limited in their perception, data uncovered by such methodologies is skewed and other important disciplines left unconsidered. So, Pike is perfectly justified in claiming that our major problem throughout history is "separating the things-in-themselves (or abstract features of things, situations, or events) from the reality of *person*—person as observer, person as reality, person as investing every 'thing-in-itself' with an *observer relation* as its discoverer, its watcher, or its deducer."[101]

A form-meaning composite, then, is more than a linguist's analytical tool; it reflects a commitment to the personal nature of reality as having always and at every point forms bound up with meaning, both of which are necessary for personal use and interpretation, i.e., human behavior. That, in essence, is why Pike was so adamant in defending his notion of form-meaning composites. Doing away with this notion would simultaneously undercut his focus on concrete participant contexts.

Sharing as Prerequisite to Change

Pike moved from a discussion of form-meaning composites to what some might think is an unrelated discussion. Why discuss at this point the notion that "sharing" is prerequisite to change?

Understanding the pieces of Pike's language theory requires constant reference to his thought as a whole. These last three chapters

[100] Notice that even the serpent in the Garden of Eden avoided this conundrum. He knew that language is tied to people—indeed, that all of reality is tied to people. Rather than taking an impersonal approach and questioning Eve on the semantics of God's expression, rather than introduce the possibility of lexical ambiguity, he put forward the lie that God had performed an act of personal deception ("For God knows that when you eat of it . . .").

[101] Pike, *Tagmemics, Discourse, and Verbal Art*, 3.

in *LC* seem to be reflecting the beginning of his book: the PWF perspectives. Form-meaning composites are readily understood as units or particles. They are pieces of language that we can observe as being more or less static. The wave perspective comes into view when we look at how those form-meaning composites are related to each other sequentially in terms of nuclear and marginal components (in grammar, phonology, or reference).

Recall Pike's example of phonology.

> When two syllables are viewed as a pair of waves in sequence, rapid speech may make them merge at their borders. This can lead to temporary or permanent change in the phonemic content of morphemes manifested by the syllables in such a way that a new sound—not present in either, under different or slower conditions—is shared. Thus in the phrase *as you like* . . . both /z/ and /y/ may disappear and be replaced by /ž/ (as in *azure*). The two morphemes, and the two syllables, both share the one newly present sound. Here the meaning is unchanged, and no unexpected shift of attention occurs. Speed-induced fusion such as this, if retained, may lead to a permanent change of morphemic phonological shape.[102]

Here there is a sharing of a sound by each syllable, but there can also be sharing of "wave components." For example, when we consider lexical waves (waves of meaning), the central or nuclear meaning of a word such as "run" (referring to physical activity) is shared in some sense by marginal meanings of "run" in phrases such as "run a business" or "run a temperature." We considered these lexical waves earlier.

A natural question arises: how do we know what the central (nuclear) meaning for a word is? For Pike, "the *central* [nuclear] meaning will usually be considered the one which is learned earliest in life, is used most frequently, is most physical in its reference, and

[102] Pike, *LC*, 118.

is used analytically as the most convenient basis for descriptive order or rule derivation."[103] A marginal use of "run" ("He ran a business") "is found to share some component of meaning implied in the context containing it."[104] Thus, in the phrase "to run a business," the verb is sharing a semantic component with the physical meaning of the same verb (e.g., "to run a race")—indicating that the business is moving, operating according to a planned network of intentional decisions that drive it towards a specific goal.

Of course, part of the fun of language is that one person's nuclear meaning can be another person's marginal one. Pike offered the example of the child who grew up in an urban area and was always scolded by his mother for eating sloppily: "Don't be a pig!" Upon seeing a real pig later in life, the child witnessed it eating from a trough and said, "Oh, so that's why they call them pigs." What has happened, in essence, is that the child's nuclear meaning for "pig" (i.e., a human who eats sloppily) was the opposite of most people's nuclear meaning for "pig." We take the animal as the original and humans as the metaphorical derivative, whereas this child took humans as the original and the pig as the metaphorical derivative.

In addition to change involving the sharing of linguistic particles and the extended semantics of a single word, it also involves shared field components. The matrix of relationships that we find in language and human behavior are built upon for the furtherance of communication. This is clear in a simple physical example. Ask me where I live, and I will not simply give you a latitude and longitude, nor will I give you a direction in relation to our current physical location. Instead, I will begin relating the location of my house to the locations of other places that may be known to you: malls, restaurants, gas stations, schools. The end result will be that you not only know where I live but you also know what surrounds me. You will learn the point of my home within a web of relations.

[103] Ibid., 120.
[104] Ibid.

Universes of Discourse

Pike ends his book with a chapter that reflects the field perspective: "Universe of Discourse." By *universe of discourse* he meant

> the general or temporary or somewhat permanent *frame of reference*, either tacit or explicit, within which social interchange is taking place; it can include topic, style, genre, discipline, or general speaker or hearer expectancies. It can reflect the cohesion component of any tagmeme of the referential hierarchy, in relation to truth or falsehood, specific history, or specific or particular encyclopedic background; or it can include general relation to the situation in respect to space, time, society, or personal psychology; or it can include phonological cohesion factors of voice quality controlled by style or emotional situation; or it can include grammatical cohesion factors which control or are controlled by literary form.[105]

A universe of discourse, in other words, really *is* a universe: it is inexhaustibly deep and broad and yet always concrete and determinative of more specific meanings in human behavior. Pike was aware of this, noting that when we are considering a universe of discourse that stands behind a linguistic unit under focus, "we are at a very high level of coherence of the human being in his joking or lying, his fears and his hates, his biography or his social immersion, his explicit assumptions or his unstated but controlling beliefs. Beyond the pure mathematician in his abstractions lies person in commitment to the sheer joy of the pattern chase."[106]

One of the perceptive and practical ways in which Pike develops his thought on universes of discourse is to draw our attention to speaker and hearer expectations. These expectations reveal the universe of discourse that underlies their exchange.

[105] Ibid., 126.
[106] Ibid.,127.

> When a speaker addresses his audience, he may expect it to expect something of what he himself expects. If the hearer does not do so, then communication may fail completely or go awry. By Ciardi (1959:847) this expectation is called the *sympathetic contract* in relation to poetry. For him, the relation between the one who writes the poem and the one who receives it must include a shared belief or value system, permanent or temporarily in the imagination, if the *artistic* event is to *occur*. . . . But the same expectancies affect prose writing and ordinary conversation.[107]

A faulty or confused sympathetic contract can result in miscommunication or humor. Pike offered the following joke as an example.

> *Mr. Whippletree*: Alex, what did you give yr'old cow when she was sick?
> *Mr. Axelgrease*: Turps.
> *Two weeks later . . .*
> *Mr. Whippletree*: Alex, what d'you say you gave yr'old cow when she was sick?
> *Mr. Axelgrease*: Turps.
> *Another two weeks later . . .*
> *Mr. Whippletree*: Alex, what d'you say you gave yr'old cow when she was sick?
> *Mr. Axelgrease*: Turps.
> *Mr. Whippletree*: Well I gave turps to mine, and she died!
> *Mr. Axelgrease*: So'd mine.

The joke hinges on a confusion in the universe of discourse. Mr. Axelgrease thought that Mr. Whippletree was simply asking him to recount a past experience, hence he keeps relaying the same information. Mr. Whippletree, however, assumed that Mr. Axelgrease

[107] Ibid.

would know that he was seeking a medicinal solution for his sick cow and would not propose a plan of action that he knew by experience would fail. The two men are like communicative ships passing in the night, and we laugh at them.

But a universe of discourse is critical for more than just our use of humor. A shared universe of discourse is the context for *every* communicative exchange. What's more, it is the base upon which we learn our native language. "The way we normally learn the meaning of new words is by hearing them in contexts."[108] As we hear the word used in more and more contexts, we pick up more and more marginal meanings. Pike rightly recognized what this implies: "a *context has a very high power to determine or to change a meaning*—vastly greater than would be suspected until we have studied the matter. That contexts can form or change meanings is a very legitimate and valuable (in fact crucial) characteristic of language."[109]

Perhaps Pike placed his discussion of universes of discourse at the end of his book because it undergirds all of language and is the foundation of his own theory. He ends his book with a deceptively terse conclusion, subtitled "Unit-in-Context within Context." As we would predict, he re-emphasizes the fact that "no unit relevant to human beings exists without its having a relation to a system of interlocking types of context. The units exist in a vast matrix of n-dimensional intersecting relations within which the specific unit is distributed and which comprise our universe with our cognitive frames of reference."[110] For him, the units-in-context "comprise part of the warp and woof of every grammatical, generalized linear pattern of verbal or nonverbal patterns of behavior."[111]

[108] Ibid., 132.

[109] Ibid. He notes on the following page that "such contextual power can appear to an observer as damaging or constructive, or as diabolical or heavenly, depending on his estimate of the legitimacy and local usefulness of the change elicited."

[110] Ibid., 135.

[111] Ibid.

He ends *LC* with a rejection of simplicity and reductionism, the theological significance of which we will note in the following chapter.

> No hierarchy exists except in relation to the others. No *simple* necessary single mapping relation is present between the hierarchies of tagmemes. No simple set of rules is adequate to capture all the possibilities or to predict at one particular moment which choice will be made by the observers involved. If one wishes his theory to handle human flexibility, he must allow his theory to have some *indeterminacy of choice* at the moment under observation. The theory must be able to *describe* any one variation of interaction, after it has occurred, without being forced to *predict* in advance which one must inevitably occur.
>
> This points up a crucial assumption of the theory: Personal interaction is given priority over identification of things or abstractions. It is *persons* who perceive, imagine, and sense relations. It is persons who talk about these concepts. But persons have limits. Therefore they *must* have hierarchy, and hierarchy intersecting with hierarchy. *Only thus* can they signal the needed complexity of their experience, and do so in a way that will not stifle them.[112]

Notice here a point that has until now been left unstated: *we need hierarchy because we are limited beings*. Hierarchy is not simply an organizational pattern; it is an unavoidable focusing structure.

My own ESL graduate students sometimes ask how they can find the main point that an author wishes to make in an essay or book chapter. My answer is, "Hierarchy." A hierarchy structures data so as to alert the observer to various levels of information. We can choose as observers which level we want to focus on in a given

[112] Ibid., 136.

moment, but the hierarchy is also vital in conveying the author's sense of which information is most important.

We could say similar things about our everyday communication. All communication requires structure on the speaker's part and focus on the hearer's part. This is what allows speakers to relate the "complexity of their experience" to others. The complex, intersecting hierarchies of grammar, phonology, and reference thus provide communicators with the means to express themselves in a way that is intelligible to others, but at the same time is never exhaustible. We can, in other words, say what we wish to express without expressing everything there is to say, for even if the latter were possible, the hearer would be limited by his or her focus. Language, in the end, conveys as much meaning as it does mystery and depth.

Summary

Pike's theory can seem dizzying to people when they first are exposed to it. He sometimes referenced his theory as "wheels within wheels within wheels"—triad after triad. Yet, Pike would be quick to affirm that the complexity of his theory is what makes it profoundly practical. Because of its multiple dimensions and perspectives, it allows the analyst or common man to account for and study language in a way that allows it to "breath." That is to say, his theory does not force itself on language, encouraging its adherents to fit their experience into a pre-fashioned grid. Rather, it allows us to experience and process language in a way that gives adequate attention *both* to detail in its structural context *and* to indeterminacy. Sacrificing the former would render his language theory ill-equipped in its analytical and explanatory functions. Yet, rejecting the latter would mean forcing human experience into a scientific model that is essentially impersonal and, in that sense, unnatural.

It would be helpful here to summarize what we have covered before moving on to the next chapter. We have discussed the emic-etic distinction and seen how our position as an insider or an outsider in a language community has a bearing on our perception. We also saw how the PWF perspectives provide options for observers in terms of how they will perceive the units of language. All three of these perspectives are necessary, and each interlocks with the others. When considering units of language and human behavior more narrowly, we can use the PWF perspectives to examine the CVD components of a unit under focus, simultaneously understanding that each unit is "trimodally structured" in terms of the grammatical, phonological, and referential hierarchies. The tagmemes within these hierarchies point out the necessity of context for communication, and this context can be understood in terms of form-meaning composites, sharing as prerequisite to change, and universes of discourse.

What is most compelling in Pike's theory, however, has yet to be stated. In the introduction, I argued that our view of language and theology proper are bound up with one another. If we are to be faithful in upholding a Reformed understanding of the Trinity, then we should seek out a language theory that foregrounds this biblical truth. Pike's theory has done this, I argue, in an unprecedented way. The following chapter will explore the Trinitarian nature of Pike's theory, thus showing concretely how our theology proper can be tied to a view of language that does it justice.

3

The Trinitarian Structure of Pike's Thought

We set out in this project by noting the deep relationship between language theory and theology proper. With reference to that relationship, my thesis has been that *Kenneth Pike's language theory offers us a picture of language that faithfully represents the incomprehensible, Triune God of Scripture.* In this chapter, my goal is to give explicit support to this claim by unpacking the Trinitarian structure of Pike's language theory. I aim to show how Pike's theory coheres methodologically with a Reformed view of the Trinity. In light of this, his theory should be given renewed attention in our era and brought to bear on our various disciplines, be it hermeneutics, systematics, sociology, or philosophy.

Let me first say that the novelty and brilliance of Pike's theory has been recognized by many scholars, and most notably by his students.[1] Yet, aside from one particular theologian, there has been little work done to mine his theory for its Trinitarian structure.[2] This is what I aim to take up in this chapter. My method of organization

[1] One thinks here of Robert Longacre, Ruth Brend, Mary Ruth Wise, Thomas Headland, Eugene Nida and several others. A collection of essays written in honor of Pike's legacy showcases many of his supporters: Mary Ruth Wise, Thomas N. Headland, and Ruth M. Brend, eds., *Language and Life: Essays in Memory of Kenneth L. Pike* (Dallas, TX: SIL International, 2003).

[2] Vern Poythress has done this with *In the Beginning Was the Word: Language—A God-Centered Approach* (Wheaton, IL: Crossway, 2009).

will be to follow the outline of Pike's language theory that I introduced at the start of the previous chapter, with one lacuna.[3] We can go through each element in this outline and note the connections to and implications for Trinitarian theology. At the outset, I wish to remind us of three of the basic contours of Trinitarian orthodoxy.

Basic Contours of Reformed Trinitarian Orthodoxy

There are several theologians—ancient, modern, and contemporary—who have outlined the contours of Reformed Trinitarian orthodoxy. It would be unnecessary to synthesize all of them for our purposes. Hence, I will only reference some of the mainstay Reformed theologians of the modern and contemporary eras. My goal in doing this is to bring to mind concepts and vocabulary of Trinitarian theology that can be linked with Pike's theory.

We might begin with Herman Bavinck.[4] Bavinck placed much emphasis on the doctrine of the Trinity. Statements such as the following are easy to gloss over, but we should be careful to give them their proper weight.

> The article of the holy Trinity is the heart and core of our confession, the differentiating earmark of our religion, and the praise and comfort of all true believers of Christ.
>
> It was this confession which was at stake in the warfare

[3] I will not discuss the emic-etic distinction in relation to the Trinity. I do see links between the emic-etic distinction and the immanent and economic Trinity. But because these links are my own applications of Pike's ideas and not expositions of what is inherently there in his theory, I will leave such a discussion for another time.

[4] Calvin, of course, was a staunch defender of Trinitarian doctrine, as has been repeatedly emphasized since his time. Benjamin Warfield, perhaps more than any other Reformed theologian, has reminded us of this. See Calvin's *Institutes*, 1.13 and B. B. Warfield, "Calvin's Doctrine of the Trinity," in *Calvin and Augustine*, ed. Samuel G. Craig (Philadelphia: Presbyterian and Reformed Publishing, 1956), 189–284.

> of the spirits throughout the centuries. The confession of the holy Trinity is the precious pearl which was entrusted for safekeeping and defense to the Christian church.[5]

Elsewhere he writes that "the doctrine of the Trinity is of incalculable importance for the Christian religion. The entire Christian belief system, all of special revelation, stands or falls with the confession of God's Trinity. It is the core of the Christian faith, the root of all its dogmas."[6]

As readers familiar with Reformed theology might predict, the Trinity for Bavinck is the only true God. Thus, Trinitarian doctrine is not an addendum to theology proper, a mere descriptor added to a generic deistic god; rather, Trinitarian dogma addresses *who* the Christian God is. It focuses on the very nature and identity of the one whom we serve and worship. Nothing, in other words, could be more important than correctly understanding *the identity* of God as triune, for this shapes our approach to all of reality—creation and redemption. Echoing Augustine, Bavinck notes that "the self-communication that takes place within the divine being is archetypal for God's work in creation."[7] If God were not triune, if he were incapable of internal communication, then he would be incapable of external communication. All of creation rests upon the internal communicative behavior of the Trinity.[8] Likewise, all of redemption

[5] Herman Bavinck, *Our Reasonable Faith*, trans. Henry Zylstra (Grand Rapids, MI: Wm. B. Eerdmans, 1956), 145. He later writes that "Nothing less than the peculiar essence of Christianity was at stake in this battle of the spirits. From two sides the church was exposed to the danger of permitting itself to be wrested from the firm foundation on which it was built and so to be submerged by the world" (156).

[6] Herman Bavinck, *Reformed Dogmatics*, vol. 2, *God and Creation*, ed. John Bolt, trans. John Vriend (Grand Rapids, MI: Baker Academic, 2004), 333.

[7] Ibid.

[8] As I have written elsewhere, this "communicative behavior" is the eternal expression of love and glory that is exchanged among the divine persons in eternity. For a fuller discussion of this, see Pierce Taylor Hibbs, "Imaging

rests upon the Trinity: the Father electing, the Spirit regenerating and indwelling, and the Son justifying and uniting all believers with the God who is three-in-one. Given this truth, Bavinck could write with boldness, "in the doctrine of the Trinity we feel the heartbeat of God's entire revelation for the redemption of humanity."[9]

Yet, what exactly is the content of the Trinitarian dogma that Bavinck holds in such high regard? Much could be said, but certainly nothing less than the fact that *God is one being in three persons* and that *this leads inevitably to his incomprehensibility.*[10] Contemporary Trinitarian theology has spilt much ink on the semantics of

---

Communion: An Argument for God's Existence Based on Speech," *WTJ* 77, no. 1 (Spring 2015): 44–48; "Words for Communion," *Modern Reformation* 25, no. 4 (August 2016): 5–8; and "Closing the Gaps: Perichoresis and the Nature of Language," *WTJ* 78 (2016): 299–322.

[9] Bavinck, *Reformed Dogmatics*, 2:333.

[10] For definitions of "essence" and "person" in the Reformed tradition, first consider Calvin, *Institutes*, 1.13. It was Calvin who famously said of these terms, "I could wish them, indeed, to be buried in oblivion, provided this faith were universally received, that the Father, Son, and Holy Spirit are the one God; and that nevertheless the Son is not the Father, nor the Spirit the Son, but that they are distinguished from each other by some peculiar property" (1.13.5). On the other Reformers' views of the Trinity and its terminology, see Richard A. Muller, *Post-Reformation Reformed Dogmatics: The Rise and Development of Reformed Orthodoxy, Ca. 1520 to Ca. 1725*, vol. 4, *The Triunity of God* (Grand Rapids: Baker Academic, 2003), 145–57; 167–95. Also consult Charles Hodge, *Systematic Theology* (Peabody, MA: Hendrickson, 2013), 1:443–45; Bavinck, *God and Creation*, 296–304; Berkhof, *Systematic Theology*, new ed. (Grand Rapids, MI: William B. Eerdmans, 1991), 84–90; Douglas Kelly, *Systematic Theology: Grounded in Holy Scripture and Understood in Light of the Church*, vol. 1, *The God Who Is: The Holy Trinity* (Ross-shire, Scotland: Mentor, 2008), 447–562; Robert Letham, *The Holy Trinity: In Scripture, History, Theology, and Worship* (Phillipsburg, NJ: P&R Publishing, 2004), 257–68 and Michael Horton, *The Christian Faith: A Systematic Theology for Pilgrims on the Way* (Grand Rapids, MI: Zondervan, 2011), 279–82. A brief, albeit selective, history of the term "person" is also presented in, Ángel Cordovilla Pérez, "The Trinitarian Concept of Person" in *Rethinking Trinitarian Theology: Disputed Questions and Contemporary Issues in Trinitarian Theology*, ed. Giulio Maspero and Robert J. Woźniak (New York: T&T Clark, 2012), 105–45.

"essence" and "persons."[11] That need not concern us at the moment. Suffice it to say that by "essence" we mean God's being as divine, uncreated, incomprehensible, and eternal.[12] The essence is the *substance* or "whatness" of God.[13] Each of the divine persons carries this full divine essence, and yet the persons are distinguished from one another. Hence, by "person" we mean a distinct, incommunicable, and relational hypostasis or subsistence.[14] While that definition may have the drawback of sounding impersonal, it is composed of the language that the Reformed tradition and the broader catholic church have consistently employed since the fourth century.[15]

[11] Consider the recent article by Wesley Hill on the continuous argument about the terms "persons" and "relations": "Divine Persons and Their 'Reduction' to Relations: A Plea for Conceptual Clarity," *IJST* 14, no. 2 (April 2012): 148–60.

[12] Gerald Bray, *God Has Spoken: A History of Christian Theology* (Wheaton, IL: Crossway, 2014), 988.

[13] Van Til, however, was careful to avoid considering this "whatness" as impersonal. Hence, he introduced the phrase "one person, three persons" to denote the unity of God as absolute personality. This was essentially Van Til's attempt to show that we can talk about God's unity in ways that go beyond the language of "essence." That is to say, we can speak of God's unity in terms of his consciousness. For an overview and defense of Van Til's proposal, see Lane G. Tipton, "The Function of Perichoresis and the Divine Incomprehensibility," *WTJ* 64 (2002): 289–306.

[14] Here I am intentionally blending the language of traditional Reformed orthodoxy with what I feel is a necessary and biblical supplement, taken from the work of Colin E. Gunton, *The Promise of Trinitarian Theology*, 2nd ed. (London: T&T Clark, 1997), 83–99. Because I believe that "persons" (both divine and human, though in analogically different ways) are necessarily communicative, it can be problematic to define "person" primarily in terms of a "distinct rational nature." Hence, the concept of *relationality* is critical to our understanding of persons. See also Muller, *The Triunity of God*, 182.

[15] If one is seeking a more explicitly biblical and concrete definition of "person," I would suggest that a person is "one who speaks." This is true of the entire Godhead (the Father speaking the eternal Word in the power of the Spirit; cf. Ps. 33:6) as well as of the distinct persons, who are each given speaking and hearing roles in the NT, albeit in different senses. The Father speaks (Matt. 3:17; 17:5; Mark 1:11); the Son obviously speaks throughout the gospels; and the Spirit speaks through believers (Matt. 10:20). The Son

Each of the three persons—Father, Son, and Holy Spirit—is consubstantial with the others. While there is order in the Trinity in light of their relations (the Father is unbegotten, the Son is eternally begotten, and the Spirit eternally proceeds from the Father and the Son), this is best understood as *ordered equality*. Or we could say, as Wesley Hill recently put it, that there is an *asymmetrical mutuality* among the persons.[16] Each of the divine persons is as much God as the others, but their common divine nature does not trump their distinctness. In sum, God is one being in three persons. This is perhaps the most basic contour of Reformed Trinitarian Orthodoxy.

The second contour is a sense of the equal ultimacy of God's unity and diversity, his oneness and his threeness. Muller reminds us that "the doctrine of the divine oneness or unity . . . is neither more nor less important than the doctrine of the Trinity."[17] There are, of course, theologians who would push for primacy of the unity

---

also hears (John 12:49–50), as does the Spirit (John 16:13). See Kevin J. Vanhoozer, *Remythologizing Theology: Divine Action, Passion, and Authorship* (New York: Cambridge University Press, 2010), 244–46. Admittedly, I am here giving biblical support to Van Til's language of God being "one person and three persons" (though 'person' in this phrase denotes two distinct things). See John M. Frame, *Cornelius Van Til: An Analysis of His Thought* (Phillipsburg, NJ: P&R Publishing, 1995), 68–69.

[16] Wesley Hill, *Paul and the Trinity: Persons, Relations, and the Pauline Letters* (Grand Rapids, MI: Eerdmans, 2015), 81, 99, 108, 111. The thesis of Hill's book is that "the patterns of New Testament speech about God, Christ, and the Spirit lead us to understand that triune, reciprocal web of relations as constitutive of the identities of each of the three. God the Father, the Son of God, and the Holy Spirit are constituted by and in their relations to and with one another" (167).

[17] Muller, *The Triunity of God*, 146. Also consider the statements of Vanhoozer and Hill in their recent work. Vanhoozer writes plainly, "the oneness (of substance) and the threeness (of persons) are equally ultimate." Vanhoozer, *Remythologizing Theology*, 146. Speaking of the divine persons, Hill adds that "specifying their shared essence and naming their distinct postures or directions vis-à-vis one another are tasks of equal priority in Trinitarian discourse." Hill, *Paul and the Trinity*, 103.

(simplicity) or the Trinity of God, but this desire for such primacy is, I believe, always weighted by a deeper desire to rationalize the being of God. While we can hold biblically to the truth of God's unity and the truth of the three distinct persons, we cannot plumb the depths of mystery that surrounds the relationship between these two truths. Certainly, we can say various things about God's unity and Trinity, but for those desiring a precise and univocal formulation of the relation of the oneness to the threeness, Reformed theologians have for the most part claimed that this is the heart of mystery.[18] K. Scott Oliphint is one contemporary example.

[18] There are, of course, divergences here when particular theologians in the Reformed tradition are drawn more to a Thomistic view of the Trinity. Recently, there has been a surge in Thomistic theology, especially with regards to the Trinity, even in Reformed circles. Many of the approaches I have read seem to prioritize the unity of God (divine simplicity) over the Trinity of persons, despite valiant efforts not to do so. For example, see James E. Dolezal, "Trinity, Simplicity, and the Status of God's Personal Relations," *IJST* 16, no. 1 (January 2014): 79–98. I believe that this prioritizing of God's unity or simplicity is related to Thomas's natural theology and Aristotle's philosophy, which presuppose that unregenerate (fallen) reason has access to *de Deo uno*. That God is one, in other words, can be proved rationally for Thomas, and, despite his and others' best attempts not to do so, the threeness is treated as subservient to the oneness, rather than being equally ultimate with it. More conservative Reformed theologians hold firmly to the concept of the noetic effects of sin, and thus find no precedence in natural reason for prioritizing God's oneness over his threeness. Both traditions, however, would agree that the doctrine of the Trinity is a purely revealed doctrine.

With regards to the Thomistic definition of "person," while it is true that the persons *are* the essence, I do not think that this necessitates Thomas's view that the persons be considered *only* with the language of "subsistent relations," especially when that language is linked to Aristotelian philosophy. While the language of "subsistent relations" has a history of proper usage and is part of standard orthodoxy, I find in some Thomistic approaches a usage of it that elevates the essence or simplicity of God (to varying degrees) over the persons in such a way that eclipses mystery. I am vigilant of any exposition of God's triunity that eclipses the mystery of the Godhead, for I believe that this is a sign that creatures are overstepping their bounds and have begun to rationalize the being of God.

> In his monumental work of theology, Herman Bavinck says that "mystery is the lifeblood of theology." In other words, because there is mystery *at every point* of our Christian thinking and living, it is important to give a proper, biblical account of that mystery as we think through the various truths of Scripture (cf. Rom. 11:33–36).
>
> Surely there is mystery in God's simplicity; perhaps nothing is more complex than God's simplicity! There is mystery, in other words, in God's triunity. These biblical truths, which we must affirm, go together. And yet, even as we affirm them, we have no laws of thinking or experience that show us exactly *how* these aspects of God's character actually cohere. They do cohere; there is no darkness or mystery in God. But we cannot see exactly *how*—not in this life, nor in the next.[19]

Oliphint affirms here that God is one *and* God is three, and while this unity and Trinity are to be understood in different senses, we can only go so far in articulating those senses. We must in the end be content to follow the voice of Scripture, which calls us simply to acknowledge that God is one in one sense and three in another. The Trinitarian terminology that we have used throughout the centuries is still valid and useful for guarding against heresy, but such terminology was never meant to rationalize the being of God. Thus, leaving the exact relationship between oneness and threeness a mystery is, I believe, a biblically defensible position. Scripture does, however, seem to emphasize both elements equally. That is, it treats the Godhead as one and yet constantly and consistently refers to the persons as distinctly conscious agents.

Holding the oneness and threeness as equally ultimate also has the great benefit of deepening our knowledge of reality. It is for

[19] K. Scott Oliphint, "Simplicity, Triunity, and the Incomprehensibility of God," in *One God in Three Persons: Unity of Essence, Distinction of Persons, Implications for Life*, ed. Bruce A. Ware and John Starke (Wheaton, IL: Crossway, 2015), 229.

this reason that Cornelius Van Til and Colin Gunton so adamantly defended the equal ultimacy of God's unity and Trinity, or as they put it, the equal ultimacy of *the one* and *the many*. Van Til wrote in his *Introduction to Systematic Theology*, "the whole problem of knowledge has constantly been that of bringing the one and the many together. When man looks about him and within him, he sees that there is a great variety of facts. The question that comes up at once is whether there is any unity in this variety, whether there is one principle in accordance with which all these appear and occur."[20] How can we relate the particulars of our experience to a sense of unity and thus find coherence in our experience? Van Til sees the answer to this question in the Trinity. "Using the language of the one-and-many question we contend that in God the one and the many are equally ultimate. Unity in God is no more fundamental than diversity, and diversity is no more fundamental than unity. The persons of the Trinity are mutually exhaustive of one another. The Son and the Spirit are ontologically on a par with the Father. . . ."[21] In other words, God's threeness and his oneness are not at odds with one another. The three persons are "mutually exhaustive" of one another; they are genuinely distinct and yet ineffably one. Trinity and unity are equally ultimate.

Applying this principle to creation helps us to understand the nature of reality in terms of the ancient one-and-many question: is reality comprised of unrelated particulars that we try to connect, or is reality ultimately an abstract unity, the particulars being nominal or illusory or merely temporary? Van Til suggests that neither answer is biblical, for the God who is both one and many is the creator of the world, and that world reflects him. Hence,

> If the doctrine of creation is thus taken seriously, it follows that the various aspects of created reality must sustain such

[20] Van Til, *Introduction to Systematic Theology*, 30.

[21] Cornelius Van Til, *The Defense of the Faith*, ed. K. Scott Oliphint, 4th ed. (Phillipsburg, NJ: P&R Publishing, 2008), 48.

> relations to one another as have been ordained between them by the Creator, as superiors, inferiors, or equals. All aspects being created equally, no one aspect of reality may be regarded as more ultimate than another. Thus the created one and many may in this respect be said to be *equal* to one another; they are equally derived and equally dependent upon God who sustains them both.[22]

In sum, for Van Til we hold to the equal ultimacy of the one and many in the Godhead, and

> we hold that in this universe we deal with a *derivative* one and many, which can be brought into fruitful relation with one another because, back of both, we have in God the original one and many. If we are to have *coherence* in our experience, there must be a correspondence in our experience to the eternally coherent experience of God. Human knowledge ultimately rests upon the internal coherence within the Godhead.[23]

Colin Gunton was one of a minority of other theologians to concur, at least in print. He recognized that "the tendency in much early Greek theology, with its quest to show the inherence of the 'many' in the 'one,' is to make the many in some way or other a logical implication of the one, whether as emanation or as a more strictly logical outworking . . ."[24] The many, in other words, was made subservient to the one. For Gunton, this was unacceptable because it relegated the biblical notion of personhood ('the many')—what should be central to our theology—to a subsidiary alcove of theology.

For both Van Til and Gunton, the one-and-many problem is

[22] Ibid., 50. See also Van Til, *Introduction to Systematic Theology*, 30–31.

[23] Van Til, *Introduction to Systematic Theology*, 59.

[24] Gunton, *The Promise of Trinitarian Theology*, 24.

not, in fact, a problem at all, for God is one being *and* three persons. Because "the unity and the diversity in God are equally basic and mutually dependent upon one another," we can trust that the unity and diversity of creation are held in perfect harmony by the providence of God.[25]

The third contour of Reformed Trinitarian orthodoxy is the biblical concept of *perichoresis*.[26] Simply put, when we speak of *perichoresis*, we are referring to the intimate union of the divine persons, such that "each is in each, and all are in each, and all are one."[27] How exactly is each person "in" the others? The language of "coinherence" and "indwelling" is most commonly offered for clarification. Others use more eccentric terms. Turretin, for instance, suggests "the divine persons *embrace* each other and *permeate* . . . each other."[28] However, no matter what terms are used, the mystery of this truth eschews rationalistic exposition. All that is clear from Scripture, particularly the Gospel of John, is that the persons of the Godhead interpenetrate one another, and yet "while indwelling one another, do not coalesce."[29] A plethora of definitions could be added as supplements,[30] but the idea is clear enough for our present purposes.

Putting all of this together, we have three contours to keep in

[25] Cornelius Van Til, *Christian Apologetics*, ed. William Edgar, 2nd ed. (Phillipsburg, NJ: P&R Publishing, 2003), 25. See also Frame, *Cornelius Van Til*, 71–76.

[26] For background on this concept, see Hibbs, "Closing the Gaps: Perichoresis and the Nature of Language."

[27] Augustine, *De Trinitate* 6.10.

[28] Francis Turretin, *Institutes of Elenctic Theology*, vol. 1, *First through Tenth Topics*, ed. James T. Dennison, Jr., trans. George Musgrave Giger (Phillipsburg, NJ: P&R Publishing, 1992), 257; emphasis added.

[29] Paul M. Collins, *Trinitarian Theology: West and East—Karl Barth, the Cappadocian Fathers, and John Zizioulas* (New York: Oxford, 2001), 211.

[30] For other definitions, see Augustine, *De Trinitate* 1.18; John of Damascus, *Writings*, trans. Frederic H. Chase, FC 37 (Washington, DC: Catholic University of America Press, 1958), 177; Joel R. Beeke and Mark Jones, *A Puritan Theology: Doctrine for Life* (Grand Rapids, MI: Reformation Heritage

mind as we move through Pike's language theory: (1) God is one essence in three persons; (2) the unity and diversity of the Trinity are equally ultimate; and (3) the concept of perichoresis reminds us of the biblical truth that the distinct persons interpenetrate or indwell one another.

Now, before we move into looking at the Trinitarian nature of Pike's theory, we do well to remind ourselves of precisely *why* we are undertaking this study. Why are we seeking to expose the Trinitarian structure of Pike's thought? Why is this so important to our understanding of God himself?

Reality is profoundly linguistic. God is a communicative (and in that sense, linguistic) being who used language to create and redeem. Bavinck's affirmation gets right to the core of this: "By the word God creates, preserves, and governs all things, and by the word he also renews and re-creates the world. For that reason, too, the gospel is called 'the word of God' (*logos tou theou*). John calls Christ the Logos because it is he in whom and by whom God reveals himself both

---

Books, 2012), 90–91; Collins, *Trinitarian Theology*, 209–15; Oliver D. Crisp, "Problems with Perichoresis," *Tyndale Bulletin* 56, no. 1 (January 1, 2005): 135–39; John P. Egan, "Toward Trinitarian Perichoresis: Saint Gregory the Theologian, Oration 31.41," *Greek Orthodox Theological Review* 39 (1994): 92; John Frame, *Systematic Theology: An Introduction to Christian Belief* (Phillipsburg, NJ: P&R Publishing, 2013), 479–81; Verna E. F. Harrison, "Perichoresis in the Greek Fathers," *St. Vladimir's Theological Quarterly* 35 (1991): 59–63; Kelly, *The Holy Trinity*, 489; Michael G. Lawler, "Perichoresis: New Theological Wine in an Old Theological Wineskin," *Horizons* 22, no. 1 (March 1, 1995): 52–53; Letham, *The Holy Trinity*, 365–66; John McClean, "Perichoresis, Theosis and Union with Christ in the Thought of John Calvin," *Reformed Theological Review* 68, no. 2 (August 1, 2009): 134–35; Randall E. Otto, "The Use and Abuse of Perichoresis in Recent Theology," *Scottish Journal of Theology* 54 (2001): 366; Daniel F. Stramara Jr., "Gregory of Nyssa's Terminology for Trinitarian Perichoresis," *VC* 52 (1998): 259; Lane G. Tipton, "The Function of Perichoresis and the Divine Incomprehensibility," *WTJ* 64 (2002): 292; Thomas F. Torrance, *The Christian Doctrine of God, One Being, Three Persons* (Edinburgh: ☒&☒ Clark, 1996), 169–73; and Cornelius Van Til, *In Defense of the Faith*, vol. 2, *A Survey of Christian Epistemology* (Phillipsburg, NJ: Presbyterian and Reformed, 1969), 78.

in the work of creation and that of re-creation (John 1:3, 14)."[31] God's eternal Word is the ontological ground for all existence, and because that Word was eternally spoken by the Father in the power of the Spirit, the linguistic Trinity is at the base of all the coherence in our experience. Every bit of the material world is here because the Trinitarian God "opened his holy lips."[32] Relating the doctrine of the Trinity to language theory, then, is a bedrock endeavor. By that, I mean that it lays the foundation for our understanding of the rest of reality. What we are undertaking in this chapter is not a playful synthesis of theology and linguistics. Rather, we are here coming face to face with the deepest reality known to us. So, let our exploration be circumspect and reverent.

Particle, Wave, and Field: Father, Son, and Spirit

Those familiar with Trinitarian theology might quickly notice that Pike's observer perspectives bear some analogical resemblance to the persons of the Godhead and their perichoretic relations.[33] Of course, we must keep in mind that this is an *analogical resemblance*, not a direct correlation. It would be diminutive of God, not to mention modalistic, to claim that the Trinity is simply three perspectives of one divine being.[34] But if they are ever more than

[31] Bavinck, *God and Creation*, 273.

[32] John Calvin, *Institutes of the Christian Religion: A New Translation of the 1541 Edition*, trans. Robert White (Carlisle, PA: Banner of Truth, 2014), 16. Note here that Calvin is referring to God's special revelation, not to creation. The analogy, however, is fitting for creation as well, since God spoke creation into existence. In this sense, it was also necessary for God to "reopen his holy lips" when sin entered the cosmic order.

[33] This section is a slightly modified version of that occurring in Pierce Taylor Hibbs, "Do You See How I See? The Trinitarian Roots of Human Perception," *WTJ* 79, no. 1 (Spring 2017): 65–68, used with permission. A helpful discussion of the PWF perspectives within a theological context is also presented in Poythress, *In the Beginning Was the Word*, 51–59.

[34] "While in human nature there is unity of person and plurality of substance (body and soul), in the divine nature there is unity of substance and

this, they are certainly not less.[35] So, sketching out the analogical connections serves not to identify the Trinitarian God but to help us further understand and enjoy the richness of his interpersonal communion. It also provides yet another opportunity to see how Pike's theory is truly unique in its structure, fitting felicitously with the Reformed understanding of the Trinity. Note, before we begin, that the examples that follow are sometimes linguistic but other times more general, as is appropriate for the observer perspectives in Pike's theory, used as they are for structuring both verbal and nonverbal behavior.

Particle

Throughout Scripture, God the Father is described as changeless and immovable. He is the unbegotten *I am* (Ex. 3:14). The world is a burning wick in the wind, but God is light eternal—unthreatened and steadfast. Certainly, the transience of creation was all too clear to the psalmist when he compared humanity to the eternally unchangeable God: "They will perish, but you will remain; they will all wear out like a garment. You will change them like a robe, and they will pass away, but you are the same, and your years have no end" (Ps. 102:26–27). Berkhof addresses God's immutability in the same vein, writing that God is

> devoid of all change, not only in His Being, but also in His perfections, and in His purposes and promises. In virtue of this attribute He is exalted above all becoming, and is free from all accession or diminution and from all growth or decay in His Being or perfections. His knowledge and plans, His moral principles and volitions remain forever the

---

plurality of persons." Letham, *The Holy Trinity*, 226–27.

[35] John M. Frame, "A Primer on Perspectivalism," Frame-Poythress.org, accessed November 9, 2014, http://www.frame-poythress.org/a-primer-on-perspectivalism/.

> same. . . . improvement and deterioration are both equally impossible.[36]

This, of course, is a description of the essence of the Godhead, not merely the Father. But we can see how this description would be especially noticeable in the Father. After all, James describes the Father as the one "with whom there is no variation or shadow due to change" (1:17). John Owen reaffirms the scriptural truth that even the Father's love is "unchangeable."[37] Such descriptions of the Father comport with the claim that in God "improvement and deterioration are both equality impossible." It also accords with the Father's distinct personal property of *agennetos*, unbegotten.[38]

The Father, then, can be linked to the particle perspective: the static, stable view of reality as a whole or of a constituent part of it (e.g., a specific linguistic unit). Whenever we view something in creation, including a unit of language, as a stable entity with relatively fixed properties, we are drawing upon remnant analogical capabilities in human consciousness that point back to the one in whom there is no shadow due to change. In other words, the Father's eternal, absolute stability and immutability are the ontological grounds for the temporal, relative stability of anything in creation. Whatever stability the object has is derived from the ultimate stability and immutability of the unbegotten Father. The same applies specifically within language. We draw on the particle perspective, rooted in the Father, when recognizing the stability of meaning in a given unit of language.

[36] Berkhof, *Systematic Theology*, 58. Certainly, "there is change round about Him, change in the relations of men to Him, but there is no change in His being" (59).

[37] Joel R. Beeke and Mark Jones, *A Puritan Theology: Doctrine for Life* (Grand Rapids, MI: Reformation Heritage Books, 2012), 106–7.

[38] Francis Turretin, *Institues of Elenctic Theology*, vol. 1, *First through Tenth Topics*, ed. James T. Dennison, Jr., trans. George Musgrave Giger (Phillipsburg, NJ: P&R Publishing, 1992), 80–81.

Consider one example. Reflecting on the meaning of the word *light*, Poythress writes,

> God is light (1 John 1:5). The ultimate anchorage for the word *light* is in God himself, who is light. God by his own character and faithfulness gives ultimate stability to meaning in this world. He shows himself to us in speech, including speech about light. He makes definite claims. Only God knows himself perfectly and exhaustively. But we do not need to be God in order to know him truly by receiving his speech in the Son through the power of the Holy Spirit.[39]

The semantic stability of a word such as *light* is rooted in the stability of the Father, in "whom there is no variation or shadow due to change" (James 1:17). Thus, in both nonverbal and verbal contexts, the particle perspective is tied to the Father.

Wave

The wave perspective can be linked to the Son. The Son is eternally and necessarily begotten or "generated" from the Father.[40] He is *from* the Father, not in terms of time or ontology, but in terms of personal subsistence. The Son has his subsistence in the "eternal *act* of the Father."[41] Couple this with the description of the Son as the *speech* or *word* of God: "both in creation and re-creation God reveals himself by the word. By the word God creates, preserves, and governs all things, and by the word he also renews and recreates the world."[42] The Word, as Son, is the dynamism of God.

[39] Vern S. Poythress, "God and Language," in *Did God Really Say? Affirming the Truthfulness and Trustworthiness of Scripture*, ed. David B. Garner (Phillipsburg, NJ: P&R Publishing, 2012), 104.

[40] Berkhof, *Systematic Theology*, 93–94. This generation is "not with respect to essence and absolutely as God, but with respect to person and reduplicatively (*reduplicative*) as Son." Turretin, *Institutes*, 1:281.

[41] Berkhof, *Systematic Theology*, 93; emphasis added.

[42] Bavinck, *God and Creation*, 273.

Consider also the Son's work in the incarnation. The incarnate Son is the "servant sent to effect the work of the Father, obedient even unto death and one day delivering up his kingdom to the Father."[43] Because the Son carries out the work of his Father, it is possible to view the salvific work of Christ as a wave: his life and teaching the *initial margin*, his crucifixion and resurrection the *nucleus*, and his following ascension the *final margin*. Even within that initial margin, we see the human nature of Christ in dynamic development within a field of relationships, as he "increased in wisdom and in stature and in favor with God and man" (Luke 2:52).

So, the wave perspective can be tied to the Son. Just as the distinct personal description of the Father as unbegotten lends itself to a static view of reality, the description of the Son as eternally begotten lends itself to a dynamic view of reality. When we view reality, or some component of it, as a dynamic development—some parts peripheral and accidental (margins) while others focal and necessary (nuclei)—we are drawing upon the eternal generation of the Son, and, in the incarnation, upon his active obedience to the Father in accomplishing the plan of salvation.

Again, this applies to linguistic units as well. Consider our understanding of the word "truth" before and after we received divine revelation in John 14:6. Prior to receiving that revelation, many of us may have understood "truth" propositionally, meaning "an expression corresponding to and accurately representing reality." But John 14:6 reveals that truth is ultimately a *person*.[44] This dynamically develops our understanding of the word "truth" in a profound way, such that we can say there is dynamism and growth in the word's meaning.

[43] Ibid., 276.

[44] "Beauty," as it turns out, is also a person. For a development of this idea within the context of artistic expression, see Hibbs, "Beauty Embodied," *Reformation 21*, February, 2016, accessed October 13, 2016, http://www.reformation21.org/articles/beauty-embodied.php.

Field

The Spirit *proceeds* from the Father and the Son. He is "from the Father and the Son by spiration."[45] Frame writes, "the Spirit is the member of the Trinity whom the Father and Son send, over and over again, to do their business on earth."[46] Our focus, at this point, is not merely on the procession of the Holy Spirit, but on the procession *from the Father and the Son*. The Spirit "stands in the closest possible relation to both of the other persons."[47] Hodge affirms, "the Spirit is no more said to send or to operate through the Son, than to send or operate through the Father."[48] While it is true that the Holy Spirit finds personal distinction in the triune community via "procession," it is equally as important that the Spirit's distinction is rooted in his procession from *both* the Father and the Son.[49] As such, the Spirit associates the Father and the Son in eternal fellowship—a communion so deep and penetrating that we can only understand a glimmer of it in the communion we have analogically with the Trinity through the Spirit's work in us.[50] In other words, the deep

[45] Turretin, *Institutes*, 1:281. Berkhof defines "spiration" as follows: "that eternal and necessary act of the first and second persons in the Trinity whereby they, within the divine Being, become the ground of the personal subsistence of the Holy Spirit and put the third person in possession of the whole divine essence, without any division, alienation or change." Berkhof, *Systematic Theology*, 97.

[46] Frame, *Systematic Theology*, 497.

[47] Berkhof, *Systematic Theology*, 97.

[48] Hodge, *Systematic Theology*, 1:478.

[49] The Spirit "is related to the Son as the latter is to the Father and imparts to us both the Son and the Father. He is coinherent in the Son as the Son is coinherent in him." Bavinck, *God and Creation*, 312. He we enter into the debate of the *filioque* clause, which has separated eastern and western Trinitarian views for centuries. Suffice it to say at this point that, with Gregory of Nazianzen, we affirm that the Spirit's procession from the Father and the Son does not infringe on the personal distinction of the Father as the "monarchy" of the Trinity, because the entire Trinity is the monarchy, the "sole principle, source, and cause" of itself. Letham, *The Holy Trinity*, 204, 366. Only this position safeguards us from subordinationism of one kind or another.

[50] Vern S. Poythress, "Reforming Ontology and Logic in the Light of the

association between the Father and the Son, a "mutual fellowship and indwelling," is what "reflects the character of God the Holy Spirit, who indwells us."[51]

As the Spirit brings out the communion of the Father and the Son, so he also brings out the communion between members of the body of Christ. In Christ, we are all "being built together into a dwelling place for God by the Spirit" (Eph. 2:22).[52]

The field perspective, then, can be linked to the Holy Spirit. We sometimes view components of reality as units in a network of functional relationships—a context. In fact, we must view *every* unit that way because "no item by itself has significance. A unit becomes relevant only in relation to a context. Outside such a relationship the item will be necessarily uninterpretable by the observer."[53] This is the case even with sensory data, which are not facts in themselves, but only become facts when processed and interpreted by *someone*.[54] Such a relational view of reality is an analogical capability drawn from the Holy Spirit, who provides the relational context for the

---

Trinity: An Application of Van Til's Idea of Analogy," *WTJ* 57, no. 1 (March 1, 1995): 191.

[51] Ibid., 192. "No communion with God is possible except by the Spirit. . . . By the Spirit we have communion—direct and immediate communion—with no one less than the Son and the Father themselves." Bavinck, *God and Creation*, 278.

[52] "The Holy Spirit is in himself the *enhypostatic* Love and the Communion of Love in the perichoretic relations between the Father and the Son, and as such is in himself the ground of our communion with God in the Love of the Father and the Son." T. F. Torrance, *The Christian Doctrine of God, One Being Three Persons* (Edinburgh: T&T Clark, 1996), 171.

[53] Pike, *LC*, 30.

[54] With Van Til, we affirm that you cannot separate a fact from its function in a system, for "a fact *is* its function." Cornelius Van Til, *Common Grace and the Gospel* (Nutley, NJ: Presbyterian and Reformed, 1977), 115. And "the most important fact about anything in the world is its relation to God's Lordship." Frame, *Systematic Theology*, 32. Moreover, we cannot separate facts from their interpreters. See Van Til, *Defense of the Faith*, 32; Frame, *The Doctrine of the Knowledge of God* (Phillipsburg, NJ: P&R Publishing, 1987), 70–72. This will be revisited in the next chapter.

Father and the Son as he proceeds from both, and also provides the relational context for individual members of the body of Christ.

Perichoresis

Now, just as the observer perspectives are all necessary, each interlocking with and presupposing the other two, so the persons of the Godhead interpenetrate one another. We have already discussed the concept of perichoresis. Here, we are saying that the mutual indwelling of the persons in the Godhead is the archetype that provides for the ectypal perichoresis of observer perspectives. The particle, wave, and field observer perspectives interlock and presuppose one another ultimately because each of the persons of the Trinity has intimate communion and interpenetration with the others without threatening or eclipsing the personal distinctions.[55]

So, while only the Father is unbegotten and only the Son is begotten, they are each described as immutable in certain senses. We noted that in Psalm 102, the psalmist seems to be referring to God the Father when writing, "you are the same, and your years have no end" (Ps. 102:27). Yet the writer of Hebrews attributes the same description to the Son (Heb. 1:12). Later in Hebrews 13:8, he writes, "Jesus Christ is the same yesterday and today and forever."[56] We see the immutability in the Holy Spirit as we witness him being given (or revoked), as a changeless gift, to those who accept and follow the redeeming Word of God (Ps. 51:11; Ezek. 36:26; Luke 11:13; John 20:22; Acts 2:33, 38; 5:32; 8:17, 19; 10:45; 15:8; Rom. 5:5; 1 Thess. 4:8).

[55] Frame, *Systematic Theology*, 479–81. Hodge notes that "this fact—intimate union, communion, and inhabitation of the persons of the Trinity—is the reason why everywhere in Scripture, and instinctively by all Christians, God as God is addressed as a person, in perfect consistency with the Tripersonality of the Godhead." Hodge, *Systematic Theology*, 1:462. Bavinck suggests that "the divine being *is* tripersonal; precisely because it is the absolute, divine personality." Bavinck, *God and Creation*, 302; emphasis added. See also Kelly, *The Holy Trinity*, 489–93.

[56] Turretin, *Institutes*, 1:287.

While the Son is described as the dynamic Word of the Father, we find in Scripture that the Holy Spirit not only *speaks* through Christ's disciples (Mark 13:11), but also speaks directly (Acts 21:11). And though Christ is said to be the power and wisdom of God (1 Cor. 1:24), the Holy Spirit is said to teach (Luke 12:12; John 14:26), and Paul prays that those in Rome would be filled with hope by the *power* of the Holy Spirit (Rom. 15:13). The dynamic wisdom and power of the Word is extended not just to the Spirit, but also to the Father, who defeats Israel's enemies (2 Chro. 13:15), and silences Job with an overwhelming queue of his divine actions: laying the foundations of the world (Job 38:4); building "bars and doors for the sea" (38:10); walking in the recesses of the deep (38:16); and cleaving channels for torrents of rain (38:15). And among God's acts of power is his implanting wisdom in his creatures. It is he who "has put wisdom in the inward parts" and "given understanding to the mind" (38:36). The Father, Son, and Spirit are each intimately involved in divine actions that are, on the surface, prominently attributable to the Son as the dynamic Word and wisdom of God.

Lastly, though the Spirit binds the Father and the Son in eternal fellowship, the Father and Son also play pivotal roles in intra-Trinitarian and extra-Trinitarian communion. The Father owns the mansion with many rooms, where Christ will reunite with believers (John 14:2–3). Immediately after stating that the Father dwells in him, Jesus tells his disciples that the Holy Spirit will dwell in them. In other words, "we are drawn through the Holy Spirit into the relationship that the Son has with the Father. We are raised 'into communion with the persons of the Holy Trinity.'"[57] So, the communion fostered by the Spirit is not isolated from work of the Father and the Son.

It is evident, then, that the observer perpectives in Pike's theory have ties to the persons of the Godhead, not merely in how those perspectives are understood but in how they *function* (perichoresis).

[57] Letham, *The Holy Trinity*, 353.

The PWF perspectives presuppose and interlock with one another just as the persons of the Godhead presuppose and interlock with one another.[58] In terms of Pike's theory, particles comprise waves, and waves crest and fall in fields. The particle perspective helps us to focus on a stable element of reality or language, but particles would themselves be unintelligible apart from movement and dynamism. If nothing in reality moved or developed, everything would be a particle, and so nothing would be a particle. Particles presuppose waves; they stand out as elements in contrast with movement. Particles also presuppose fields. We cannot identify or focus on something in *utter* isolation. Whether tacitly or explicitly, we draw on relationships—between words, events, emotions—in order to understand another particular word, event, or emotion. The same applies to the wave and field perspectives. Waves are composed of particles and rely on that sense of stability for their structure (i.e., having margins and a nucleus). Fields, as well, would be non-existent without relatively static particles to hold the field structure in place.

This is only the first triad in Pike's theory that we have surveyed. The Father, Son, and Spirit are also behind the contrast, variation, and distribution (CVD) of individual linguistic units. That is where we turn next.

Contrast, Variation, and Distribution: Father, Son, and Spirit

Recall that the CVD triad focuses on linguistic units themselves. All linguistic units—in fact, every unit of human behavior—has contrastive-identificational features, variation, and distribution. As we noted in the previous chapter, Pike coined the phrase "contrastive-identificational" because units of human behavior, language included, have both a *negative* and a *positive* element of identity.

[58] Vern S. Poythress, *Redeeming Philosophy: A God-Centered Approach to the Big Questions* (Wheaton, IL: Crossway, 2014), 143–44.

Negatively, "we do not know what something is unless we know something about what it is not."[59] Positively, "the same components which help us to see that one unit differs from another also help us to *recognize* the unit when it is no longer close to the one which we separated it from."[60] Contrastive-identificational features can appear within the GPR hierarchies, which we will examine next.

Variation deals with (1) difference amidst sameness and (2) particular manifestations of the same emic unit. As Pike noted, "normal social behavior requires that we be able to recognize identities in spite of change. Unless we can do so, there can be no human society as we know it."[61] Following from this principle, the same emic unit can have many manifestations (and Pike would say that there is *always* some physical manifestation), each one varying in specific ways from the others while not comprising the identity of the emic unit, defined as its functional purpose in the emic system, which includes the responses it elicits from other participants.[62] Variation, once more, occurs in terms of the GPR hierarchies. That is to say, there can be grammatical, phonological, or referential variation of an emic unit.

Lastly, distribution helps us to remember the importance of context and systematic relations within language and human behavior. More broadly, "Something must tell us where we are, beyond reference to our immediate environment. Reference to successively larger patterns of occurrence, to a larger *universe of discourse*, is necessary if one is to know the significance of a person, a thing, or a word."[63] Distinguishing these larger patterns that Pike is referring to involves an awareness of members that fit in particular classes in certain sequences.[64] Distribution also involves our awareness of

[59] Pike, *LC*, 42. See also Poythress, *In the Beginning Was the Word*, 154.

[60] Pike, *LC*, 42.

[61] Ibid., 52.

[62] Poythress, *In the Beginning Was the Word*, 156, 273.

[63] Pike, *LC*, 60.

[64] Ibid., 62.

"points" within a system, for "the distributional relation of a unit to a background system must enter the definition of every unit either as an implicit underlying assumption or as an explicit part of the descriptive mechanism."[65] Put differently, the function of a linguistic unit is only understood within a context.[66] That context has both an *internal* element (the smaller-sized units that make up grammatical, phonological, or referential matrices of which such units are members; e.g., a finite verb is part of the verb tense matrix—an intricate system of suffixes, word form changes, and structural additions we have developed to express our perspective on the action) and an *external* element (membership in a class that fills a particular slot in a hierarchy of discourse or behavior).

Keeping these things in mind, let us now turn to see how the CVD triad relates to the Trinity.

Contrast

The person of the Father seems most naturally connected to the element of contrast, in his identity, will, and action.[67] We might first note that there are numerous references to God ("Yahweh," "the Lord") in the OT, distinguishing him as separate from the pagan gods of other nations, thus providing us with the "negative" element of identification. God is *not* the gods of other nations; those gods are false.[68] Yahweh is the only true God. There are also instances in

[65] Ibid., 65.

[66] Poythress, *In the Beginning Was the Word*, 243.

[67] Remember here that *contrast* is linked with the *particle* perspective, *variation* with the *wave* perspective, and *distribution* with the *field* perspective. See Vern S. Poythress, *Perspectives Originating in the Mystery of the Trinity*, unpublished manuscript, Appendix D.

[68] For example, in the Pentateuch God is often contrasted with the pagan gods of other nations, which may ensnare Israel. See Ex. 20:3; 23:13; Deut. 5:7; 6:14; 7:4; 8:19; 11:16, 28; 13:7; 28:14, 36, 64; 29:26; and others. In Isaiah 44 and 45, there are many places where the Lord's incomparability with other gods is accented (e.g., 44:6, 8; 45:5, 14, 18, 21, and 22). See also Frame, *Systematic Theology*, 426–27.

which God is identified in a positive way. For instance, many OT texts identify God positively by attributing certain characteristics to him, e.g., righteousness, holiness, goodness, steadfast love, faithfulness, etc. One example would be God's self-identification to Moses in Exodus 34:6–7.

> The Lord passed before him and proclaimed, "The Lord, the Lord, a God merciful and gracious, slow to anger, and abounding in steadfast love and faithfulness, 7 keeping steadfast love for thousands, forgiving iniquity and transgression and sin, but who will by no means clear the guilty, visiting the iniquity of the fathers on the children and the children's children, to the third and the fourth generation."

Here, God is positively identified with certain traits and actions.

However, it is not always clear that such texts are referring to the Father specifically. Many OT texts can be interpreted as referring to the entire Godhead, some more obviously than others, as we saw with Ps. 33:6, "By the word of the Lord the heavens were made, and by the breath of his mouth all their host." We seem called to read this verse with particular attention to the roles of the Trinitarian persons in creation. The connection between a biblical passage and a particular person of the Godhead in the OT, though, is not usually this clear.[69] Rather than delve into this interpretive issue at the moment, it may be more helpful for our purposes to look at a few texts in the New Testament in which Jesus makes statements about God the Father, since these statements can be more readily understood as referring to the first person of the Godhead. In these texts, we will see that the Father takes on clear *contrastive-identificational features*.

[69] This issue is resolved with certain passages in the NT, such as 2 Cor. 1:21–22, "And it is God who establishes us with you in Christ, and has anointed us, and who has also put his seal on us and given us his Spirit in our hearts as a guarantee." Here "God" (*theos*) is a clear reference to the Father as distinguished from Christ and the Spirit.

Let us first consider Jesus' prayer in Matthew 11:25–27, which "provides a window into Jesus' own insight into the Father-Son relationship."[70]

> At that time Jesus declared, "I thank you, Father, LORD of heaven and earth, that you have hidden these things from the wise and understanding and revealed them to little children; [26] yes, Father, for such was your gracious will. [27] All things have been handed over to me by my Father, and no one knows the Son except the Father, and no one knows the Father except the Son and anyone to whom the Son chooses to reveal him.

Notice that there both negative and positive descriptions of the Father here. That is, he has both *contrastive* and *identificational* features. Perhaps the most obvious contrastive feature is Jesus' assertion that *no one* knows the Father but the Son. Negatively, the Father is he whom only the Son knows exhaustively;[71] thus, the Father is *not* known exhaustively by his creatures, though he is certainly known truly by them according to their limited capacity as image bearers. It is also being implied that there are those who do not know the Father because the Son has not chosen to reveal him to them. The Father, in other words, is in part identified negatively for God's creatures as the one whom we cannot see except by the revelation of the Son. This is the case because "Jesus possesses an intimacy and knowledge of the deep things of his Father that excels all created beings."[72]

This contrastive element of the Father's personhood, however,

[70] Brandon D. Crowe, "The Trinity and the Gospel of Matthew," in *The Essential Trinity: New Testament Foundations and Practical Relevance*, ed. Brandon D. Crowe and Carl R. Trueman (London: Apollos, 2016), 31.

[71] This is linked to Van Til's assertion that the divine persons are "exhaustively representational" of one another. Cornelius Van Til, *A Survey of Christian Epistemology*, 78.

[72] Crowe, "The Trinity and the Gospel of Matthew," 30.

is supplemented with positive identificational features regarding his identity, will, and action. In terms of the Father's identity, he is marked by the appositive phrase, "Lord of heaven and earth," which labels the Father not in terms of what we cannot know but in terms of what we *do* know. The Father is sovereign over the celestial and earthly realms. This is part of the *identity* of the Father that we recognize even when we are not specifically considering the Father in his relationship to the Son.[73] In addition, the Father is distinguished by Jesus as having a unique will, for he has desired (willed) to hide certain things (i.e., the sending of his own Son as a precursor to divine judgement, Matt. 11:20–24) "from the wise and understanding and revealed them to little children."[74] Why did the Father do this? It was his "gracious will." The Father has a will that is distinct from, though in exhaustive harmony with, that of Jesus. Lastly, the Father is set apart by his action. He is the one who hands all things over to Jesus. The Father, as divine agent, hands over to the Son what he has made.[75]

These contrastive-identificational features of the Father, of course, must be understood in a certain way. Such features do not serve to segregate him from the other divine persons; rather, they actually allow for unity, since "unity" is an empty term if there is not diversity. We see this unity brought to our attention when some of the actions that are prominent in the personhood of the Father do not exclude the Son. For instance, in Matthew 11:25–27 "a

[73] Pair this with Pike's statement, "The same components which help us to see that one unit differs from another also help us to *recognize* the unit when it is no longer close to the one which we separated it from." Pike, *LC*, 42. In other words, what helps us to identify the Father in relation to the Son also allows us to recognize the Father when we are not explicitly relating him to the Son.

[74] We can also think of these hidden things as "the realities of eschatological salvation in Christ." Crowe, "The Trinity and the Gospel of Matthew," 30.

[75] The Son will hand back to the Father all things at the completion of his ministry, as Paul tells us in 1 Cor. 15:28, "When all things are subjected to him, then the Son himself will also be subjected to him who put all things in subjection under him, that God may be all in all."

comparable revealing function is attributed to both the Father and the Son."[76] And because Matthew clearly expresses that "Jesus' position is squarely on the Creator side of the Creator-creature divide," we know that the Son shares in the LORDSHIP of the Father (as passages such as 1 Cor. 15:28 make plain). Thus, while we see the Father given contrastive-identificational features, those features serve the gloriously deep harmony of the Godhead.[77]

Several other passages in the New Testament link Pike's element of contrast to the personhood of the Father, but we can focus on a select number of texts in which the Father is identified by his actions in relation to Jesus, particularly in raising him from the dead. Wesley Hill has done helpful work in bringing this to the surface of Pauline studies.[78]

The Father is contrastively identified as "the one who raised Jesus from the dead."[79] Hill notes that Paul frequently uses a substantival participial construction that serves to identify the Father as the agent who raised Christ from the dead. Hill and other scholars have seen these constructions as "identity descriptions." "The aim of such formulations is not merely to reference some divine action but also to 'name' God or specify his unique character by that action."[80]

[76] Crowe, "The Trinity and the Gospel of Matthew," 30.

[77] There is also a sense in which all of the contrastive-identificational features that we might have of the Father are in some sense related to the Son and the Spirit, since the very word "Father" presupposes sonship. This has been evident at least since the time of Augustine. He addresses this issue in the first few books of *De Trinitate*.

[78] Hill, *Paul and the Trinity*.

[79] Hill, *Paul and the Trinity*, 52. He discusses Gal. 1:1, Rom. 4:24, Rom. 8:11a, and 8:11b as examples. Similarly, Francis Watson writes, "Paul's God is the one who raised Jesus from the dead, but this God is also the one who did not spare his own son but gave him up for us all (Rom. 8:32): the death and the resurrection of Jesus are two sides of the single yet complex action in which God defines who God is." Francis Watson, "The Triune Divine Identity: Reflections on Pauline God-Language, in Disagreement with J. D. G. Dunn," *JSNT* 80 (2000): 107.

[80] Hill, *Paul and the Trinity*, 53.

Hill goes on to argue that "Paul discerns the character and actions of the God of Abraham only through the lens of his act of giving up (Rom. 4:25) and raising (4:24) Jesus."[81] In other words, the action of the Father serves to *contrast him with* and *identify him in relation to* the Son.

Again, the contrastive-identificational nature of the Father does not sunder his identity from the Son and the Spirit. As Bruce Marshall put it,

> The persons of the Trinity . . . can only be identified together. Thus in order to pick out the Father as a particular person—to grasp his unsubstitutable personal uniqueness—we have to be able to pick out the Son and the Spirit as particular persons; the same goes, *mutatis mutandis*, for identifying the Son and the Spirit as well. The reason for this is that the persons of the Trinity have their personal uniqueness only in their relations to and interactions with one another.[82]

Still, the element of contrast can be seen as more prominently displayed in the Father, especially in light of what Jesus says concerning the Father's work. As Bray reminds us, "when Jesus spoke about his Father, it was often in the context of what the Father was doing, either in and through the Son or independently of him."[83]

The work of the Father in sending the Son and Spirit to reconcile the world to himself, along with the Father's ceaseless providential care over all that has been made (and, through Christ and the Spirit, is being re-made) serves to set him apart not just from

[81] Ibid., 71.

[82] Bruce D. Marshall, "Christ and the Cultures: The Jewish People and Christian Theology," in *The Cambridge Companion to Christian Doctrine*, ed. Colin E. Gunton (New York: Cambridge University Press, 1997), 96. Hill brought this passage to my attention (Hill, *Paul and the Trinity*, 73.)

[83] Gerald Bray, *God Has Spoken: A History of Christian Theology* (Wheaton, IL: Crossway, 2014), 188.

other divine persons, but from the created world.[84] In other words, the Father can be linked to Pike's element of contrast in light of the Creator-creature distinction. True, the Creator-creature distinction encompasses the *triune* God. Yet, there is also a sense in which the tenebrous light of a created and contingent reality contrasts with the radiance of "the Father of lights" (James 1:17).

The Father's relationship to contrast seems especially evident when we consider the other elements of Pike's triad in relation to the Son and the Spirit. That is where we turn presently.

Variation

Remember that for Pike variation encapsulates the truth that "normal social behavior requires that we be able to recognize identities in spite of change."[85] When examining linguistic units, variation brings into focus "those features of a unit which may change *without causing the loss of recognizability* of the unit. The appropriate observer readily recognizes that certain changes do not affect deeper identities."[86]

The person of the Son seems most prominently connected to the element of variation, especially if we consider the entire Godhead to be a "linguistic unit" of sorts.[87] We must be careful in drawing

[84] Ibid., 152, 175.

[85] Pike, *LC*, 52.

[86] Ibid.

[87] Though we do not have the space to develop it here, there may be something to the notion of God's unity as communicative. By that, I mean the unity of God is *more than* a unity of essence, though certainly not less. In addition to the unity of essence, the unity of the Godhead can also be understood as an outworking of perichoresis, whereby the divine persons eternally and ceaselessly communicate with one another in such a way that they foster exhaustive unity among themselves. Gisbert Greshake seems to hint at this in his article, "Trinity as 'Communio,'" in *Rethinking Trinitarian Theology: Disputed Questions and Contemporary Issues in Trinitarian Theology*, ed. Giulio Maspero and Robert J. Woźniak (New York: T&T Clark, 2012), 331–45. Again, I want to be careful not to adopt social Trinitarianism, but there are biblical truths to Greshake's argument and to the notion that God is one in the sense of his

connections here, especially because the CVD triad is a maturation of the FMD *modes*. The Son is not merely a "mode" of the one God.[88] He is an eternally begotten and truly distinct person of the Trinity. We must be vigilant in guarding against the ancient heresy of modalism.[89] Still, if we keep charry in our exposition here and remember that the CVD triad is a *reflection* of the Trinity, we can in some senses talk about the Son as a "variant" or "manifestation" of the divine essence, particularly with reference to the Son being the eternal Word of the Father (John 1:1). Some explanation is in order before we look at this more specifically.

The Son can be understood as a variant of the Godhead in the sense that he is a concrete manifestation of the divine essence, eternally begotten (or spoken) by the Father. Bavinck highlights this by drawing our attention to the "fecundity" of God, which he sees as tied to the eternal generation (begetting) of the Son.

> Generation occurs also in the divine being. God's fecundity is a beautiful theme, one that frequently recurs in the church fathers. God is no abstract, fixed, monadic, solitary substance, but a plentitude of life. It is his nature (*ousia*) to be generative (*gennaetikae*) and fruitful (*karpogonos*). It is

eternally unifying intra-Trinitarian communication. However, this needs to be *added to* the traditional teaching of the unity of God's essence, rather than being substituted for it.

[88] For this reason, I have never been quite comfortable with defining the divine persons as "modes of subsistence," though that language has been part of the orthodox tradition for some time. See Frame, *Systematic Theology*, 482; and Turretin, *Institutes*, 1:253–55, 278.

[89] Part of the reason why it is difficult to associate elements of Pike's triad with the divine persons is the fact that *no* analogy between created reality and the triune God is perfect. Because we are moving from creation to Creator, there will always be elements of discontinuity between the worldly referent and the Trinity. This is simply a result of the Creator-creature distinction. For a brief discussion of this, see Hibbs, "A Note on Trinitarian Analogies," Place for Truth, January 4, 2015, accessed October 18, 2016, http://www.placefortruth.org/content/note-trinitarian-analogies-1.

> capable of expansion, unfolding, and communication. Those who deny this fecund productivity fail to take seriously the fact that God is an infinite fullness of blessed life. All such people have left is an abstract deistic concept of God, or to compensate for this sterility, in pantheistic fashion they include the life of the world in the divine being. Apart from the Trinity even the act of creation becomes inconceivable. For if God cannot communicate himself, he is a darkened light, a dry spring, unable to exert himself outward to communicate himself to creatures.[90]

We might phrase Bavinck's point here with the language of Pike's theory. God's ability to manifest himself and produce the eternal "variant" of the Son is part of what makes God Trinitarian and what allows for creation.

Consider this point in reference to John's analogy of the Son as the eternal Word of the Father. What exactly does it mean for the Son to be the Word of the Father? An answer to this question could, in itself, fill volumes. For our purposes, we might consider what Geerhardus Vos has suggested in volume 1 of his *Reformed Dogmatics*. The Son is the Word of the Father in the following senses.[91]

1. The word is something caused by the speaker.

2. Nevertheless this word is not created out of nothing. Its rationale is already inherent in the speaker.

[90] Bavinck, *God and Creation*, 308–9.

[91] Geerhardus Vos, *Reformed Dogmatics*, vol. 1, *Theology Proper*, ed. Richard B. Gaffin, Jr., trans. Richard B. Gaffin Jr. (Bellingham, WA: Lexham Press, 2014), 57. We are focusing here on the linguistic analogy for the Trinity. "God the Father is speaker, God the Son is the speech, and God the Spirit is the breath carrying the speech to its destination. The Spirit is also the power who brings about its effects." Poythress, *In the Beginning Was the Word*, 21. This biblical truth, again, must be parallel with the truth that the divine persons also speak to each other as conscious agents.

3. The word reproduces an image of the speaker; it is an imprint of his personal existence. There is equivalence between the speaker and his word.

4. Speaker and word remain tied to each other in the most intimate way. Even after it has been spoken, the word lives on in the consciousness.

There is much we could unpack here, but we can at least note how Vos's language is related to Pike's concept of variation (or, in his earlier work, manifestation). The Word of the Father is eternally brought forth by the Father as speaker. In terms we have already used, the Word of the Father is eternally *generated* or *begotten*. That is, the Father as Speaker is the logical cause (*not* the ontological cause) of the Son as Word.[92] The Son is thus an eternally begotten manifestation (or variant) of the divine essence. The logical relationship between the Speaker (Father) and the Word (Son) points to the Son as a unique manifestation (variant) of the Godhead who has an unfathomably intimate relationship with the Father and shares in the one divine essence.

Again, let us be careful. The Son is not a reduplication of the Father. In fact, in some ways it would be theologically inaccurate to say that the Son is a manifestation or variant of the Father, as Gilles Emery does.[93] The Son does "manifest" the Father in the sense of

[92] To speak of the Son as being ontologically caused by the Father—i.e., as if the Son's being were brought about by the Father—smacks of subordinationism. In contrast with the eastern tradition, the west has commonly affirmed that the Son logically proceeds from the Father (for there is an order in the Godhead), but this logical procession does not mean ontological derivation. Hodge, *Systematic Theology*, 1:445; Turretin, *Institutes*, 1:280. All persons of the Trinity are, in Calvin's words, *autotheos*, i.e., underived.

[93] This is the language that Emery uses: "The Word reveals and manifests the Father, by nature, the word is a manifestation." Gilles Emery, *The Trinity: An Introduction to the Catholic Doctrine on the Triune God*, trans. Matthew Levering (Washington, DC: Catholic University of America, 2011), 129.

being his perfect image, but to say that the Son is an *ontological* manifestation of the Father (a manifestation of the Father's essence) is problematic, since it suggests that the Father is the "fountain of deity," and that the persons of the Godhead are not each *a se*.[94] It is worth noting here that Calvin was an important figure in establishing the aseity of each of the divine persons, especially the Son, as has been recently noted.[95] Van Til followed him and emphasized that unity and diversity (or unity and plurality) are equally ultimate in the Godhead; neither can be reduced to the other. Thus, I would say that the Son is an eternally generated variant or manifestation *of the one divine essence*.[96]

[94] I was given helpful direction here by Carlton Wynne with regards to why Emery may have used the language that he did. In light of his Thomistic background, Emery does not truly distinguish the nature and the personhood of the Son; in other words, for him the Son's personal generation from the Father simply *is* a generation of the Son's essence. This is an outgrowth of Thomas's "methodological emphasis on divine unity as epistemologically foundational to his discussion of divine triunity (i.e., his nature/grace dualism)." For some of us in the Reformed tradition, this seems to at least partially erode the "distinctions among the persons as self-conscious agents." Carlton Wynne, email message to author, October 19, 2016.

[95] Brannon Ellis, *Calvin, Classical Trinitarianism, and the Aseity of the Son* (New York: Oxford University Press, 2012).

[96] We can affirm, in other words, that "the Father is proposed in Scripture as the first person, who is from no one; the Son as the second, who is from the Father; and the Holy Spirit as the third who is from the Father and the Son." Turretin, *Institutes*, 1:280. Yet, this logical order is with regards to the personal relations—the persons as they relate to themselves—not with regards to the essence. Thus, we must clarify or slightly revise Bavinck's words, "divine generation implies that the Father begets the Son out of the being of the Father." Bavinck, *God and Creation*, 309. It is important to focus solely on the word "being" here (i.e., the one divine essence). The "being" of the Father should be understood as a reference not to what belongs properly *only* to the Father but to that which belongs properly to all three divine persons. In Frame's language, following John Calvin, "what the Son receives from the Father is not his being, not his divine essence, but his *person*." Frame, *Systematic Theology*, 492. The essence is that which the Father, Son, and Spirit share equally. And "as the same divine essence with all its infinite perfections is common to the

As such, the Son is described by Paul as "the radiance of the glory of God and the exact imprint of his [the Father's] nature" (Heb. 1:3). The exactness of the imprint can be understood with the language of variation. The Son is the eternal, wholly divine variant of the divine essence and the *perfect* image of the Father. He is "the image of the invisible God" (Col. 1:15), "the perfect expression of the Father."[97] All of this deepens our understanding of what it means for the Son to be the Word.

Let us now return more specifically to how we understand the languagc of thc Son as "Word." Vos was by no means the only one who expounded on the Son as the Word of the Father. Theologians both within and outside the Reformed tradition have done this for centuries. A prime example in the Catholic tradition is Gilles Emery, the Thomistic scholar previously referenced, who devoted much space to expositing Aquinas's thought on this very topic. In his popular work *The Trinity: An Introduction to Catholic Doctrine on the Triune God*, he writes,

> In naming the Son "*Word*," one signifies a twofold aspect in the Son himself. First, the Word comes forth from the one who speaks him or pronounces him. A word is spoken by someone. The tradition flowing from St. Augustine meditated on the divine Word by considering, by analogy, the "interior word" that a human being forms or conceives by his mind and that remains in his mind. This "likeness" allows one to show believers that the Word is characterized by a relation of origin to the One who speaks him from all eternity: the Father. Second, the Word is the perfect and

---

Father, Son, and Spirit, there can be no inferiority of one person to the other in the Trinity. Neither does it imply posteriority; for the divine essence common to the several persons is self-existent and eternal." Hodge, *Systematic Theology*, 1:460–61. This solidifies the biblical maxim that in the Godhead unity and plurality are equally ultimate.

[97] Emery, *The Trinity*, 131.

> full expression of the Father. We can see this by considering the following: by the human interior word, which the vocal word signifies exteriorly, our human mind *expresses what it conceives*. By analogy, the Father, by knowing himself in a personal and fruitful act, pronounces a Word who expresses all that he is.[98]

Like Vos, Emery draws our attention to the Son as a manifestation (or variant) of the divine essence that is intimately related to the Father, who eternally speaks him. Recall Vos's language: "The word reproduces an image of the speaker; it is an imprint of his personal existence. There is equivalence between the speaker and his word. . . . Speaker and word remain tied to each other in the most intimate way. Even after it has been spoken, the word lives on in the consciousness." The Son as the eternal Word is "an imprint" of the Father's personal existence, as that existence emerges from the one essence and lives eternally in the Father's consciousness. So, there is "equivalence between the speaker and his word," and "speaker and word remain tied to each other in the most intimate way." All this is to say that the Word is *both* fully equal to the Father as Speaker and yet distinct from him as a unique manifestation of the divine essence.

That the Son is a variant eternally spoken by the Father is perhaps easier to perceive when we consider the Son in his incarnation. As theologians have long been aware, the intra-Trinitarian relationships are the basis of their work *ad extra*. That is why Frame defines the phrase "word of God" as "(1) an attribute of God, identical to his being, (2) the second person of the Trinity, and (3) any and all of

[98] Ibid., 129. Directly after this quotation, Emery writes, "The Word is the full expression of the whole divine being of the Father." Again, we would need to revise this, as we revised Bavinck's words above. The Word is the full expression *of the divine being*, and he is the perfect image of the Father. This is an important place in Trinitarian theology where the Reformed should part ways with the Thomistic tradition.

his specific communications, addressed either to Trinitarian persons or to creatures."[99] There is an undeniable link between the eternal Word of the Father and the words God speaks to creatures.[100] There is also a link between the eternal Word of the Father and the incarnate Son. The Son is, in fact, the only one who could have become incarnate.[101] Why is that? There is great mystery here, and Francis Turretin, among others, has offered several reasons, all of which are biblical and theologically valid. However, that does not preclude us from answering this question in light of what we have said about the Son as the eternally begotten variant of the divine essence. The Son, as the eternal spoken variant of the divine essence, is uniquely suited to be a temporal variant of humanity. Throughout church history, orthodoxy has stood firmly on the claim that Christ is *both* fully divine and fully human. Another way of putting this would be to say that the Son as eternal variant of the divine essence takes on the temporal variant (or manifestation) of our human nature, such that he is both fully God and fully man, and yet his divine and human natures are never mixed or confused.

In his humanity, he undergoes the variation that all of us undergo. Pike once used the following illustration to express the

[99] Frame, *Systematic Theology*, 524.

[100] On this relationship, see Vern S. Poythress, "God and Language," in *Did God Really Say? Affirming the Truthfulness and Trustworthiness of Scripture*, ed. David B. Garner (Phillipsburg, NJ: P&R Publishing, 2012) and Poythress, "Reforming Ontology and Logic," 188.

[101] Turretin's discussion is helpful here. For him, only the Son could be incarnate because the Father could not be sent by the Son, for that would contradict their interpersonal relations. Nor could the Spirit become incarnate, since the Spirit would be sent by the mediator. The Son, and only the Son, could become incarnate, "(a) that he who is between the Father and the Holy Spirit should be Mediator between God and men. (b) It was fitting that he who was the Son by nature should make us adoptive sons by grace . . . . (c) It was his to recreate whose it was to create; that the Word, by which all things were made in the first creation, should reform us after his image in the second." Turretin, *Institutes*, 1:304–5.

notion of variation with regards to human persons.[102] He provided two pictures side by side, the left one showing a girl with her hair down and the right one showing the same girl with her hair in a bun.

Yesterday

Boy: I promise to take you to the party.
Girl: Great! I can't wait!

Today

Boy: I can't take you to the party.
Girl: Why not?
Boy: You're not the same girl I promised to take to the party—you're wearing your hair in a bun!

Pike's point is obvious, and humorous. Variation does not mean the loss of basic identity. Indeed, "refusal to acknowledge identity within variability would stop all normal behavior."[103]

During the incarnation, Christ experienced the same sort of daily variation that the rest of us experience as humans. Each day, he awoke as a slightly different and yet essentially same person. We are even told in Luke's Gospel that Jesus "increased in wisdom and in stature and in favor with God and man" (Luke 2:52). This is another way of saying that he underwent the sort of variation and growth that constitutes humanity, for he was fully human. This is what makes Christ *Immanuel*, God *with* us.

We do not need to spell out all of the ways that Christ's own language would demonstrate the principles of Pike's theory, but it is important to at least notice them. The words that Jesus spoke and

[102] Pike, *LC*, 53. I have filled in some minor details to make the illustration more intelligible.
[103] Ibid.

the behaviors he performed all had elements of contrast, variation, and distribution. Yet, we can group all his words and actions together and say that Christ is a unique manifestation or variant of humanity. There will never be another human like him, though we would do well to remind ourselves that Scripture often calls us *to be like him*; we are called upon to conform to the image of Christ (Rom. 8:29). Each of us, as creaturely words spoken by the triune God, must conform to the incarnate Word of the Father, and we do so through the power of the Spirit, who is the breath of God (Gen. 2:7; Job 33:4)! Another way of putting this biblical truth is to say that we are called upon to conform the variant of our own life to the perfect variant of Christ. This has been ordained for us by the Father and will be carried out through the Spirit.

In sum, the eternal Son, as a variant of the one divine essence, and the incarnate Son, as a variant of temporal humanity, link the Son to the concept of variation in Pike's theory. We have only one element in this triad yet to develop.

Distribution

Distribution, you will remember, refers to the importance of context and integrated sub-systems of language within the grammatical, phonological, and referential hierarchies. Once again, for Pike, "reference to successively larger patterns of occurrence, to a larger *universe of discourse*, is necessary if one is to know the significance of a person, a thing, or a word."[104] Distribution is what binds the actual occurrence of linguistic units to a holistic and complex system of patterns. The existence of such patterns is what allows for clear communication.[105]

Predictably, the Spirit can be linked to the element of

[104] Ibid., 60.

[105] "Beyond the pure mathematician in his abstractions lies person in commitment to the sheer joy of the pattern chase." Ibid., 127. In other words, humans are creatures that interpret the world only through recognizing patterns. "Man without pattern is not man." Pike, *LC*, xiii.

distribution, for the Spirit is the *context* for the relation between the Father and the Son. In fact, "without the personality and deity of the Spirit there can be no true oneness between the Father and the Son."[106] The Father and the Son are in harmony *through the Spirit*, who proceeds from them both. Without the Spirit, whom theologians have called "the bond of love" between the Father and the Son, God would be incomplete.[107] As Bavinck wrote,

> The Trinity only completes itself in the divine person of the Holy Spirit. Only through that person does the unity of being in the "threeness" of the persons and the "threeness" of persons in the unity of being, come into being. The entire dogma of the Trinity, the mystery of Christianity, the heart of religion, the true and genuine communion of our souls with God—they all stand or fall with the deity of the Holy Spirit.[108]

Thus, from the time of the early church, the Spirit was identified by his relationship to the Father and the Son.[109]

This relationship was given particular expressions. Bavinck writes that "the relation that exists between the Holy Spirit and the Father and the Son is suggested by his name 'the Holy Spirit' as well as by many verbal forms, such as 'given,' 'sent,' 'poured out,' 'breathed out,' 'proceeded,' 'descended.' Christian theology in turn described this relation in terms of projection, procession, outgoing, spiration,

[106] Bavinck, *God and Creation*, 312.

[107] Matthew Levering, "The Holy Spirit in the Trinitarian Communion: 'Love' and 'Gift'?," *IJST* 16, no. 2 (2014): 129–30.

[108] Bavinck, *God and Creation*, 312.

[109] Just as the other persons, likewise, must be understood with reference to the other two. As Watson notes, this is part of "Trinitarian grammar": "discourse concerning God, Christ or the Spirit should only occur within the framework of discourse concerning God, Christ *and* the Spirit; for 'these three are one'." Francis Watson, "The Triune Divine Identity: Reflections on Pauline God-Language, in Disagreement with J. D. G. Dunn," *JSNT* 80 (2000): 123.

emission, outpouring."[110] The vocabulary can be dizzying, but what I want to point out amidst the array of lexical choices is the common notion of *joint givenness* by the Father and the Son.[111]

Now, how exactly is this related to Pike's notion of distribution? Well, given that the west has embraced the *filioque* clause in the Nicene Creed (procession from the Father *and* the Son), we believe that the work of the Spirit "is dependent on [the Father and the Son] equally and cannot reflect one without the other."[112] The eternal procession of the Spirit is as necessary to the Father as it is to the Son. In this sense, wherever we see the Father and wherever we see the Son, the Spirit is there as well. In terms of Pike's language theory, we might say that the Holy Spirit establishes the distribution—the divine, relational placement of the persons, if you will—of the Godhead. The Spirit ensures that when we say "Father," Son and Spirit are presupposed; and when we say "Son," Father and Spirit are presupposed; and when we say "Spirit," Father and Son are presupposed. The person of the Spirit unites the Father and the Son such that God is three-in-one. God, in other words, is always and everywhere the distribution of three divine persons. The Spirit is thus the *context* for the Father-Son relationship, since the Father-Son relationship flourishes in an eternal bond of Spirit-wrought love. As written by the Greek Orthodox theologian Dumitru Stăniloae, "The Father and the Son unite as Father and Son even more through the Spirit. They are three Persons, but the third does not stand to the side of the other two; He unites Them. He is in each, uniting Them and reinforcing Them in Their distinct qualities even when they speak with us."[113] Especially noteworthy

[110] Bavinck, *God and Creation*, 313.

[111] On the joint giving of the Spirit by the Father and the Son, see J. van Genderen and W. H. Velema, *Concise Reformed Dogmatics*, trans. Gerrit Bilkes and Ed M. van der Maas (Phillipsburg, NJ: P&R Publishing, 2008), 155–56.

[112] Bray, *God Has Spoken*, 726.

[113] Dumitru Stăniloae, *The Holy Trinity: In the Beginning There Was Love*, trans. Roland Clark (Brookline, MA: Holy Cross Orthodox Press, 2012),

for our purposes is the fact that Stăniloae reaffirms that the Spirit is united to the Father and the Son *through divine language*.

> Both the Son and the Spirit speak with the other—and the Father—in Themselves. This is why we say that the Spirit is not a "He" about whom the Father and Son speak, but each speaks of the other two inseparably. Neither the Father nor the Son speaks about the Spirit as about a third who is apart from Them, but the Father has the Spirit within Himself when he speaks with the Son, and the Son has the Spirit within Himself when He speaks with the Father, just as when He speaks with us.[114]

The Spirit is thus the divine person fostering and partaking in the divine speech among the persons of the Godhead—a speech of love and glory that is indicated in Scripture but which transcends our cognitive capacities as creatures.[115]

The Spirit is also the context for divine personal identity, which analogically parallels what Pike wrote about the identification of units in the context of communicative human behavior: "reference to successively larger patterns of occurrence, to a larger *universe of discourse*, is necessary if one is to know the significance of a person, a thing, or a word."[116] To know the significance of the Father and Son as persons, we must know them in the context of the Spirit.

Consider now what we have said in relation to the economic

---

65. Of course, given Stăniloae's theological tradition, Reformed readers must guard against the subordinationism that still lies in eastern theology, since they have never accepted the *filioque* clause of the Nicene Creed. Nevertheless, Stăniloae's work is helpful in showing the bond of love that unites the Father, Son, and Spirit.

[114] Ibid.

[115] On the mutual love and glorification of the divine persons, see Frame, *Systematic Theology*, 480–81.

[116] Pike, *LC*, 60.

Trinity. As Hill notes, "the Spirit raises Jesus at God's initiative, thereby binding God and Jesus together in such a way that their relationship may be said to involve his agency. God and Jesus are who they are only in relation to this action of the Spirit, just as the Spirit is who the Spirit is only as the Spirit of God and of Jesus."[117] In the work of salvation, the Spirit is the agent responsible for raising Christ at the Father's beckoning.

In an analogous manner, we are adopted in Christ and reconciled to the Father by the internal work of the Spirit. The holy bond of union that we have with Christ and the Father is brought about by the Spirit. In this sense, the Spirit is the *context* of our reconciliation, and as such he moves deeply within us. As Kuyper put it, "the Father remains outside of the creature; the Son touches him outwardly; by the Holy Spirit the divine life touches him directly in his inward being."[118] Of course, once we have been touched by the Spirit and brought into union with Christ, the Father and the Son make their home in us (John 14:23); they do not remain outside of us. The Spirit, however, is nevertheless the personal context in which we come to know the significance of the Father and Son.

The Spirit is also linked to Pike's concept of distribution in the sense that, for Christians, the Spirit is the context for all of our actions and thoughts. Paul prayed that the Corinthians would have *fellowship* in the Holy Spirit (2 Cor. 13:14)—that they would associate with one another in the loving bond of the Holy Ghost. In Galatians 5:16, Paul adds that we are to *walk* in the Spirit, that is, carry out all human behaviors in prayerful reliance on his guidance, as that guidance is expressed in God's Word. We are to *speak* in the Spirit of God (1 Cor. 12:3). In fact, Paul goes so far as to say that we simply *are* in the Spirit: "You, however, are not in the flesh but in the Spirit" (Rom. 8:9). Every part of a Christian's behavior is to happen

[117] Hill, *Paul and the Trinity*, 163.

[118] Abraham Kuyper, *The Work of the Holy Spirit*, trans. Henry De Vries (Chattanooga, TN: AMG Publishers, 1995), 45.

in the context of the Spirit, who unites us to Christ and reconciles us with the Father.

The Spirit, in sum, is tied to the concept of distribution in that he is the context for the loving relationship among the intra-Trinitarian persons and the bond uniting us to Christ and the Father. In order to interpret human behaviors correctly—that is, in accordance with the truth—we rely on the Spirit. We might say that for the Christian the Spirit is the ultimate *universe of discourse*; he is the context for all that we do, say, and think. All of the patterns of our behavior, including human language, are ultimately meaningful only because of his presence.[119]

Perichoresis

Before moving to the next triad, we should note the place of perichoresis in the CVD triad. What I have argued for above is a connection of prominence between one of the elements of the CVD triad and a person of the Trinity. But in light of the truth that the persons of the Godhead exhaustively interpenetrate and indwell one another, there are bound to be overlaps.

For instance, the Father can be tied to the element of contrast, but the Son is also described in Scripture with contrastive language. Colossians 1:15–20 is a prime example.

> He is the image of the invisible God, the firstborn of all creation. [16] For by him all things were created, in heaven and on earth, visible and invisible, whether thrones or dominions or rulers or authorities—all things were created through him and for him. [17] And he is before all things, and in him all things hold together. [18] And he is the head of the body, the church. He is the beginning, the firstborn from the dead,

[119] As the reader will see, I will also highlight the Father as the universe of discourse in a different sense. This may appear inconsistent, but it is possible because of perichoresis and the exhaustive representation of the Trinitarian persons.

> that in everything he might be preeminent.[119] For in him all the fullness of God was pleased to dwell, [20] and through him to reconcile to himself all things, whether on earth or in heaven, making peace by the blood of his cross.

Christ is identified here as having unique contrastive-identificational features. He is the firstborn, the medium of creation; he precedes all things and holds all things together. He is the one head of the body, and the firstfruits of the resurrection. In *everything* he is preeminent. Surely this is strong contrastive language, separating the Son from all of creation.

The Spirit, also, is sometimes discussed with contrastive language, particularly as he works within human agents. In Genesis 41:38, Joseph is set apart from his peers because he has "the Spirit of God." In Job 33:4, there is an implied contrast between Job and dead creatures or lifeless things: "The Spirit of God has made me, and the breath of the Almighty gives me life." In John 3:5, being born "of water and the Spirit" is what grants a person access to the kingdom of God, i.e., what contrasts him from those in the kingdom of the world.

Nevertheless, Scripture seems to reference the Father most prominently with contrastive language, as has Reformed theology. The Spirit proceeds from the Father and the Son; the Son is eternally generated by the Father, but the Father is himself *unbegotten*. He is given a unique, logical identity as *origin*. That is, he is contrastively identified as the one who is neither begotten nor proceeding.

The same applies to the concepts of variation and distribution. There is certainly a sense in which we could say that each of the divine persons is a variant or manifestation of the divine essence, but the Son, as the Word and image of the Father, is most appropriately linked with this element; word and image are by nature manifestations of something logically prior (a speaker and an original). Remember Vos's language, "the word reproduces an image of the speaker; it is an imprint of his personal existence."[120] Likewise, there are senses in which we could discuss the Father and the Son as a context for the personhood and work of the Spirit or as the context for Christian behavior (especially given Paul's frequent use of "in Christ"), but the Spirit's joint procession from the Father and the Son naturally pairs him with the element of distribution because this procession is distributed in the Father and the Son.

One of the additional elements that perichoresis brings out here is the equal ultimacy of the one and many, which Van Til was very careful to uphold. As he put it in *Defense of the Faith*, "we contend that in God the one and the many are equally ultimate. Unity in God is no more fundamental than diversity, and diversity in God is no more fundamental than unity."[121]

Applying this to our discussion, we might say that just as every linguistic unit has contrast, variation, and distribution, so the one divine essence has clear expressions of contrast, variation, and distribution in the Father, Son, and Spirit. Oneness and threeness are equally ultimate in the Godhead, and thus oneness and threeness are equally ultimate for linguistic units. This is summarized in figure 3.1.

Our theological associations here are actually confirmed by Pike himself in his later work. In fact, the CVD triad is the only one that Pike ever explicitly associated with the Trinity. Bringing out his 1958 discussion on this triad is thus a fitting end to this section.[122]

It was not until 1958 that Pike drew special attention to what he called the "tristructural" nature of units of human behavior, linking them explicitly to the Trinity via the CVD triad.[123] But before

[120] Vos, *Reformed Dogmatics*, 1:57.

[121] Van Til, *Defense of the Faith*, 48.

[122] The following discussion is taken directly from Pierce Taylor Hibbs, "Where Person Meets Word Part 2: The Convergence of Personalism and Scripture in the Language Theory of Kenneth L. Pike," *WTJ* 78, no. 1 (Spring 2016): 129–32, used with permission.

[123] Kenneth L. Pike, "Language and Life 4: Tristructural Units of Human Behavior," *Bib Sac* 114, no. 456 (January 1958): 36–43.

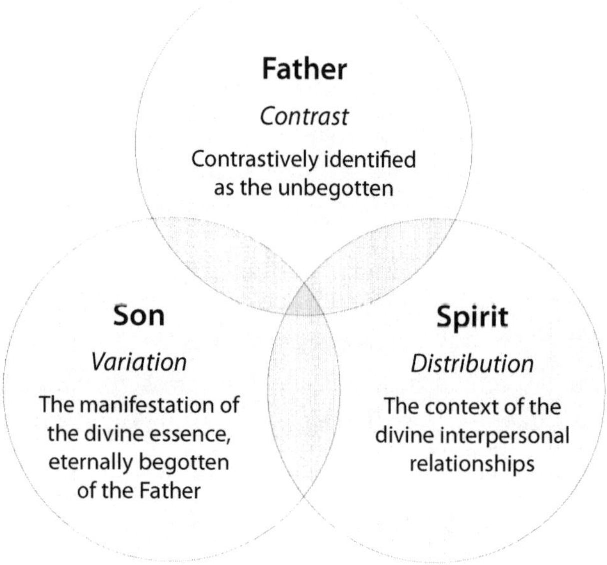

Fig. 3.1. CVD as Father-Son-Spirit

we get to his exposition of that connection, note his circumspection when he defines his key term—"tristructural"—markedly reminiscent of the vigilance of the early church in defining the triunity of God:[124]

> This tristructural theory is sharply distinct from a tripartite view. In the latter, the tripartite one, a unit would be conceived as having sections like an orange, or parts; the substance of the unit could be analytically split, divided, parceled out into these sections or parts, and then the parts added together would make up the whole. If one part of a tripartite unit

[124] Take, for example, the language of the Nicene Creed: [I believe] "in one Lord Jesus Christ, the only-begotten Son of God, begotten of the Father before all worlds; God of God, Light of Light, very God of very God; begotten, not made, being of one substance with the Father . . ."

> were removed, two parts would be left. A chain with three links might symbolize the tripartite view. In the tristructural view none of these things are true. If only one of its three structures is removed from a tristructural unit the entire unit has disappeared, since each structure includes within it all the other substance of that unit. A tristructural unit is not comprised of three parts, but of one whole, with the whole structured in three different ways at once.
>
> A tristructural analysis is crucially different, also from a triaspectual or tridimensional view of a unit. A triaspectual approach may look at a single unit from three different angles, see it from three different vantage points, study it in relation to three different functions, even though the unit is treated as having a single set of structural parts. A tridimensional view of an object may consider it as having three dimensions at the very time that it is assumed to be solid and with no internal macroscopic parts. A cube may be viewed as having height, length, and breadth, for example, but this says nothing about the internal structure of the cube. A tristructural analysis does not look at the same set of parts from different viewpoints or in different dimensions as such, but sees a single large unit divided into three sets of hierarchically arranged subunits such that each hierarchical set comprises the whole, just as the layers of a cake and the slices of that cake each include all of the substance of the cake.[125]

Now, Pike is not making a direct correlation to the Trinity here. As noted earlier, there is no direct correspondence between a physical object and God's triune nature that does not tend to heresy on one end or the other (usually modalism or tritheism). Given his theological upbringing, Pike knows that the Trinity is incomprehensible, so he knows that he must use analogous language when

[125] Pike, "Language and Life 4," 37.

relating human behavior to the Trinity.[126] We may say more broadly, however, that his tristructural approach is Trinitarian in that it clearly resembles a key feature of the Trinity that we have already discussed: perichoresis—threeness in oneness, and the interlocking and overlapping of hierarchies.

Pike did, however, at least venture to associate his theory with the Trinity.[127] For instance, he wrote, "in the Christian understanding of God's nature there are three persons which, in order to show the analogy, might be called personal 'structures.' Each has its own personal individuality and function without constituting a new part of God or an additional God; each is the whole."[128] Christian readers might have predicted this analogy based on the description of "tristructural" alone. But he does go a bit further in his analogy, confirming what we have discovered in our theological exposition of the CVD triad:

> If one seeks for linguistic analogies for some facts of the Christian Trinity, the identificational-contrastive structure with its basic priority of meaning and purpose and communication from individual to individual would be suggested as illustrative of the relationship of the person of God the Father to the Trinity as a whole—inasmuch as ultimate purpose seems to reside in Him (Eph. 1:9, 11), He has taken

[126] On Pike's upbringing, see Hibbs, "Where Persons Meets Word: Part 2," 118–20.

[127] "For the Christian theologian the postulation of tristructural features in human behavior may well prove to be one of the most interesting of all linguistic phenomena. If this analysis can be sustained in some detail . . . there would be available a number of illustrations of a Trinitarian type which could be used to help students grasp with more intellectual clarity some restricted components of the doctrine of a Trinitarian God (note that we *do not* say 'proofs' of the nature of deity. The knowledge of the structure of deity must come from revelation grasped by faith or it cannot come at all." Pike, "Language and Life 4: Tristructural Units of Human Behavior," 39.

[128] Ibid.

> the initiative to communicate and to reveal Himself to us (Heb. 1:1–2), and the Sonship of Christ implies the Father's priority of rank in some sense (John 14:28; Col. 1:15). On the other hand, as the manifestation structure of linguistic units is the audible, concrete form which can be directly apprehended by us, and is the medium through which all linguistic meaning is communicated, so the second person of the Trinity, the Son, was made concretely available to the senses of man, to be seen, heard, touched (Col. 1:15; 1 John 1:1) and it was through the manifested Word become flesh (John 1:1, 14) that the purposes of God were effected (John 1:3). Similarly, as the distributional-functional structure in the sentence forms the matrix within which the words of the sentence occur, in formal units that are obscure and hard to find of themselves because of their function in making vividly present before us the more concrete sounds and lexical units, so the third person of the Trinity may perhaps be viewed as the structured distributional personal matrix for the work of God (as the Spirit works in us with the love of God which "is shed abroad in our hearts by the Holy Ghost").[129]

Here, perhaps more than anywhere else in his corpus, Pike was unabashed about the connections he saw between his theory of human behavior and the doctrine of the Trinity.

Grammar, Phonology, and Reference: Son, Spirit, and Father

The Trinitarian connections for the next triad in Pike's theory have already been highlighted by Vern Poythress in *In the Beginning Was the Word: Language—A God-Centered Approach*. In this work, he also shows how the CVD triad can be derived from the PWF

[129] Ibid., 42–43.

perspectives.[130] We can draw on his work here in relation to the GPR hierarchies and keep the discussion in this section brief, since our goal in this chapter is merely to show how Pike's theory has a Trinitarian scheme.

Grammar

The grammatical hierarchy for Pike is more than simply a system of "chunks" of language that can be coherently constructed. The levels within the grammatical hierarchy—morphemes, words, phrases, clauses, sentences—are not recognized solely for their structure. Rather, they are predominantly recognized for their *function*. Within the grammatical hierarchy, "each major type of level has some *kind of function* in behavior. Its structural arrangement, its form, has simultaneously a general kind of impact on the hearer (which we call the *meaning* of that level)."[131] This coheres well with Pike's emphasis that language finds its meaning, in large part, with regards to participant response.

Nevertheless, Pike would never deny the systematic nature of any of the hierarchies, especially the grammatical. Each level of the grammatical hierarchy only has "*relative independence*, or *relative isolatability*" because it is always understood within a context of broader or larger grammatical structures or networks of such structures (e.g., paragraphs).

In light of this, Poythress links the system of grammar to the Son, who is the "systematic wisdom of God."[132] Commenting on the example sentence, "I am going to the store to get more bananas," he writes, "The sentence has a grammatical structure. Each word can be classified as a noun, or a verb, or a preposition, and so on. The words fit together into a grammatical construction to make a whole sentence. I express myself with structure, in conformity with

[130] Poythress, *In the Beginning Was the Word*, 56–57, 154.
[131] Pike, *LC*, 72.
[132] Poythress, *In the Beginning Was the Word*, 265.

the grammatical rules. In doing so, I imitate God, whose Son is the systematic wisdom of God."[133] In what sense is the Son the "systematic" wisdom of God? God is incomprehensible to man. "God is so much greater than we that the prospect of coming to know him can often seem daunting. How can we, with all our ignorance, weakness, and sin come to know the LORD of the universe?"[134] Of course, we come to know the transcendent God by his immanence, his accommodating presence with us. "God's incomprehensibility follows from his transcendence over us, and his knowability follows from his immanence."[135] This knowability of God comes through revelation, and Jesus Christ is the climax of God's revelation; Christ is Immanuel, God *with us*, the transcendent God tabernacling with his people in the flesh.

In this sense, the Son is related to the grammatical hierarchy as the systematic exposition of the knowledge of God. To know the Son *is* to the know the Father (John 8:19; 14:7). We know God the Father through the Son (by the power of the Spirit) because the Son systematically structures the identity of God in functional levels of human behavior.

An example may help here. What is the *grammar* of God's love? How are we to understand what it means to say, "God is love" (1 John 4:8)? We understand this on a number of hierarchical levels in the behavior of the incarnate Son. John himself links the love of the Father with the work (the behavior) of the Son in that passage memorized by many children, "For God so loved the world, that he gave his only Son . . ." (John 3:16). The Son is the expression of the Father's love. All that the Son does expresses the love of God systematically, on a great number of levels. Just think of all the smaller and larger behaviors of the Son that express the love of God. Some of these are suggested in figure 3.2.

[133] Ibid., 268.
[134] Frame, *Systematic Theology*, 702.
[135] Ibid., 704.

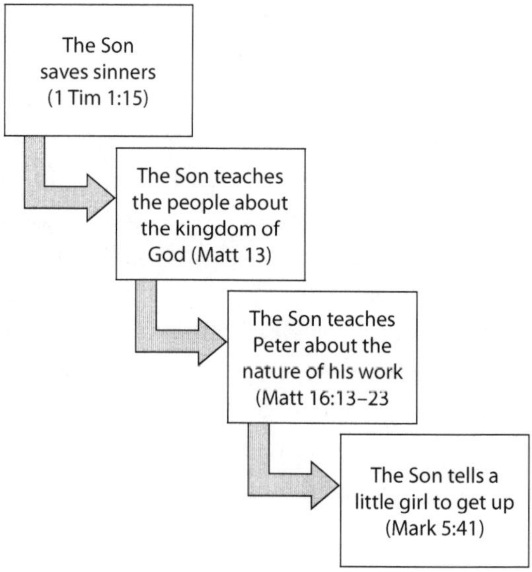

Fig. 3.2. Hierarchy of the Son's Expressions of Love

Each of the Son's actions is, to one degree or another, a hierarchical and systematic expression of the love of God the Father. *Jesus*—in all of his behaviors—is the grammar of God's love. He systematically represents how deep the Father's love for us is. Thus, we look to Jesus in order to understand how God loves us and how we can love others. In this way, the Son is linked to the grammatical hierarchy. He structures the love of God into coherently related chunks of human behavior.

A Trinitarian Revision of the Tagmeme

Now, in the midst of our discussion of the grammatical hierarchy, it may be appropriate here to introduce a revision to Pike's theory, one that has been anticipated by a former student of his.[136]

[136] See Poythress, "Hierarchy in Discourse Analytics"; "A Framework for Discourse Analysis: The Components of a Discourse, from a Tagmemic Viewpoint," *Semiotica* 38, no. 3/4 (1982): 277–98. My revision here is by no means as robustly developed as that of Poythress, but it serves the theological goals of this chapter.

Recall that Pike's tagmeme contained four boxes: *slot*, *class*, *role*, and *cohesion*. The final element, cohesion, seems to me to deal with a unit in context at a broader level. In other words, slot, class, and role focus on a linguistic unit at a narrow level, but then cohesion focuses on the broader patterns within a chunk of discourse, the patterns surrounding the linguistic unit. Such patterns are certainly an important and necessary consideration, but I question whether cohesion belongs properly in the definition of a tagmeme.

I propose that tagmemes are comprised of slot, class, and role. The cohesion of a tagmeme with its surrounding environment is noticed when we take a step back from the immediate context of the tagmeme. This revision would have the benefit of more consistently defining the components of a tagmeme while at the same time cohering with the triadic structure of Pike's theory. It also has the benefit of suggesting associations with the persons of the Trinity.

The Father might be associated with class, since his personal attribute of being unbegotten and his comprehensive plan for redemption sets the divine apart from all other creaturely classes. All creatures are by very definition *begotten*; the Father thus draws our attention to the unique glory and authority of the divine class in the Creator-creature relationship.

The Son could be associated with the slot, since his eternal generation from the Father, along with his incarnation, show us where and when the divine essence is manifested—both in eternity and in time. Just as the slot component of a tagmeme tells us about the specific place of a linguistic unit, the Son reveals a specific manifestation of the Godhead in relation to the Father and the Spirit.[137]

The Spirit would then be associated with role, since one of the Spirit's primary functions (roles) is to serve as the personal bond of union between the Father and the Son. In redemption, the Spirit also serves the critical role of regenerating those who are dead in sin and uniting them with the Father in the Son.

[137] Pike, *LC*, 75.

Each of the divine persons could also be linked with one of the practical questions that Pike proposed for the tagmeme. This is illustrated in figure 3.3.

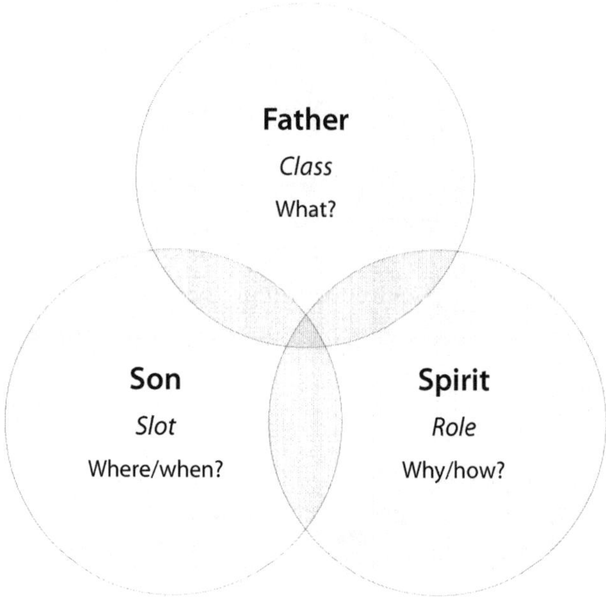

Fig. 3.3. Father, Son, and Spirit as Class, Slot, and Role

Class, slot, and role are inseparable and overlapping. They presuppose one another. Thus, this revision to the tagmeme would theologically cohere with the notion of perichoresis and serve to make Pike's theory more methodologically consistent. Details, of course, would need to be worked out here based on actual examples, but that will be the occasion for another project.

Phonology

For Pike, the phonological hierarchy (along with the referential and grammatical hierarchies) is a simultaneous restructuring of the same data.[138] In grammar, the levels of the hierarchy represent

[138] Pike, *LC*, 84.

systematically arranged functional strata, and the same is the case with phonology. However, in the latter the hierarchical levels exist in terms of speech rather than grammar. Common to all of the hierarchical levels in phonology is the exertion and manipulation of breath. This breath produces the phoneme, the syllable, the stress group, etc. This feature of the phonological hierarchy, especially when considered in the context of John 1:1, lends itself to a connection with the Holy Spirit, "who breathes out the speech of God."[139]

With regards to the economic Trinity, the Holy Spirit is the breath of the Father (the divine Speaker) that carries the Son (the divine Word) to his destination and makes it effectual. In an analogous manner, every person as speaker exerts breath to produce words. "Human speaking with sound imitates God's utterances, which he utters through the power and 'breath' of the Holy Spirit."[140]

It can be easy to dismiss phonology as a less important hierarchy—perhaps in a manner that parallels how western theology functionally dismissed the Holy Spirit for a time in its history.[141] But Pike has taken some steps to show just how critical the phonological hierarchy is. By extension, this reminds us of the importance of the Holy Spirit.

A case in point is Pike's emphasis on the significance of intonation. It seems easy to study language with regards to reference (semantics) or grammar, but this is not the case with intonation. Intonation bridges the world of speech and writing in a way that, frankly, can intimidate many students of language. Bringing phonology to bear on written words seems to introduce unnecessary complexity into the analysis of human language. Yet, as Walter Ong wrote some time ago, phonology is not absent from written language, for *we speak when we read*. "What the reader is seeing on this page are not real words but coded symbols whereby a properly informed

[139] Poythress, *In the Beginning Was the Word*, 268.
[140] Ibid., 267.
[141] Bray, *God Has Spoken*, 607–11.

human being can invoke in his or her consciousness real words, in actual or imagined sound."[142]

Now, pair the truth that Ong has noticed with one of Pike's statements: "Part of the meaning of what a man says—often the most important part—is in the intonation."[143] Pike goes on to show how intonation is what marks the difference between sincerity and sarcasm, hubris and humor, statements and questions, etc. Apart from intonation, many of our utterances (and thus many of our written words) would be misinterpreted or ambiguous. Considering this on a corresponding theological level, we might say that our understanding of the Son and the Father would be compromised apart from the person of the Spirit, who allows us to hear the truth of God because he is the Spirit of truth (John 14:17). Let us never forget that the Spirit is just as necessary and important a person of the Godhead as the Father and the Son. Analogously, the phonological component of language is just as necessary and important as reference and grammar.

Reference

Lastly, the referential hierarchy deals with real-world identity, meaning, and semantic sameness amidst lexical variation.[144] Poythress reminds us that "language has resources for talking about the world: for making statements, for issuing commands and requests, and for carrying out innumerable human purposes. These resources for talking about the world are the *referential* subsystem."[145]

This hierarchy (or subsystem) is tied to the Father. The Father has a purposive plan for all of reality. "The plan of God is the plan preeminently of the Father."[146] That plan includes the purpose of every

[142] Walter J. Ong, *Orality and Literacy: The Technologizing of the Word* (New York: Routledge, 2002), 74.

[143] Pike, *LC*, 92.

[144] Pike, *LC*, 97.

[145] Poythress, *In the Beginning Was the Word*, 266.

[146] Ibid., 265.

reference in existence—physical, theoretical, or spiritual. Thus, when we speak and reference the real-world and the purposes each reference within that world has, we are imitating on a creaturely level "God's purposes, and more specifically the purposes of God the Father."[147]

The referential hierarchy (and the work of the Father) is critical to uphold in our day, since Derrida and his supporters in the twentieth and twenty-first centuries have attempted to undermine the ability of language to refer to events in the real world. The ability of language to make such references reliably is sometimes called *logocentrism*, which Vanhoozer reminds us is

> the belief that there is some stable point *outside* language—reason, revelation, Platonic Ideas—from which one can ensure that one's words, as well as the whole system of distinctions that order our experience, correspond to the world. It is the desire for a center, for a point of reference, for an ultimate origin—anything on which we can non-arbitrarily hang our beliefs and values. In short, *logocentrism* stands for the fundamental presupposition that it is possible to speak truly: that our talk will be about reality, and not merely talk about talk.[148]

Logocentrism is clearly linked to Pike's referential hierarchy. It is the Father's control over all of created reality—every physical, theoretical, and spiritual referent—that guarantees our words (via grammar and phonology) have the ability to correspond to the real world.[149]

[147] Ibid., 267.

[148] Kevin J. Vanhoozer, *Is There a Meaning in This Text? The Bible, the Reader, and the Morality of Literary Knowledge* (Grand Rapids, MI: Zondervan, 1998), 53.

[149] Part of the reason for this is that the referential world was created by God's divine speech. Human speech, as a creaturely analogue of divine speech, can thus reliably reference the physical and spiritual worlds that are themselves the products of God's Word.

This is not to segregate the referential hierarchy from the grammatical and phonological hierarchies, for we cannot segregate the Father from the Son and the Spirit. The referential component of language is accessed and expressed by the grammatical and phonological components of language, just as, analogously, the Father is accessed and expressed by the Son in the love of the Spirit. On the spiritual level, we have access to the Father by the Son and through the power of the Spirit. So, by extension, we refer reliably to the world outside of ourselves (reference) through the systematic structures of our language (grammar) that are expressed with the power of our breath (phonology).[150]

Perichoresis

Our discussion here has been brief, but intentionally so. Before moving on to Pike's final triad, we would do well to remind ourselves of the perichoretic nature of these hierarchies, which again mirror the perichoretic nature of the Godhead.

Pike constantly reinforced his claim that the hierarchies were overlapping and interlocking. This does not by any means lead to an

[150] It is worth noting here that Poythress has recognized the partial truth with which deconstructionists took issue. While Vanhoozer opposes the deconstructionist movement as an assault on a biblical understanding of logocentrism, Poythress notes that this critique may go too far. "It may sound as if deconstruction is directly attacking Christian doctrine. But that impression in superficial. Rather, deconstruction plays on the different possible allusions of the term 'logocentrism.' The target of its critique is first of all the practice in Western philosophy of using reason as the way to conduct a quest for final wisdom. The quest has the aim of attaining a godlike, transparent, rational, final vision of truth, a truth of pure thought. In this context, the Greek word "logos" is associated with reason rather than specifically with Christian thought. The philosophical quest relies on reason and has reason at its center. At the same time, the term "logocentrism," by alluding to Christian thought, suggests that this Western quest is a secular transmutation of religion. Deconstruction uses the term as a provocative label, and intends to suggest that the rationalist tradition in the West is a substitute religion." Poythress, *In the Beginning Was the Word*, 378.

understanding of the hierarchies as "modes." Rather, it establishes their distinctness, for the units of one hierarchy are not necessarily coterminous with the units of the other hierarchies. Recall an earlier example. *I'm* is a simple unit of the phonological hierarchy and yet a complex unit in the grammatical hierarchy, consisting of a subject and a linking verb: *I am*. It would be helpful here to reproduce Pike's own thoughts on the nature of the relations among the hierarchies. After briefly commenting on this, we can turn to the final triad and conclude this chapter.

> Interlocking between hierarchies may relate two or three of the hierarchies as a whole, but when it does so the actual linking must take place between one particular unit or layer of one of the hierarchies and one particular layer or unit of one of the other hierarchies. Multiple linking at the borders and/or nuclei of units of the hierarchies makes up the interlocking of the hierarchical system as a whole.
>
> Language constitutes a system but no language system can occur unless some kind of interlocking also occurs. Lower-layers within one modal hierarchy must somehow be fused into or integrated with larger units of activity on a higher level of that hierarchy, or else there is no structure joining these units.
>
> Structure, in this sense, is in part a function of the interlocking and interpenetration of levels or layers of a hierarchy. The various hierarchies of such a system, furthermore, must also be relevant to and interlocking with one another or else no structural organization of them occurs. On the one hand there must be certain points or regions at which some of the units of the hierarchy *are* coterminous or co-nuclear, in order for the units of the various hierarchies to be relevant one to another. On the other hand there must be certain points in the system at which some of the units on various levels of the hierarchies of the modes are *not* coterminous or co-nuclear.

> If all units of all hierarchies were always coterminous and co-nuclear then there would be no trimodal structuring at all, but merely a single structure which could be looked at from three different points of view.[151]

Pike is here recognizing the need for both continuity and distinction. In order for the unified structure of a language to hold, there must be *both* overlap and distinction. The Trinitarian connections are apparent here. "The glory of the confession of the Trinity consists above all in the fact that that unity, however absolute, does not exclude but includes diversity."[152] Pair this with the fact that Pike emphasizes the *necessity* of interlocking for any language system. Louis Berkhof carried on a long tradition of the church affirming that God is *necessarily* triune, *necessarily* one and three, *necessarily* a harmony of unity and diversity. God's "tripersonal existence is a necessity in the Divine Being, and not in any sense the result of a choice of God. He could not exist in any other than the tripersonal form."[153]

I end this section by picking up a thread of Pike's comments that we will weave into the following discussion: a unified system of language must have both overlap (interpenetration) and non-coterminus units or hierarchical layers. This will be important in our discussion of the final triad where Pike asserts that change presupposes sameness. At this point, we turn our attention to that triad.

Form-Meaning Composites (Son), Sharing as Prerequisite to Change (Spirit), and Universe of Discourse (Father)

As of yet, there has not been a discussion of the Trinitarian elements of Pike's final triad. In what follows I hope to balance

[151] Pike, *LRUT*, 566.
[152] Bavinck, *God and Creation*, 300.
[153] Berkhof, *Systematic Theology*, 84.

circumspection with creativity. However, before I begin I would point out that I am not making the connections that might seem consistent with the previous discussion. Form-meaning composites are tied to the particle perspective and the element of contrast, so it would seem natural to link form-meaning composites with the Father. However, I am linking them with the Son. Sharing as prerequisite to change is tied to the wave perspective and to variation, so it would seem we should link it with the Son, but I am linking it with the Holy Spirit. Lastly, the field perspective and distribution were tied to the Spirit, so we might assume a connection between universe of discourse and the Spirit (which is certainly warranted), but here I am connecting it with the Father. I hope the reasons for the connections I have drawn are evident by the end of this section. After all, we want our connections to be based on substantive overlap rather than on rote consistency. The perichoretic structure of Pike's theory also must be factored into our exploration.

Form-Meaning Composites Rooted in the Son

The relationship between form and meaning was deeply important to Pike, in his earlier theory as much as in the later.[154] He

[154] Consider some of Pike's critiques of other linguists: (1) "we reject the theory of signs of de Saussure (1931) and of Hjelmslev—who says that 'A "sign" functions, designates, denotes; a "sign," in contradistinction to a nonsign, is the bearer of a meaning' (1953:27); our present theory would not allow us to say . . . that a linguistic item 'is the bearer of a meaning,' since there would be no available linguistic units to 'bear' meanings, in view of the fact that there are only form-meaning composites"; (2) "As more and more materials in speech begin to appear structured, the view that 'language' as a structure differs from 'speech' as an activity is threatened. In behavioremics, furthermore, the structural units always retain substance as relevant to their manifestation mode. Under the impact of these two factors, we abandon the distinction between *la langue* and *la parole* proposed by de Saussure"; (3) "Chomsky attempts to present a grammar theory which is 'completely formal and non-semantic' (1957a:93; cf. also 94, 97, 99–104"; (4) "A tagmemic view would feel that a rigid transformationalist approach does not give adequate theoretical attention to the nature of units in general (contrast, variation, distribution); to

states his position on this in the very first sentence of the opening chapter on form and meaning: "In this chapter I am rejecting all views of language or life which claim that *abstract* forms comprise basic reality."[155] He continues,

> Here, as over against centuries of work by some scholars, *form* is a term used to refer to concretely structured elements which include a physical component, not idealized disembodied realities, essences, or ideas—or even rules or relations. In addition to form, a meaning, relevance, value, significance, deduced cause, result of a deduced cause, of some other *observer-related component* is always demanded in our affirmation of the existence of any unit of rational behavior, of the existence of the observability of any concrete object or event, or of any object or event as deduced by man or imagined by man.[156]

Every emic unit of language and behavior must have a physical component for Pike.[157] Thus, by "form" he means a concrete, physical manifestation. Even human thoughts have a physical manifestation in being connected to synapses in the brain.

---

emic levels such as clause; to patterning by way of field theory (experience of pattern is not merely perception of a role); the necessity for more persistent attention to the correlation of form with meaning in a unit of grammar (a tagmeme); to etic versus emic elements of units or levels; to the structure of units beyond the sentence; to partially-independent but partially-overlapping hierarchies of lexicon, of phonology, and of grammar, in reference to particle, wave, and field; to the relation of verbal to nonverbal structure." Pike, *LRUT*, 63, 536, 97, 149, 496.

[155] Pike, *LC*, 111.

[156] Ibid.

[157] "No item of human behavior can be completely abstracted from all physical settings, or from all physical components; no purely abstractional system can serve in it, whether of ideas or of postulated systemic relational elements. Each must have its physical component." Ibid., xii–xiii.

Why was he so adamant about this? It is difficult to say for certain, but it is likely related to his insistence that his language theory be practical, fit for the man on the street. Everyday life suggests that there is really no such thing as "pure form" or "pure meaning"; the two cannot be abstracted from one another. Pike's emphasis on form-meaning composites, as I have argued elsewhere, is also related to the personalism in his theory.[158] *People* never abstract form and meaning in their use of language.

Yet, there may also be a more explicitly theological reason for maintaining Pike's emphasis on form-meaning composites. When we think about it, the connection between form and meaning is not so foreign to Trinitarian theology. The incarnate Son, after all, is in some sense a divine form-meaning composite. This might seem strange at first, but all of us are form-meaning composites of a sort. This language is not meant to depersonalize humanity, but merely to draw out how we are structured as creatures. Let me explain how this applies to us before drawing out the Trinitarian connection.

People are, of course, physical forms. Certainly, we are much more than that, since we are body-*spirit* image bearers of God. But the "body" component of that phrase is important. God did not create us body-less, and when we are resurrected, we will have a *bodily* resurrection, not merely a spiritual resurrection. Our bodily form is thus a divine gift that is inextricable from our identity as persons. We are born, re-born, and resurrected *with a body*.

At the same time, we are all *meaningful* persons within God's plan of redemption. There is no human body (and thus no person) that is not meaningful to God. Bodily form and divinely endowed meaning go hand in hand. Persons are thus *form-meaning composites*; we are spiritually animated bodies that have special meaning to God in his all-encompassing plan for redemption.[159] There is no

[158] Pierce Taylor Hibbs, "Where Person Meets Word Part 1: Personalism in the Language Theory of Kenneth L. Pike," *WTJ* 77, no. 2 (Fall 2015): 366–69, 374–77.

[159] We will explore this notion more in the final chapter.

such thing as a "mere human body" and no such thing as meaning that is truly abstracted from persons.[160]

Let us now bring this to bear on Trinitarian theology. The eternal Son was sent by the Father and became incarnate by the power of the Holy Spirit (Matt. 1:18; Luke 1:35). In terms that we used earlier, we would say that the eternal manifestation of the divine essence (the eternally begotten Son) took on a temporal manifestation at the incarnation. The eternal Son, in other words, became a form-meaning composite. He took on a body in order that he might sympathize with his people in every way, apart from sin (Heb. 4:15). Likewise, he took on an unparalleled meaning within God's divine plan of redemption. In fact, he *is* God's divine plan of redemption!

Thus, the relationship between form and meaning can be tied to the Son, particularly in his incarnation. This has implications not just for language theory, but for broader semantic theory. There are theological implications for attempting to divorce meaning from concrete forms. By extension, there are theological implications for attempting to divorce meaning from *persons*, i.e., treating meaning as purely propositional. Because form-meaning composites are linked to personhood, separating one from the other is quintessentially impersonal. Not only must linguistic units be related to persons (given that humans are form-meaning composites of a higher order), but all meaning must, in the end, be traced back to its value for persons.

While this has clear associations to the incarnation of the Son, it is also rooted in eternity, since the eternally begotten Son is a

[160] As an aside, this is one of the reasons why the pornographic industry is such a destructive evil. To treat human bodies as "mere bodies," used only for sex, is to deny what makes us truly human. When our bodies are abstracted from the meaning and use they are given in covenantal relationship with God, our soul suffers inexpressible anguish. This has a crippling effect that grows worse with time, for those who struggle with pornography grow more and more accustomed to objectifying human bodies and treating others as, in a very real sense, less than human.

foundationally meaningful manifestation (and thus a type of form) of the divine essence. The relationship between form and meaning, then, goes back to the ontological Trinity.

Our discussion here needs to be related also to the language theory of Ferdinand De Saussure, whose distinction between *la langue* and *la parole* Pike openly opposed. Let us discuss this briefly before moving on to the next element in the triad.

Pike, Saussure, and Calvin: The Signifier and Signified

Strange as it may seem, we will need to bring together Pike's thought, Saussure's language theory, and John Calvin's theology to address the relation between form and meaning at its deepest levels. Let us begin with Calvin and then move to Pike before bringing what we have seen to bear on Saussure's approach to language.

Why, one might ask, do we need to reference John Calvin in a debate concerning modern language theory? Calvin, of course, is a landmark Trinitarian theologian, as Warfield reminded us decades ago.[161] And because Calvin sometimes wrote in French, the native language of Saussure, it is helpful to see some of the correlations between the use of certain terminology in that language.

The issue before us is this: what is the nature of the Son as the Word of the Father? We have asked this question before and provided some answers in light of Vos's theology, but we find new insight in chapter thirteen of Calvin's *Institutes*. In this chapter, Calvin refers to the eternal Son as *la Parolle éternelle de Dieu*, the eternal Word of God.[162] At another place in the same section he calls him *la Parolle essentielle et éternelle du Père*, the essential and eternal Word of the Father. While this Word is clearly distinct from the Father, he remains *une et immuable en Dieu*, one and the same with God. The Son, as *la Parrolle*, signifies God the Father perfectly in the power

[161] B. B. Warfield, "Calvin's Doctrine of the Trinity," in *Calvin and Augustine*, ed. Samuel G. Craig (Philadelphia: Presbyterian and Reformed, 1956), 189–284.

[162] Calvin, *Institutes*, 1.13.7.

of the Holy Spirit. He is both the personally distinct *form* (eternally generated by the Father) and yet essentially identical *meaning* of God, tied in loving communion to the Father and the Spirit. As the divine Word, the Son is a form-meaning composite of the Godhead. This is merely to repeat what we said earlier, now in terms of Calvin's French, which has a bearing on Saussure's language theory.

Now, though we cannot get into the details of such a complex discussion, the nature of linguistic signification is where Pike would take issue with Saussure. In *LRUT*, Pike writes,

> we reject the theory of signs of de Saussure (1931) and of Hjelmslev—who says that "A 'sign' functions, designates, denotes; a 'sign,' in contradistinction to a nonsign, is the bearer of a meaning" (1953:27); our present theory would not allow us to say . . . that a linguistic item "is the bearer of a meaning," since there would be no available linguistic units to "bear" meanings, in view of the fact that there are only form-meaning composites.[163]

A bit more needs to be said about some of the assumptions of Saussure's theory of signs, which will clarify Pike's critique.

For Saussure, signs (spoken and written words) are arbitrarily associated not with objects in reality but with what he called a "sound image." "The linguistic sign unites, not a thing and a name, but a concept and a sound image. The latter is not the material sound, a purely physical thing, but the psychological imprint of the sound, the impression that it makes on our senses."[164] Whereas for Pike every linguistic unit has a physical manifestation that is tied to the grammatical form and its referent, for Saussure every linguistic unit (every word, in this case) is tied to a psychological impression that

[163] Pike, *LRUT*, 63.

[164] Ferdinand De Saussure, *Course in General Linguistics*, ed. Charles Bally and Albert Sechehaye, trans. Wade Baskin (1959; repr., London: Forgotten Books, 2012), 66.

has been *arbitrarily* associated with it. Vanhoozer summarizes his approach.

> The meaning of a sign or "signifier" for Saussure is not some actual thing to which the sign refers, but rather a concept or "signified" that has come to be arbitrarily associated with it. It is only arbitrary convention that the letters G-o-d signify a divine rather than a canine entity. A word, after all, does not resemble anything but another word. "Red" means what it means because it is *not* "bed," "fed," or "wed," and because it is not "blue," "green," "crimson," "maroon," or "pink." In other words, "red" is an arbitrary sign that takes its meaning from its place in a system of linguistic differences.[165]

Vanhoozer points out that this is essentially the same position as that of Derrida. The arbitrary nature of signs means that they are internally labyrinthine: we are trapped within a system of signification in which arbitrary signs can only ever refer to other arbitrary signs.[166]

[165] Vanhoozer, *Is There a Meaning in This Text?*, 61.

[166] Kevin J. Vanhoozer, "A Lamp in the Labyrinth: The Hermeneutics of 'Aesthetic' Theology," *Trinity Journal* 8 (1987): 25–56. "Language is a system of interdependent terms in which the value of each term results solely from the simultaneous presence of the others." Saussure, *Course in General Linguistics*, 114. Poythress has done a fine job in reading deconstructionists such as Derrida and Saussure charitably. Deconstructionists such as Derrida commonly claimed that we cannot get *outside* the text of our own language: it is a labyrinth of signification. When we consider what Derrida and Saussure have articulated from a *redeemed* theological perspective, we can say that "there is nothing outside the text of God's speech." Poythress, *In the Beginning Was the Word*, 372. In other words, deconstructionists have stumbled across a truth in God's common grace, though they have distorted it. They claim that we cannot get *outside* the text of our own language. That is not true, for God is a participant in all languages and thus allows for us to refer to his truth in a way that glorifies him. It is true, however, that we cannot get outside the text of God's language, which created all things (Gen. 1) and upholds all things (Heb. 1:3).

This is problematic in a number of ways, not least of which is the fact that this view undercuts the ability of language to reliably reference the external world. However, what is even more relevant for our current discussion is how Saussure connects the arbitrary nature of signification with the language system as a whole. If signification is an arbitrary abstraction built upon the psychological impressions that have been socially imposed on the human mind, then language as a system is an arbitrary abstraction. Meaning, in this sense, is filtered through the language system and is grasped as such only in particular instances. Thus, "Saussure distinguished the system of language (*langue*) from particular acts of saying or speaking (*parole*)."[167]

This distinction underscored his assumption that there is no *necessary* connection between a word and its referent. The word is an arbitrary abstraction, known only in its relation to other arbitrary abstractions. His distinction also suggests that concrete acts of speech should be considered separately from language as an interrelated system of signification shared by those in a common social setting. He tells us, "In separating language from speaking we are at the same time separating: (1) what is social from what is individual; and (2) what is essential from what is accessory and more or less accidental."[168] This separation, however, is both practically and theologically problematic.

First, in terms of pragmatics, if signs are arbitrarily associated with "sound impressions," then "words are thus unreliable guides to the nature of things."[169] Words are, in this sense, untrustworthy since there is nothing that holds them in place throughout time. Language is always changing, so arbitrary signifiers that we use are never stable. The communicative world is in flux, which means that it is inherently unreliable as a vehicle for communicating anything

[167] Vanhoozer, *Is There a Meaning in This Text?*, 61.
[168] Saussure, *Course in General Linguistics*, 14.
[169] Vanhoozer, *Is There a Meaning in This Text?*, 17.

of lasting significance. This has obvious repercussions for our view of Scripture, and of literature more broadly.

What is even more disturbing, however, is the theological problem Saussure's theory raises. When John calls the second person of the Trinity "the Word" (*la Parole*), he is *not* indicating that the Son is an arbitrary signification. Rather, the Son as Word is an exhaustively intentional, unfathomably meaningful, and eternally reliable representation of the Father in the personal presence of the Holy Spirit; the Son manifests the divine essence in perfection and glory and is the place where signifier and signified ultimately meet. As Poythress writes,

> God the Father is in a sense the ultimate Signified. But the Father exists in eternal relation to the other persons in the Trinity. The Father is known through the Son. By analogy with the subsystems of language, we can say that the Father is like the Signified, the Spirit is like the signifier, and the Son is the Word, in whom Signifier and Signified are eternally united and mutually indwelling. The three persons exist in unity and diversity, in fellowship with one another rather than in conceptual isolation. . . . Relations of signification within language derive from the final relation of signification among the persons of the Trinity.[170]

By implication, the Word cannot be considered in isolation from the loving and glory-giving interpersonal language of the Trinity.[171] In

[170] Poythress, *In the Beginning Was the Word*, 376. "Jesus, one might say, is both signifier and signified; he does not only represent God but is himself God's presence." Vanhoozer, *Is There a Meaning in This Text?*, 86.

[171] Remember here that the Trinity has a divine language all its own. "Not only is God a member of a language community that includes human beings, but the persons of the Trinity function as members of a language community among themselves. Language does not have as its sole purpose human-human communication, or even divine-human communication, but also divine-divine communication." Poythress, *In the Beginning Was the Word*, 18.

eternity, *la Parole* is inextricably bound up with the divine essence, which is the context for what we might consider *la langue divine*, the divine language, i.e., the intra-Trinitarian communication that is proper to God as God. Just as *la Parole* cannot be torn from *la langue divine*, so we cannot tear language from speech. In other words, the eternal form-meaning composite of the Son binds temporal form and meaning together. *Langue* and *parole*—language system (form) and concrete manifestation (meaning)—are knotted together in the being of God himself, and no one can untie that knot.

Pike's critique of Saussure thus has theological grounds—perhaps unnoticed by Pike himself, but nevertheless true. We cannot divorce signs from meanings, or treat signs as the "bearers" of meanings, since human signs are based on the eternal signification of the Word, who (together with the Father and the Spirit) is the union of Signifier and Signified. Form-meaning composites, in this sense, are actually related to the tripersonality of the communicating God. Form and meaning, signifier and signified, are bound up together, ultimately because the Father, Son, and Spirit are bound up together.

Much more can and should be said about this, but developed discussion will need to wait and be the subject of future research. At this point, we can move on to discuss the Spirit's relation to Pike's concept of sharing as prerequisite to change.

Sharing as Prerequisite to Change, and the Relating Spirit

Pike noted throughout his career that any worthwhile language theory must account not only for the stability of the world around us (particle) but also for its dynamism. We must be able to account for "physically flowing, merging, smearing, overlapping perceived entities."[172] We see this in linguistic units when sounds are blended, e.g., *as you like* can be pronounced *az-y-like*. We even use such blending or overlapping in phonology and reference when telling a joke, such as the one Pike references concerning the sound "catt'll."

[172] Pike, *LC*, 118.

'Why is a mouse like a pile of hay?'
'The cat'll eat it.' Or 'The cattle eat it.'

There can also be the sharing of wave components. We examined semantic waves in which a nuclear meaning for a given word can be expanded for the use of marginal meanings (e.g., *run a race* vs. *run a business*). A sense of sharing or overlap is also common from the field perspective, when a given linguistic unit or human behavior is seen as a *part* of a *whole*. Common to these linguistic and behavioral phenomena—the overlapping or sharing of sounds or meanings or relational systems—is the notion that *change, distinction, and nuance happen within a relational environment*. In other words, there is no such thing in reality as "pure change," i.e., change which does not begin with some components or elements of a previous thing. We never have complete segmentation of one linguistic unit or event from the preceding and following linguistic unit and event.[173]

This may be startling to some readers, but it is apparent even in ordinary life. We typically consider *wood* and *fire* as separate entities. No one mistakes wood for fire or vice versa. They are clearly distinct. But what about when we are looking at the fire in a wood stove? In a traditional wood stove, such as I had growing up, we would see not two clearly distinct elements in isolation but two distinct elements in a dynamic relationship of change. The fire feeds on the wood for fuel. Without the wood, there would be no fire. So, if we look through the window pane of a wood stove and see a burning fire, are we looking at wood or at fire? Of course, the answer is that we would be looking at some elements that are clearly wood, and other elements that are clearly fire, and other elements that seem to be somewhere in the middle, such as the charred parts of a log that

[173] This phenomenon is linked to what Colin Gunton considered the relational nature of reality, which is rooted in the Trinity. "The world and all in it takes its creation and recreation from the Trinitarian relatedness of Father, Son and Spirit." Colin E. Gunton, *The Promise of Trinitarian Theology*, 2nd ed. (London: T&T Clark, 1997), 99.

are being consumed by the flame. The point is that the change from wood to fire is a *relational change*—a change in which each element is related to the other as there is movement from one distinct entity to another.

Certainly, this example is limited, and I do not in any way mean that everything is at base one relational blob, changing forms in an endless process. Rather, I am saying that change and distinction cannot be understood atomistically, as if there were perfectly clear and infinitely precise borders between one thing and another. That is simply not the sort of universe in which we live. Ours is a universe with simultaneous unity and diversity, one and many, sameness and change, relationality and distinction.

Given this, we are prevented from making the sort of atomistic distinctions that certain scientific approaches to language and human behavior demand. Instead, we must learn to be content with—indeed, to revel in—the fact that sharing is prerequisite to change.

Now, recall our earlier discussion about the Spirit being the bond of union between the Father and the Son, as well as between all believers. The Spirit has a unique place in the Godhead as proceeding jointly from the Father and the Son. The Father and the Son *share* the procession of the Spirit. The Spirit, in this sense, can be understood as the sharing that is necessary for distinction between the person of the Father and the person of the Son. The Father and the Son can never be divorced from one another, and one of the many reasons for this is that they *share* in the eternal act of the Spirit's procession. What I am saying, in other words, is that the Spirit is the necessary shared component of the Godhead that allows for sustained personal distinction of the Father and the Son. Some further explanation may be needed here.

Why, exactly, is it necessary for the Spirit to be the shared person of the Father and the Son if there is to be distinction between persons of the Godhead? Well, rudimentary Trinitarian theology assumes that each of the divine persons bears the full divine essence. There is thus necessary *ontological* sharing that is prerequisite to personal distinction, for if personal distinction had no shared ontological base in the Trinity, we would have not three persons in one essence, but three persons with distinct essences. That is, we would have tritheism rather than the historic Trinitarian faith. The sharing between the Father and the Son that comes through the joint procession of the Spirit is thus a natural, relational outworking of the ontological sharing that underlies the divine persons. This, however, does not mean that there is not an order in the Trinity, as if the Father could be sent by the Son, or the Son could be spirated from the Father rather than being eternally begotten. There is order in the Godhead. That order is expressed in the personal uniqueness of the Father as unbegotten, the Son as eternally begotten, and the Spirit as eternally proceeding. Yet, there must also be a way to express the equality that underlies the order. While the church has traditionally used the language of essence to express that unity, that does not prevent us from noticing additional means by which the unity of the Godhead can be expressed. One of these means, I argue, is the element of sharing between persons, particularly the shared procession of the Spirit from the Father and the Son.

At its heart, the argument above is really no different from affirming the necessity of the third person of the Trinity. If anything is novel in our discussion, it is simply the fact that *sharing* is not typically brought into discussions of change, difference, or distinction. But perceiving the Spirit as the shared procession from the Father and the Son, which simultaneously allows for unity and personal distinction, would explain much about how and why reality is structured as it is—*without* infinitely precise borders and *with* a constant presence of relationality, of sharing. We live in a world of overlap and sharing that allows for difference and distinction. This would make perfect sense if the same relationship is found analogously in the ontological Trinity, who created the cosmos to reflect his own glory.

In sum, the Spirit who relates the Father and the Son through his joint procession simultaneously allows for interpersonal distinction in the Godhead. Analogously, in human language and behavior, there is always an element of sharing that undergirds change, difference, or distinction.

The Father as Universe of Discourse

Let us now bring the Father into our discussion.

On the one hand, a universe of discourse is staggeringly complex. It includes a many-faceted "*frame of reference*, either tacit or explicit, within which social interchange is taking place."[174] It reflects the multi-layered speaker or hearer expectancies in relation to each person's history and background. Within any universe of discourse, there is always more going on and more being assumed than meets the eye. This can make analyzing a universe of discourse fairly intimidating.

On the other hand, a universe of discourse is so cohesive that it is easily recognizable and appears to be quite simple. Within a given universe of discourse there are elements of cohesion with regards to the grammatical, phonological, and referential hierarchies. Grammatically, there are cohesive factors controlled by literary form. For example, we expect to witness a principled use of verb tense when someone is telling a story. We also expect logical connecting phrases or chronological cues (*so*, *then*, *after that*). These grammatical features tell us almost instantly that a story is being told. Phonologically, there are cohesive factors in voice quality, pacing, and volume that reflect the situation. As someone tells a story, we may expect the problem and solution to be articulated at a slower pace, the climax to be expressed with higher volume, etc. Referentially, we expect the story teller to draw on shared assumptions of truth and falsehood, known history, or popular background.[175] These cohesive factors

[174] Pike, *LC*, 126.
[175] Ibid.

within the GPR hierarchies help us to grasp a social exchange—a universe of discourse—with relative ease and confidence.

The universe of discourse is thus both complex and simple, deep and yet recognizable. A similar truth is found in the person of the Father. The Father is both inexpressibly deep—and thus incomprehensible to creatures—and yet easily recognizable (cf. Rom. 1). He is the universe of discourse for the Son and the Spirit—not *ontologically* but *logically* and *relationally*, in a way that is distinct from how the Spirit is context of the Father-Son relationship. The Father is neither begotten nor proceeds. He is the first in order. As such, he is the universe of discourse—the frame of reference—for our understanding of the Son and the Spirit. Both Son and Spirit can "look back," as it were, to the logically prior person of the Father. Mind you, this looking back is *logical*, not *ontological*.

This means that we cannot understand the person and work of the Son or the Spirit in isolation from the Father, for there is "one God and Father of all, who is over all and through all and in all" (Eph. 4:6). To attempt to do so is, in fact, an attempt to identify and comprehend a divine person *out of context*. This notion is basic to all Trinitarian discussions, and has been for centuries. If we want to know *who* the Son is and the relevance of his work for us, we must place the Son in relation to his Fatherly context, likewise with the person and work of the Spirit.

This profound theological truth is expressed on a creaturely level in Pike's language theory when he writes that "a context has very high power to determine or to change a meaning—vastly greater than would be suspected until we have studied the matter."[176] In an ultimate sense, the Father is the context for the meaning of the Son and the Spirit—both in their eternal identity and in their work through creation and redemption. The Son reconciles us *to the Father* (2 Cor. 5:18).

[176] Ibid., 132.

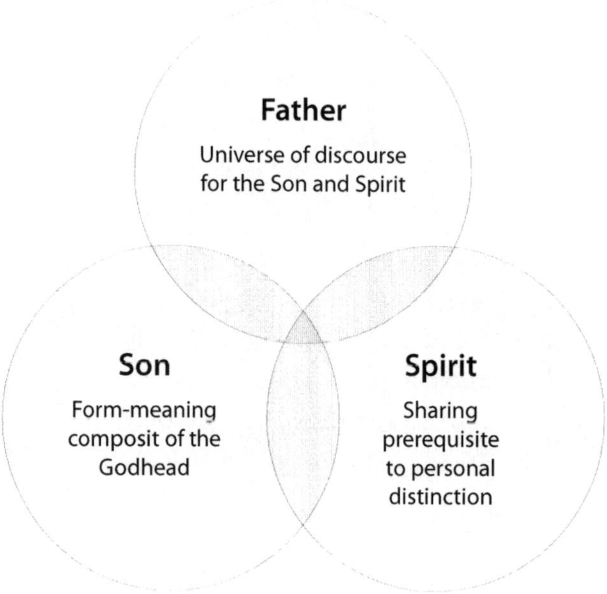

Fig. 3.4. Trinitarian Connections for Form-Meaning Composites, Sharing as Prerequisite to Change, and Universe of Discourse

Conclusion

Perichoresis, of course, would need to be applied to this final triad. It should be evident based on our earlier discussion that the Spirit has clear ties to the universe of discourse, as the context for the relationship between the Father and the Son. Since we have developed the concept of perichoresis and applied it in other parts of the chapter, I leave it to the reader to recognize the perichoretic relationship between these elements.[177]

[177] For example, the Son as form-meaning composite is always functioning within the Fatherly context and in the personally distinctive power of the Holy Spirit. Analogously, every human form-meaning composite occurs within a universe of discourse and is part of a relationship that both connects it with and distinguishes it from other form-meaning composites. All three elements

This chapter has been a crucial one in supporting the thesis for this project. I hope to have shown the deeply Trinitarian scheme of Pike's language theory. But that is only part of my concern. My thesis has been that *Kenneth Pike's language theory offers us a picture of language that faithfully represents the incomprehensible, Triune God of Scripture*. I hope to have sufficiently explored this in the current chapter. But I am not content to end there.

This chapter is, in part, a call to action, a call to understand language and, indeed, all of human reality from a Trinitarian perspective. To my knowledge, there has never been a linguistic theory that is so markedly reminiscent of the Trinitarian God as that of Kenneth Pike. This does not mean that his thought is merely *theologically interesting*; it means that he has presented us with a biblically grounded perspective on language and reality that should, in some way, become fundamental to how we see and interpret the world.

At the very least, I hope that Reformed scholars revisit his thought in light of the ongoing revival of Trinitarian theology. Pike's language theory is able to give Reformed scholars and pastors—indeed, all of Christendom—an approach to language and human behavior that aligns with the biblical truth of who God is as triune.

To solidify this last point, I will summarize a few of the fascinating ways in which Pike's theory overlaps with the theology of Cornelius Van Til, a benchmark of Reformed orthodoxy. Given the connections between these two great thinkers, we have many reasons to continue exploring Pike's language theory in the context of Reformed theology. This next and final chapter also revisits one of the questions I posed at the outset: What do a Connecticut-born linguist and a Dutch Reformed apologist have in common? A great deal, as it turns out.

---

are always present and are mutually informative and mutually necessary.

4

Kenneth Pike and Cornelius Van Til

Up to this point, I have held off on a discussion of the fascinating connections between Kenneth Pike and Cornelius Van Til, though I have assumed and relied upon such connections in the previous chapters. It is now time to have this discussion. Yet, such a discussion is more than an exercise in comparison. I draw out the connections between these two thinkers to further support my contention that serious adherents of the Reformed faith would do well to familiarize themselves with Pike's language theory.

However, though this discussion is important to have, it will also be brief. More in-depth development will be an avenue for additional research. I have discerned four areas where Pike's and Van Til's thought overlap: (1) the interpreter/observer dynamic; (2) personalism; (3) a rejection of autonomy; and (4) the definition of facts according to their functions (or meaning in light of participant responses). I will discuss each of these in turn before concluding the project. But first, it is important to mention one philosophical maxim that Van Til and Pike draw upon.

Immanuel Kant's "Copernican Revolution"

Countless books and articles have been written about Immanuel Kant's philosophy; indeed, Kantianism is a field of study in its own right. So, my comments on Kant here are meant to be selective and simple. I wish only to point out a common notion in Kant's thought that Van Til and Pike rely upon in their respective disciplines.

Immanuel Kant's (1724–1804) philosophy is described by John Frame as a "convulsion" in the history of human thought.[1] It shattered previous philosophical models and led to a new foundation for inquiry and interpretation in continental philosophy. There are many reasons for this, but I choose to focus on perhaps the most important one: Kant's argument for the existence of synthetic *a priori* knowledge.[2] Kant's Copernican revolution was in suggesting that philosophers had been going about philosophy the wrong way. They had assumed that knowledge was a matter of having the external world shape the mind, but Kant proposed that the opposite was the case: the mind shaped the external world. Of course, we must be careful in how we understand this. As Frederick Copleston notes,

> Kant's 'Copernican revolution' does not imply the view that reality can be reduced to the human mind and its ideas. He is not suggesting that the human mind creates things, as far as their existence is concerned, by thinking them. What he is suggesting is that we cannot know things, that they cannot be objects of knowledge for us, except in so far as they are subjected to certain *a priori* conditions of knowledge on the part of the subject.[3]

In other words, for there to be any "objects of knowledge," they must be filtered through the perceptual framework of the mind—a

[1] John M. Frame, *A History of Western Philosophy and Theology* (Phillipsburg, NJ: P&R Publishing, 2015), 251.

[2] For background on the notion of synthetic *a priori* statements, see K. Scott Oliphint, *Reasons for Faith: Philosophy in the Service of Theology* (Phillipsburg, NJ: P&R Publishing, 2006), 63–72; and Frame, *A History of Western Philosophy and Theology*, 254–55.

[3] Frederick Copleston, *From Wolff to Kant*, A History of Philosophy 6 (Westminster, MD: Newman Press, 1964), 225.

framework that is built into us as humans.[4] The genius of Kant's conclusion was that

> Our most basic knowledge comes about not by the world's impressing it on the mind, but by the mind's impressing it on the world. Experience is the result of the mind's imposing various concepts on the raw data given to it by the noumenal world. . . . As Copernicus argued that the earth revolves around the sun, reversing centuries of geocentric astronomy from such great thinkers as Aristotle and Ptolemy, so Kant now argues that man, not nature, is the source of the synthetic *a priori* truths that constitute genuine knowledge.[5]

There are many implications of this conclusion, but in the context of our current discussion, it means that all knowledge is *personal* in the sense that knowing subjects—persons—always impose categories on raw data and then convert that data to knowledge. Epistemology, the process of knowing, is thus intrinsically *personal*. We are deceived if we think that there are objects of knowledge, facts, just floating in the universe, waiting for humanity to discover them. There is always a knowing subject. There is no such thing as self-existent, autonomous knowledge detached from persons.

Now, neither Van Til nor Pike embraced Kant's notion uncritically; they adapted it and reformed it from a biblical perspective before it surfaced in their respective work. This was necessary since Kant's thought was deeply imbedded in secular philosophy, which assumed the autonomy of humanity from the outset.[6] For Van

[4] This framework is composed of twelve types of judgments and corresponding "categories" that allegedly cover all of the sorts of judgments a person could make about anything. Frame, *A History of Western Philosophy and Theology*, 258–59.

[5] Ibid., 256–57.

[6] "Man's autonomous mind, for Kant, not only *knows* the world, but makes the world intelligible." Ibid., 268.

Til, Kant's thought emerged in his teaching that creatures are re-interpreters of God's interpretation; for Pike, it was manifested in the role of the observer in the context of language and human behavior.

The Interpreter/Observer Dynamic

Kant claimed that persons were central to the knowing process. Van Til would adapt this idea in asserting that there was no such thing as "brute facts," i.e., facts that are not tied to an interpreter, facts that exist by themselves. All facts are interpreted facts. Creatures are thus *interpreters*, but Van Til does not stop there. They are actually *re-interpreters*. Why the "re" prefix? Because all of reality has already been interpreted by the ontological Trinity. All knowledge is what it is because of its relation to the mind of the tripersonal God. He writes,

> As human beings we must know or interpret the facts after we look at the facts, after they are there and perhaps after they have operated for some time. In the case of God, on the other hand, God's knowledge of the facts comes first. God knows or interprets the facts before they are facts. It is God's plan of his comprehensive interpretation of the facts that makes the facts what they are.[7]

In other words, "Christian theism says that there are two levels of interpreters, God who interprets absolutely and man who must be the re-interpreter of God's interpretation."[8]

Now, whether we are talking about the triune God as the original interpreter or man as a re-interpreter, the fact remains: there is

[7] Van Til, *Defense of the Faith*, 32.

[8] Ibid., 70. Or, as Oliphint put it more recently, "Every fact and experience is what it is by virtue of the covenantal, all-controlling plan and purpose of God." K. Scott Oliphint, *Covenantal Apologetics: Principles and Practice in Defense of Our Faith* (Wheaton, IL: Crossway, 2013), 53.

no such thing as knowledge detached from persons—not from the tripersonal God of the Bible, and thus not from persons created in his image.

This led Van Til to a profound appreciation for the Trinity's incomprehensibility and for man's dependence on the God who is wholly rational to himself.[9] We do not have time to unpack all of this here, but part of what this brings into view is the fact that man is a creature made in God's image and, as such, reveals God and is exhaustively dependent upon God for all things. That is why Van Til makes statements about man such as, "Being himself exhaustively revelational of God, he is in all his activities dependent on God."[10] Our dependence on the incomprehensible triune God therefore means that mystery—not an irrational mess of facts, but a gloriously covenantal mystery—pervades reality. Exhaustive knowledge is a divine attribute rather than a human goal. As he put it,

> It is as impossible for man to know himself or any of the objects of the universe about him exhaustively as it is impossible for man to know God exhaustively. For man must know himself or anything else in the created universe in relation to the self-contained God. Unless he can know God exhaustively, he cannot know anything else exhaustively.
>
> It is only if these two points are taken together—the fact that man knows something about everything, including the very essence of God, and on the other hand the fact that he does not know anything exhaustively—that the doctrine of the incomprehensibility of God can be seen for what it is.[11]

[9] For a discussion of Van Til's understanding of God's incomprehensibility, see Lane G. Tipton, "The Function of Perichoresis and the Divine Incomprehensibility," *WTJ* 64 (2002): 289–306.

[10] Cornelius Van Til, *Introduction to Systematic Theology: Prolegomena and the Doctrines of Revelation, Scripture, and God*, ed. William Edgar, 2nd ed. (Phillipsburg, NJ: P&R Publishing, 2007), 266.

[11] Ibid., 269–70.

Humans are thus finite re-interpreters of the triune God's exhaustive interpretation of reality. At every time and in every place we stand in the presence of the Trinity, who alone knows all things from every perspective imaginable. As John Frame would put it, we live in the presence of the incomprehensible, omniperspectival God.[12]

Pike, of course, was no stranger to the notion of perspectives. Central to his particle, wave, and field observer perspectives was his maxim that "personal interaction is given priority over identification of things or abstractions."[13] He was dead-set on reaffirming this throughout his career. "It is *persons* who perceive, imagine, and sense relations. It is persons who talk about these concepts."[14]

The relation to Kant's thought is evident here. In fact, Pike makes Kant's influence on him explicit in an edited volume on emics and etics, each of which is a sort of perspective on human behavior, as we discussed previously:

> Kant said, "We can attain to a knowledge of *appearances* only, never to that of the *things in themselves*." My view of emic structure is related to this affirmation of Kant in that emic structure, it seems to me, is essential to see how thing is tied to thought and knowledge. "Person" is integrated with the "outside world" when we emically categorize our perceived environment.[15]

For Pike, the emic structure of culture is prerequisite if we are to understand how reality is connected to human knowledge. To put it

[12] Frame, "A Primer on Perspectivalism."

[13] Pike, *LC*, 136.

[14] Ibid.

[15] Kenneth L. Pike, "On the Emics and Etics of Pike and Harris," in *Emics and Etics: The Insider/Outsider Debate*, ed. Thomas N. Headland, Kenneth L. Pike, and Marvin Harris, Frontiers of Anthropology 7 (London: Sage, 1990), 34.

the other way around, all emic units of human behavior presuppose that knowing subjects are engaging with reality in order to interpret it, manipulate it, or discuss it. If for Van Til there is always an interpreter, for Pike there is always an observer. We can say also that for Pike, the ultimate observer is the triune God himself, who sees and understands all—every unit of every emic community. This mirrors Van Til's claim that the ontological Trinity is the original interpreter of all facts.

Personalism

The second area of overlap for Van Til and Pike is that of *personalism*.[16] This follows conceptually from the previous area of overlap. Personalism as an official movement, however, is difficult to define, not only because there are many schools and applications of it (depending on the setting—historical and geographical), but because it carries core values common to other philosophical movements.[17] We can try to limit ourselves to what Simon Blackburn calls the "older usage" of the term: "personalism is the theistic stress on the existence of divine personality or any philosophy according to which the individual person is the starting point of theory."[18] Better yet for our context is the definition provided by Alistair Hannay, "the

[16] Material in this subsection is taken from Hibbs, "Where Person Meets Word: Part 1," 364–67, used with permission.

[17] Personalism, according to the Stanford Encyclopedia of Philosophy, has roots recognizable in Europe, America, and Asia; its proponents range from F. D. E. Schleiermacher to Walt Whitman, its forebears as diverse as Boethius, Thomas Aquinas, Immanuel Kant, Jean Lacroix, and Emmanuel Mounier. With so many figures attached to a single movement, whether to its historical foundation or contemporary expression, we must be careful in committing to a definition without qualification. See "Personalism," Stanford Encyclopedia of Philosophy, accessed August 3, 2014, http://plato.stanford.edu/entries/personalism/.

[18] Simon Blackburn, *The Oxford Dictionary of Philosophy* (New York: Oxford University Press, 1994), 284.

finite individual is somehow grounded in and seeks its fulfillment in an infinite spirit, or God, understood as personal."[19] This, in part, is in accord with the American strand of personalism brought out in the work of Borden Parker Bowne (1847–1910) and Edgar Sheffield Brightman (1871–1960), which was "both idealistic and theistic. . . . and had as its foundational insight the view that all reality is ultimately personal. God is the transcendent person and the ground or creator of all other persons; nature is a system of objects either for or in the minds of persons."[20] Speaking more particularly of Bowne's personalism, we can say that it "maintains that reality is a society of selves and persons with a Supreme Person (God) at its center. Person was, for Bowne, the fundamental principle of explanation, capable of explaining all other principles but itself."[21]

However, we can and must improve and clarify these definitions within the Reformed tradition, as Van Til himself did.[22] In distinction from the so-called "Boston personalism," Van Til affirmed that all of reality is grounded in the Triune personal God who reveals himself objectively and yet personally in revelation to man as his image-bearer. In this sense, we can say that reality is ultimately personal, and that if nature is a system of objects in the minds of

[19] Alistair Hannay, "Personalism," in *The Oxford Companion to Philosophy*, 2nd ed., ed. Ted Honderich (New York: Oxford University Press, 2005), 692.

[20] Robert Audi, ed., "Personalism," in *The Cambridge Dictionary of Philosophy*, 2nd ed. (New York: Cambridge University Press, 1999), 661.

[21] Rufus Burrow, Jr., *Personalism: A Critical Introduction* (St. Louis: Chalice Press, 1999), 11.

[22] Van Til was clear in articulating the theological chasm between "Boston personalism" and what he called "orthodox personalism." Proponents of the former, namely Bowne and Brightman, ran into serious trouble because they sought to make finite personality the "fulcrum for the operations of the laws of thought. But finite personality can be thought of intelligently only on the presupposition of the idea of the self-intelligent God. And on the basis of the idea of this God alone is it possible to avoid both rationalism and irrationalism, both determinism and pure contingency, or a combination of them." Van Til, "Boston Personalism" (lecture delivered at Boston University School of Theology, March 6, 1956), 55–56.

persons, then the ultimate mind is the mind of God.[23] Personalism in this sense is not relativism or subjectivism. When couched in the appropriate language, it is nothing more than a representation of Scriptural truth. Reality is not an impersonal conglomeration of material, facts and data; there is nothing that exists apart from God's creating and sustaining Word, and because God is personal, all of reality is as well.

Theologically, personalism falls into the field of general revelation. God "reveals himself in the history of nations and persons (Deut. 32:8; Pss. 33:10; 67:4; 115:16; Prov. 8:15, 16; Acts 17:26; Rom. 13:1). He also discloses himself in the heart and conscience of every individual (Job 32:8; 33:4; Prov. 20:27; John 1:3–5, 9, 10; Rom. 2:14, 15; 8:16)."[24] Or, as Calvin put it, "there is a sense of divinity engraved in the hearts of all *people*. . . . it cannot be erased from the human spirit."[25] God reveals himself not only in the world around us, but also in each person's conscience,[26] and by nature of the fact that all people are made in God's image.[27] People are walking

[23] "Man's surroundings are shot through with personality because all things are related to the infinitely personal God." Cornelius Van Til, *A Christian Theory of Knowledge* (Nutley, NJ: Presbyterian and Reformed, 1961), 208. Van Til is quick to point out that though there is continuity between man's mind and God's mind, there is not identity of content. Van Til, *Introduction to Systematic Theology*, 270–71. God's mind is ultimate in the sense that there can only be analogical knowledge for man, but the fact that this is the case means there is continuity between God's mind and man's mind, since "God is the original knower, and man is the derivative re-knower" (ibid., 274). For man to be a "re-knower," he must have a mind in analogical correspondence to that of his Creator.

[24] Bavinck, *Prolegomena*, vol. 1 of *Reformed Dogmatics*, ed. John Bolt, trans. John Vriend (Grand Rapids, MI: Baker Academic, 2003), 310.

[25] John Calvin, *Institutes of the Christian Religion: 1541 French Edition*, trans. Elsie Anne McKee (Grand Rapids, MI: William B. Eerdmans, 2009), 26; emphasis added.

[26] Douglas Kelly, *Systematic Theology: Grounded in Holy Scripture and Understood in Light of the Church*, vol. 1, *The God Who Is: The Holy Trinity* (Ross-shire, Scotland: Mentor, 2008), 144. See also Romans 2.

[27] The *imago dei* is far too rich a subject to breach here. Suffice it to say that

testaments to the nature of reality as created and sustained by a triune, personal God.

The above definitions of personalism and its place in general revelation will help us to understand Pike's personalism. His strand of personalism was not an explicit acceptance of an official movement but a manifestation of his theological convictions within the field of linguistics. Pike, like many figures in the Reformed tradition, is wary of treating reality as an impersonal, mechanistic system rooted in pure physicality. Yet, the uniqueness of Pike's strand of personalism comes to the fore in what we have already explored in earlier chapters: his embrace of observer perspectives (particle, wave, and field) and the rejection of abstract categories or concepts that are either divorced from concrete manifestation or skew the data of language by being reductionistic.[28] In light of these concepts, his

---

the *imago dei* is reflected in everything we do as human beings. In Oliphint's words, "all that we are, think, do, and become is derivative, coming from or out of something else; we depend on, as well as mirror, the real, the Original, the *Eimi*. In classical terminology, we are 'ectypal.' The *kind* or *type* of people we are, knowledge we have, thoughts we think, things we do, is always and everywhere a copy, pattern, impression, image, taking its metaphysical and epistemological cue from the only One who truly *is*, that is, from God himself." Oliphint, *Reasons for Faith*, 178–79. Berkhof suggests that we are always "God-related," that we do not simply *bear* the image of God occasionally; we *are* the image of God. He adds to this general truth the traditional features of the *imago dei*: knowledge, righteousness, holiness, spirituality, immortality of the soul, and dominion over "lower creation." Berkhof, *Systematic Theology*, 203–5. These aspects echo Turretin's (among others') earlier conclusions. Francis Turretin, *Institutes of Elenctic Theology*, 1:466.

[28] Rémy de Gourmont stated that "the only excuse a man has for writing is to write himself—to reveal to others the kind of world reflected in his individual mirror." Commenting on this, Pike writes, "The world mirrored in each man's mind is unique. Constantly changing, bafflingly complex, the external world is not a neat, well-ordered place replete with meaning, but an enigma requiring interpretation. This interpretation is the result of a transaction between events in the external world and the mind of the individual—between the world 'out there' and the individual's previous experience, knowledge, values, attitudes, and desire. Thus the mirrored world is not just the sum total of eardrum rattles, retinal excitations, and so on; it is a creation that reflects the peculiarities

critiques of other linguists were spent on those who either (1) bifurcated aspects of language that he felt must be tied together (such as form and meaning); or (2) reduced linguistics to a particular hierarchy (e.g., grammar or reference) rather than focusing on its interlocking hierarchies as perceived by observers. Both critiques are tied to his personalism—the notion that *people are central to inquiry and investigation*. This is back of Pike's critiques of the *structuralist* movement within American descriptive linguistics (a movement of which he was a part), as it was based on the foundations laid by Ferdinand de Saussure, Leonard Bloomfield, and Noam Chomsky.

In terms of Pike's own teaching, both theological and linguistic, we find that even from its genesis in the mid-1930s, people remained his central focus. This might be attributed to his initial experience with the Summer Institute of Linguistics (SIL), where he worked on his own among the Mixtecs, an isolated and agrarian people of Mesoamerica, translating the New Testament into a tongue to which he had no prior exposure.[29] In such a setting, relationships are the bedrock of survival, both physically and socially. When you are several days' journey by donkey to the closest train

of the perceiver as well as the peculiarities of what is perceived. In a very real sense there are as many interpretations of the world as there are people in it." Richard E. Young, Alton L. Becker, and Kenneth L. Pike, *Rhetoric: Discovery and Change* (New York: Harcourt, Brace, & World, 1970), 25. In Pike's later work, *LC*, he begins the preface by saying, "In this volume *person* (and relation between persons) is given theoretical priority above formalism, above pure mathematics, above idealized abstractions." He goes on, "the hopeless attempt to eliminate the observer in favor of scientific detachment or of objectivity is dismal. Units must be experienced or observed or deduced or imagined. . . . When man studies 'things,' he injects part of himself into their definition. What is a chair, if there is no man to sit on it? A flute, with no player? A concert, with no listeners? A saw, with no carpenter? The relevance of intended use of a thing is part of its nature as experienced by an observer" (*LC*, xi, xii, 3).

[29] Pike's boss at the time, W. Cameron Townsend, even had him avoid learning Spanish before living among the Mixtecs, so as to help his immersion and subsequent functionality in the language. See Eunice V. Pike, *Ken Pike: Scholar and Christian* (Dallas, TX: Summer Institute of Linguistics, 1981), 18–48.

station, linguistic ideals and abstractions do little to fill your stomach or break the language barrier isolating you from substantive human contact. Pike cut his teeth on practical linguistics, choosing to live among a foreign people, to think in their language, and to study both its structure and pronunciation. The experience showed him early on that compartmentalizing aspects of language such as grammar and phonemics was an exercise in abstraction and did not adequately represent the linguistic community under consideration. Thus, in 1947, he writes, "If a language structure is to be described realistically, the interweaving of grammatical and phonemic facts must not be ignored. A language system represents a structural whole which one cannot compartmentalize mechanically without doing violence to the facts."[30] Pike's theory of language was always tailored to the behavior of *persons* in the real world.

Thus, Van Til and Pike, in their own ways, were staunch adherents of personalism.

A Rejection of Autonomy

The third area of overlap between these two thinkers is their rejection of autonomy. At the outset, I should say that autonomy for Van Til usually refers to the alleged "self-control" of the covenant breaking unbeliever, whereas for Pike autonomy is the falsely perceived independence of one fact or set of facts from everything else. We might say that for Van Til autonomy is willful rebellion against the sovereign God, while for Pike autonomy is a refusal to recognize the interconnectedness and complexity of the reality that God has created. Still, though the two thinkers rejected autonomy in different senses, there is nevertheless a common conceptual core to autonomy that they both took issue with.

[30] Pike, "Grammatical Prerequisites to Phonemic Analysis (1947)," in *Kenneth L. Pike: Selected Writings to Commemorate the 60th Birthday of Kenneth Lee Pike*, ed. Ruth M. Brend (The Hague: Mouton, 1972), 48.

As is well known by Reformed theologians, Van Til was adamantly opposed to the idea that humanity is in any way independent of the tripersonal God of Scripture who has clearly and authoritatively revealed himself. He would write, "The sinner seeks to be *autonomous*. He will, therefore, seek to set himself up as a judge over that which presents itself to him as revelation."[31] Elsewhere he claims, "The revelation of a self-sufficient God can have no meaning for a mind that thinks of itself as ultimately autonomous."[32] For Van Til, autonomy is willful rebellion against a sovereign God and is therefore utterly futile. Only the Trinity is autonomous.

Pike brought this truth out within his own field, applying it to language theory and linguistics. He showed his opposition to autonomy most clearly in his 1985 article "The Need for the Rejection of Autonomy in Linguistics." In this article, Pike rejects the concept of autonomy on a number of levels.

In terms of his observer perspectives (and this goes back to our discussion of Kant), he rejected the notion that language could be understood as a behavior in isolation from people (the observer). For him, there is no such thing as purely propositional language—language that can be interpreted or analyzed in complete isolation from the person who produced it. He writes,

> A crucial characteristic of tagmemic linguistic theory . . . is its insistence upon a relation between observer and observed; between knower and the item known. Knowledge of autonomous items is denied. Knowledge is seen as a "composite" of an observer component and a component of item as observed.
>
> Tagmemics bridges the gap between person and thing by the concept of emic units [units of human behavior with

[31] Cornelius Van Til, *Introduction to Systematic Theology: Prolegomena and the Doctrines of Revelation, Scripture, and God*, ed. William Edgar, 2nd ed. (Phillipsburg, NJ: P&R Publishing, 2007), 225–26.

[32] Cornelius Van Til, *The Defense of the Faith*, ed. K. Scott Oliphint, 4th ed. (Phillipsburg, NJ: P&R Publishing, 2008), 112.

> socially-significant contrasts to other units based on their use]. . . . The emic approach . . . leads to a rejection of observer autonomy and a rejection of thing autonomy.[33]

He would go on to argue that none of the elements of his own language theory was autonomous in relation to the others: the PWF perspectives overlapped and interlocked, as did CVD components of a linguistic unit and the GPR hierarchies. We have shown this in the previous chapters. For Pike, "We need . . . to reject the autonomy of any single perspective of particle, wave, or field (or autonomous static, dynamic, or relational views). . . . Instead we seek a set of complementary approaches."[34] Again, as we have seen, the ultimate reason for this overlapping and interlocking of perspectives is the truth that each of the persons of the Trinity has intimate communion and interpenetration with the others without threatening or eclipsing the personal distinctions.

Likewise, the GPR hierarchies could not be understood in isolation from one another (i.e., autonomously). Each hierarchy is integrated with and presupposes the others. Remove the grammatical units, and there is no phonological or referential data. Remove the phonological units, and there is no grammatical or referential data, and so on.[35]

Thus, Pike would end up making statements about language that were markedly reminiscent of Van Til's theology. "Things are not autonomous. Ideas are not autonomous. The universe is not autonomous. Linguistics is not autonomous. We are hooked—together."[36] For both Pike and Van Til, autonomy is a conceptually alien notion to the fabric of reality as spoken into being by the sovereign Trinity.

[33] Kenneth L. Pike, "The Need for the Rejection of Autonomy in Linguistics," in *The Eleventh LACUS Forum, 1984*, ed. Robert A. Hall (Columbia, SC: Hornbeam Press, 1985), 42–43.

[34] Ibid., 38. See also Poythress, *In the Beginning Was the Word*, 57.

[35] Pike, "The Need for the Rejection of Autonomy in Linguistics," 41.

[36] Ibid., 49.

Fact and Function, Meaning and Participant Response

The fourth and final area of overlap between Van Til and Pike is particularly unique, and, from what I can see, seldom given the attention it deserves in broader academia.

In a climate in which Aristotle's ontological categories of "substance" and "accidence" were (and still are) in widespread use, Van Til seemed to suggest a different view of ontology—of what things *are*. He wrote, "a fact *is* its function."[37] What he meant was that things are not what they are abstractly. They are ontologically defined in terms of their function in God's creative and redemptive speech (i.e., God's plan for creation and redemption). As one of Van Til's disciples put it, "every fact and experience is what it is by virtue of the covenantal, all-controlling plan and purpose of God."[38] Oliphint continues,

> In order for someone to understand one fact properly, that fact needs to be seen in the context of God's plan and purposes. The explanation of the fact itself is not sufficient unless and until the context and purpose of that fact is known and acknowledged. For example, it is not enough simply to say that lions instinctively seek their prey because they are such good hunters; the real story includes the fact that "the young lions roar for their prey, seeking their food from God" (Ps. 104:21). It is God who provides for the animals, not instinct.[39]

I do not think that many people understand just how counter-cultural—we might say "counter-philosophical," if we are thinking

[37] Cornelius Van Til, *Common Grace and the Gospel* (Nutley, NJ: Presbyterian and Reformed, 1977), 115.

[38] K. Scott Oliphint, *Covenantal Apologetics: Principles and Practice in Defense of Our Faith* (Wheaton, IL: Crossway, 2013), 53.

[39] Ibid., 54.

purely of the secular philosophical tradition—that claim is. The revolutionary truth of this statement is drawn right from the pages of Scripture. It is God who has made all things and given life and breath to his creatures (Gen. 1; Acts 17:25). All of reality *is* only because of him. Everything we can see, think, or imagine only has ontological significance with reference to its function in the Triune God's plan for the cosmos. In other words, every fact *is* its function in that plan. Therefore, attempting to hold any ontological or metaphysical discussion apart from God is amaurotic; it reflects the blindness that comes along with the lethal spiritual injury inflicted on every person by sin (2 Cor. 4:4). This turns the philosophical world upside-down; it is, in its own way, a Copernican revolution on par with that of Kant. The being of a thing is not discussed first and then related to the question of God's existence. Rather, God's existence is presupposed for there to be any discussion of being at all—and once such a discussion begins, it must always and everywhere have reference to the Trinity, for it is only in the Trinity that anything *is*. To use a phrase from Robinson Jeffers, there is nothing in existence that has managed to escape the *seine-net* of the sovereign Trinity.[40] All is captured and held and defined by *him*.

That remarkable truth is met by a similar one in Pike's language theory. Meaning is perhaps as basic to language studies as ontology is to philosophy. To get into the bog of semantics is unnecessary at this point, but we can and should at least mention that *meaning*—in its vast array of senses—can sometimes be understood impersonally. That is, meaning can be considered a propositional brute fact. For example, the utterance "The door is open," could be understood in a given context as an assertion or observation. While this may be true, it does not really get at the significance of that utterance. John Lyons wrote that "the meaning of words and sentences is learned

[40] Robinson Jeffers, "The Purse-seine," in *The Wild God of the World: An Anthology of Robinson Jeffers*, ed. Albert Gelpi (Stanford: Stanford University Press, 2003), 157–58.

and maintained by the use to which language is put in communicative situations."[41] The *use* in communicative situations is critical here. Better said, "meaning depends on persons who communicate, and persons depend on a situation and norms about which to talk."[42] Meaning, in fact, is not purely propositional; it is, at its heart, *relational.* It is established between and among persons. Meaning, in this sense, does not reside "in" words or even in patterns of usage for a given language or subculture. Rather, meaning lies in purposive interpersonal exchange.

That is where Pike introduced his teaching that meaning is found in the emic responses one has to an utterance in a specific situation. Consider again the example, "The door is open." If I uttered that sentence while I was in a room with my wife, she might have various responses, depending on the context. If I were trying to have a private conversation with her, she might respond by getting up to close the door. If I had just closed the door, she might look at me with a puzzled expression as to why the door is now open. My utterance would thus be calling her to consider the dysfunction of the door. If we were having an argument, I might instead be asking her to leave the room, which would be very nasty of me! The point is, the meaning of linguistic units is found in the participant responses to those units. Apart from the participant response, meaning cannot be determined. This foregrounds the *relational* nature of meaning—the nature of meaning as an elicitation-and-response behavior between persons.

For Pike,

> The intention of the speaker along with the understanding of the hearer, and the eliciting activity of the speaker along with the responding activity of the hearer together make up the behavioral context of communication in a society. The

[41] John Lyons, *Semantics* (New York: Cambridge University Press, 1977), 1:4.

[42] Vern S. Poythress, *God-Centered Biblical Interpretation* (Phillipsburg, NJ: P&R Publishing, 1999), 208.

> various components of this communicating situation of eliciting activity and responding activity, of intention and of understanding, constitute the social components of language meaning.[43]

Now, as with Van Til's claim that facts *are* their functions, it can be easy to overlook the Copernican nature of Pike's position. Meaning, for centuries, has been viewed as propositional or more strictly referential. The notion that meaning is found in participants' responses suggests that semantics is far more contextually complex and even mysterious than we might first recognize. Pike's theory, of course, was built to deal with contextual complexity, so it is fitting for him to take this position. Yet, not every theory of language—in fact, I would say that *no other* theory of language—is capable of dealing with such complexity in a systematic and fruitful way. Meaning, for Pike, was only discovered in a massive network of hierarchical and situational complexity. And, in fact, our understanding of meaning cannot be exhaustive precisely because of this. The triune God is the only one who knows the relation of every fact to every other fact, the relation of every hierarchically situated and trimodally structured (CVD) language unit in relation to every other hierarchically situated and trimodally structured language unit—past, present, and future. God alone is master of meaning. He alone knows how every fact functions in his plan, in relation to every other divinely purposive fact.[44] As Van Til wrote, "all the facts of nature and of history are what they are, do what they do, and undergo what they undergo, in accord with the one comprehensive counsel of God."[45] The facts of linguistic meaning are known truly by us but not exhaustively.

Of course, non-Christians despise this idea. Since they operate on the basis of autonomy, the complexity of human behavior

[43] Pike, *LRUT*, 598.
[44] Van Til, *Common Grace*, 115.
[45] Van Til, *Christian Apologetics*, 127.

is not representative of God's covenantal control and Lordship; rather, it is a threat to their own claim of self-sovereignty. Thus, non-Christians are forced to take up two disconcerting assumptions.

> One assumption is that unless one knows the terms or objects of propositions in the fullness of their relationships, one does not know them at all. A second assumption is that the terms of propositions are not merely unknown but ultimately unknowable in all their relationships. And what is called scientific knowledge is a cross between knowing everything about nothing and knowing nothing about everything.[46]

For non-Christians, and for Christians who have been influenced by a secular way of thinking, Pike's language theory is unnerving. It presents us with methods for accessing and analyzing the richness of language in context, but not the key for mastering meaning in its fullness. The latter is a privilege of the Trinity, not a prerogative of finite creatures. Our duty is, as Pike would put it, to "jump into" the staggering complexity of language and strive to serve God in the particularities of our historical context, working out our salvation with fear and trembling (Phil. 2:12).

Much more could be said about the fascinating connections between these two great thinkers, but this brief chapter has at least shown that, in God's providence, a Connecticut-born linguist and a Dutch Reformed apologist came to strikingly similar conclusions about the nature of reality and our place within it. This should be no surprise when we consider that both men were deeply devoted to understanding and spreading the truth of God's Word.

It is time now to conclude this project with some implications of what we have discovered.

[46] Van Til, *Defense of the Faith*, 141.

5

Conclusion

We have learned much in these pages about the relationship between language and the Trinity, and about the theory of a man who devoted himself to studying and teaching language under the sovereign Lordship of the triune God. In many ways, language became Pike's *lens for life*. It would not be an exaggeration to say that by the end of his life everything was perceived through it. Indeed, one of his final books was an adaptation of his language theory to philosophy in general.[1]

In this concluding chapter, we end by taking the language theory of Kenneth Pike and applying it epistemologically to human metaphysics. By this, I mean that we can use Pike's language theory to shape how we think about who we are.[2]

In the final chapter of *LRUT*, Pike himself began walking down this path. He starts this chapter by noting that "the structure of language shares many kinds of characteristics with the structure of a society (or with the structure of an individual or of a 'thing' in the society)." Thus, "man has certain structural traits which are more pervasive than have previously been suspected, and which therefore

[1] Kenneth L. Pike, *Talk, Thought, and Thing: The Emic Road toward Conscious Knowledge* (Dallas, TX: Summer Institute of Linguistics, 1993).

[2] I am anticipated in this discussion by Vern Poythress, especially in chapters 9 and 10 of his *Redeeming Philosophy: A God-Centered Approach to the Big Questions* (Wheaton, IL: Crossway, 2014).

tell us something important about man himself."[3] Pike is hinting here that people themselves might be considered linguistic units—each society of persons being, in a sense, a *language*.

> The structure of a particular society comprises a set of relationships in a network. Individuals having relationships in this network have relevant contacts with other persons not only in a hierarchical ordering of groups within groups, but across such hierarchical lines—the lowest commoner may wave to a passing king. In addition, since a single individual may act in several roles—as father of a son, son of a father, husband of a wife, etc.—the individuals are not members of a single hierarchy but form a network of crisscrossing hierarchies and relationships. In this sense a society constitutes a system of individuals within a network—a matrix or field—just as a language has a network of sounds all in contrast directly one with another, of syllables likewise in contrast, of words and sentences in contrast, and so on. As language utterances in sequence form a hierarchy of parts, whereas the language units as an abstract system constitute a network of intersecting hierarchies, so society likewise has the activities of its individuals sequentially but hierarchically structured while the relationships between those individuals themselves are integrated into a total network.[4]

Societies can thus be conceived as trimodally structured units woven into multiple, intersecting hierarchies.

Pike first focuses on society as trimodally structured (CVD), before moving on to discuss how this applies to individual persons. Contrastive-identificational features of a society may include "self-awareness as a group . . . ; shared, articulated goals, values,

[3] Pike, *LRUT*, 641.
[4] Ibid., 643–44.

and cognitive orientations giving direction, sustaining motivation, preventing the on-set of disintegrating apathy . . ."[5] Each of these features serves to set the society apart from others. For example, the United States had (and still has) a profound sense of its self-awareness since the September 11th attacks on the Twin Towers. The assault by Islamic extremists targeted two buildings in a single city, and yet all Americans responded as if *they themselves* had been attacked. That is part of the dynamics of group identity for a country. Another way of saying this is that the attacks stimulated our self-awareness as a contrastive-identificational feature of American English society.

The variation of a society can be seen in "the grouping of individuals in a structure rather than a pattern of grouping abstracted from their relationships. Our units of society would then always involve a physical component, the individuals organized."[6] The groups within societies are composed of real persons, not merely of ideological factions. Those groups vary in their precise manifestation each day—because the persons within those groups are continuing to change and develop and because some members leave a given group and are replaced by others.

Lastly, the "distribution mode of society in reference to its internal structuring would involve the relevant slots or positions in the society which are appropriately filled by individuals or groups of individuals."[7] Every society has a plethora of slots filled by appropriate classes of individuals, each serving a particular function. We do not go to a barber shop to report a crime, nor do we seek out a grocery clerk when we are feeling ill. There are persons at certain places who are trained and responsible to manage particular problems and offer specific services. Another way of putting this would be to say that every society has functional slots that are filled by appropriate classes.

[5] Ibid., 644.
[6] Ibid., 645.
[7] Ibid.

Societies thus are trimodally structured. They are also composed of intersecting hierarchies, and the groups and individuals that make up those hierarchies have features of contrast, variation, and distribution.

Given what we have said, it is not difficult to imagine how people themselves are marked by contrast, variation, and distribution. This could be deduced from the previous discussion we had concerning Christ as a variant or manifestation of humanity, since he took upon himself a human nature. Pike tells us in this final chapter,

> We assume, to begin with, that *the individual is at least as complex in his internal structure as the language is which he speaks*—otherwise, how could he speak a language which is complex? Something within his structure, furthermore, is presumably responsible for the structuring of his language and of his other behavior. It would seem possible, then, that some of the structuring phrases of the individual himself might be analogous to structured components of language.[8]

Indeed, they are analogous. Every person is unique; each of us has peculiar contrastive-identificational features that set us apart from others. We each have a special purpose and meaning in God's redemptive plan.[9] Each of us has nuanced "beliefs, values, desires, ideals, standards, and the like."[10] It is in this sense that persons can be viewed from the particle perspective. Simultaneously, when we wake each day, we are a new variant of ourselves—we have changed and yet remain the same. We have fewer hairs and perhaps more wrinkles, but we are still ourselves.[11] This would represent a wave

[8] Ibid., 655.

[9] Pike labels these as "I-purpose" and "I-meaning" ("I" referring to "Individual"). Ibid.

[10] Ibid.

[11] Ibid., 656. Pike uses the prefix "allo" before a person's name to refer to the

perspective of persons. We are dynamically developing creatures driven by waves of experience (margins and nuclei). Lastly, we are all distributed in space and time, connected to a web of personal and functional relationships that help shape and define us. This has both an *internal* and *external* sense. Internally, each person "is a bundle of roles, in which the roles on the one hand constitute part of his contrastive-identificational features as an individual, and on the other hand reflect the internal structuring of his social personality."[12] Externally, every person is "distributed in a physical matrix, geographically, climatologically, and in reference to the particular kind of physical objects which surround him."[13]

Now, there are many ways in which we can explore the analogical relationship between a person and a type of linguistic unit in Pike's theory (e.g., a phoneme, morpheme, tagmeme), and I hope to explore such relationships in the future. However, it might be a fitting end to this project if we simply think of persons as *words*.

The analogical connection between persons and words has the advantage of being clearly biblical. God spoke creation into existence; he breathed life into Adam and, in a sense, spoke Adam into being. Adam was a word uttered by his heavenly Father in the power of the Holy Spirit. Likewise, every person can be understood as a word fitly spoken by the Trinity. This connection is all the more reasonable when we consider the Son as the eternal Word of the Father. If we are meant to conform ourselves in every way to Christ (Rom. 8:28), are we not meant in some ways to see ourselves as creaturely words spoken by God?

Now, certainly humanity and the rest of creation is, strictly speaking, a multidimensional description produced *by* the divine Word. We are the *products* of divine speech, not divine speech itself.

---

same individual in a unique manifestation. For example, today I am a new allo-Pierce. This afternoon, I will be yet another allo-Pierce. Time, in this sense, is factored into our stability and growth as individuals.

[12] Ibid., 657.

[13] Ibid.

Making this point ensures that we uphold the Creator-creature distinction on all fronts.

However, if we are careful, there is a metaphorical sense in which we can see ourselves as words spoken by the Trinity. Of course, we are not words in the same sense that the Son is the eternal Word—we are *creaturely* analogues. Yet, the analogical relationship is striking in many ways. Just as the eternal Word reflects the thought of the Speaker (the Father), we are meant to reflect or image God in all that we do. Our entire life, in this sense, is a single word uttered before God, meant to reflect him on a creaturely level in knowledge, righteousness, and holiness.

Now, as words, what do we *mean*? What is our semantic value in God's eyes? Biblically speaking, it would seem that we find our meaning in our participant response to the eternal Word who took on a human nature. Every creature, in the end, is either in Adam or in Christ (Rom. 5:12–19; 1 Cor. 15:22)—*outside* of the Word or *in* the Word. Our meaning is found within the Trinity, who knew us before we were made (Jer. 1:5; Ps. 139:13) and foresaw (Rom. 8:29) who would respond in faith to the eternal Word of the Father come in the flesh: Jesus Christ. That response, of course, would be the work of the Holy Spirit; the very breath of God that brought us to physical life is the same breath that brings us to spiritual life. Our meaning as creaturely words is found in our participant response to the eternal Word.

As words spoken by the Trinity, we are each in a sense part of the GPR hierarchies. These hierarchies, remember, can be linked to the divine persons. Grammatically, my entire life is a word that fits into a systematically functional role in God's plan for redemption—a plan that is structured around the person and work of his Son. All of the relationships I form, the feelings I experience, the expressions I voice—these can be viewed cumulatively through the particle perspective. Taken together, all of them put me in a multifaceted and glorious position in God's providential grammar—his structured plan—that reconciles the world to himself. My life, however, fits into a hierarchy. I am a word; my family is a phrase; my relations with other persons constitute a sentence; my generation is a paragraph, helping others to interpret my behaviors contextually; and so on. I am a part of a systematically structured and hierarchically arranged whole. In that whole, I have CVD, for God has specified me with his speech, which itself has CVD.

Phonologically, my behavior looked at cumulatively has a certain sound. The sound evokes a response in the emic participants of my life. When my name is pronounced in the presence of one of my brothers, for instance, a certain interest or disposition might be stirred within them, similar to the way in which our ears perk up at sounds that have special significance to us. The same is the case when I hear someone mention their names. Just as sounds (combining with grammar and reference) can be sharp and cutting or gentle and empathetic, so my entire life can take on a similar dimension when I am brought to someone's mind. In this sense, it is helpful to repeatedly ask ourselves, *how do I sound?* This question, of course, can be asked about each of our utterances, but it can also be asked about the trends in our behavior and even about our entire life. How do we tend to sound to others? When we die, will we be remembered as a word spoken in grace or in hostility, in Christ-like love or in selfish ambition? These questions, however, must be asked and answered in specific and hierarchically situated contexts. As a word, I am a composite of consonants and vowels,[14] which may form multiple syllables, which are then put together into stress groups, which comprise thought groups, which

[14] Though I do not want to press the analogy too far at the moment, we might think of consonants and vowels as routine and personally unique mannerisms, thoughts or behaviors, respectively. Thus, my morning routine may include reading Scripture and then making some coffee (two consonants). The way in which I do those things, however, is unique (the vowel that joins the consonants). Just as a vowel sound affects the pronunciation of consonants, so my personal uniqueness affects the routine thoughts and actions that people might label as "ordinary."

comprise thought "paragraphs," and so on. The sound of my life, in this sense, cannot be segregated from the context of concrete personal relationships and events that God has used to shape and define me.

Referentially, my life is woven into the fabric of space-time reality. As I type these words, I sit in a navy-blue leather armchair in front of a black desk. There is a stack of books on the left corner and a computer tower on the right. A corded phone is between the books and the computer screen. The blue cover of Pike's magnum opus, which over the years has been marked with stains and fingernail scratches, is just to the left of me, mirrored by a cup of coffee to the right. All of these objects are part of the reality that the triune God has spoken into being. I am *here* within it. I engage with these objects almost every day for various purposes. They are marked by the oils from my skin and by my finger prints. The same is the case, of course, anywhere I go. As a creature with a body and spirit, I am part of the referential world that God has made. I interact with that world in exercising my body, in forming my relationships, in working out my salvation with fear and trembling before the God whose breath gave birth to every molecule.

As mentioned earlier, my ultimate reference, my meaning, is found in relation to the person of Jesus Christ. I am a disciple of Christ on this referential earth, following in his footsteps. When I am taken into glory, my meaning will still be found in him, as a worshiper no longer impeded by the snares and bramble of sin.

And, to complete the triad of triads, I am simultaneously particle, wave, and field. I have a unique, God-given identity. My life will be like no other's. In the midst of that stable identity, I will develop as I go through peaks and valleys, each day encountering margins and nuclei of physical and spiritual activity. But I am also a field of relationships. I have been and am who I am not in isolation, but in my relationships to other people and to other physical components of reality.

Thus, Pike's language theory can be a sort of window into

biblical anthropology, informing who we are and how we think. But the rabbit hole runs deeper. Beneath the Trinitarian structure of humanity is the Trinitarian structure of all things. Pike's theory has thus paved the way for a unique, Trinitarian metaphysics established through divine speech. To put it tersely, *every element in creation is trimodally structured ultimately because it is the linguistic product of the Trinitarian God.*

We have taken space in the previous chapters to show how the CVD triad can be linked to the divine persons of the Trinity: contrast with the Father, variation with the Son, and distribution with the Spirit. Now, it is *this* Trinitarian God who "through his word of command and through his comprehensive rule over the universe specifies every dimension of the world that we enjoy."[15] That is to say, divine speech *is* true metaphysics; divine words brought about the creaturely world, so the metaphysics of every part of created reality reflect the self-communicating Trinity in its contrast, variation, and distribution. "Divine specification"—that is the ultimate foundation for all being.[16] This flies in the face of centuries of philosophical inquiry, but it is difficult to overlook the biblical roots of this position. As Poythress notes,

> This approach is like saying that there is *no* metaphysics of the kind that most philosophers have sought—there is nothing within creation that serves as a final foundation. No "ultimate" system of abstract categories reaches down and makes transparent to human reason the foundations of existence. That is because creation as a whole and every individual creature have their foundation in God's plan, his commands, his governance, and his presence. We can know God, but we cannot comprehend him.[17]

[15] Poythress, *Redeeming Philosophy*, 137.
[16] Ibid., 144. See also 153–54, 161–62, 170–71.
[17] Ibid., 137.

All of reality is linguistic in nature and reflective of the Trinity.

This is precisely where we began this project. Because of the richly linguistic nature of reality, spoken into being by the Triune God, it makes perfect sense for us to use language as a lens for life and to see the Trinitarian structure of God's self-communication impressed on every fiber of creation. This is especially evident with persons. We are by nature communicative beings made in the image of the self-communing Trinity. As such, our identity is deeply related to the nature, structure, and trends of our communication. We can learn much about ourselves and about the world in which God has placed us when we pay attention to language as a part of human behavior—its functions, its effects, its blessings and curses. If language was Pike's lens for life, I see no reason why it should not be so for Reformed theologians today, given the theological discussions we have had in the previous pages.

Let me end by saying that Kenneth Pike and his disciples have shown that language is trimodally and hierarchically structured because persons are trimodally and hierarchically structured, and persons are trimodally and hierarchically structured because they are reflective of the Trinity. In fact, we have just seen how all of reality is trimodally and hierarchically structured!

My thesis has been that Pike's thought presents us with a picture of language that faithfully represents the incomprehensible, Trinitarian God of Scripture. Perhaps it would be more accurate to say that Pike's theory gives us a lens for life. Perhaps more than anything else, Pike points out the breadth, depth, and complexity of human communication and behavior. The structure of his thought brings us to glorify the incomprehensible, self-communing Trinity in a way that aligns especially well with the Reformed faith. I hope and pray that other theologians and teachers in our time will recognize the genius of his thought and see how it can help us better serve and worship the God who speaks.

Appendix 1: An Implication for Trinitarian Terminology

In this appendix, I offer one implication of a component of Pike's theory. It is an implication for the use of the word "person" in Trinitarian theology. Certainly, there are several of such implications for Pike's theory, many of which I hope to explore in the future, but this is at least one concrete example of how Pike's genius engages with current debates in contemporary theology.

In what follows, I draw on Pike's language theory to better understand how the Trinitarian term "Person" is understood. By reintroducing Pike's teaching on "conceptualized hypostasis," I hope to point out how language is embedded in participant contexts and how this fact influences our terminological debates. In the end, I conclude that Pike's notion of conceptualized hypostasis may lead to further developments in a "dogmatic model of natural theology."

Introduction

Much of the recent debate about the Trinitarian language of "Person" has yet to properly account for a theory of language that gets at the heart of the issue.[1] Oftentimes scholars butt heads about

[1] Throughout church history, discussions on the precise meaning of "Person" abound. Broadly speaking, there seems to be a consensus that "*Person* is simply a label for the ways in which Father, Son, and Spirit are alike, in distinction from the Godhead as a whole." John M. Frame, *Systematic Theology: An Introduction to Christian Belief* (Phillipsburg, NJ: P&R Publishing,

lexical semantics or pragmatics. "What does 'Person' mean, especially with regards to 'relation'? How can we use the term with confessional and biblical integrity? Where does the analogy between divine Persons and human persons begin, and where does it end?"[2]

2013), 484. Understood more narrowly, "Person" connotes relationality. And for Colin Gunton, the relational nature of the term is critical to maintain. "A person, we must learn and relearn, can be defined only in terms of his or her relations with other persons, and not in terms of a prior universal or non-personal concept like species-being, evolution or, for that matter, subsistent relation." Colin E. Gunton, *The Promise of Trinitarian Theology*, 2nd ed. (London: T&T Clark, 1997), 96. Gerald O'Collins similarly contends that "authentic personhood does not spring out of one's private experience but is given and received within relationships. To be a person is to be an interpersonal subject, sharing love and giving oneself in love." Gerald O'Collins, *The Tripersonal God: Understanding and Interpreting the Trinity*, 2nd ed. (New York: Paulist Press, 2014), 177.

One could argue that the term's popularity throughout the ages has been its "analogy in the life of creatures. . . . we make a distinction between the nature [essence] of persons and the persons themselves." Herman Bavinck, *Reformed Dogmatics*, vol. 2, *God and Creation*, ed. John Bolt, trans. John Vriend (Grand Rapids, MI: Baker Academic, 2004), 299. Yet, part of noting the bounds of such an analogy, as Bavinck points out, is that the three persons are ever tied to the unity of the Godhead: "The three persons are the one divine personality brought to complete self-unfolding, a self-unfoldment arising out of, by the agency of, and within the divine being." Bavinck, *God and Creation*, 303. Amidst this unity, "although Father, Son and Holy Spirit coinhere in one another, their distinct conscious subjectivity is not lost in one another or merged into an impersonal unity." Douglas Kelly, *Systematic Theology: Grounded in Holy Scripture and Understood in Light of the Church*, vol. 1, *The God Who Is: The Holy Trinity* (Ross-shire, Scotland: Mentor, 2008), 494. In other words, "God's oneness is always and at the same time to be understood in terms of his threeness. . . . the oneness *requires* the threeness, and vice versa." K. Scott Oliphint, "Simplicity, Triunity, and the Incomprehensibility of God," in *One God in Three Persons: Unity of Essence, Distinction of Persons, Implications for Life*, ed. Bruce A. Ware and John Starke (Wheaton, IL: Crossway, 2015), 224. This truth should, as Oliphint notes, lead us to worship God in his incomprehensibility (229–33; see especially Oliphint's poignant critique of Barth on this issue).

[2] I recommend a helpful and lucid article by Wesley Hill, "Divine Persons and Their 'Reduction' to Relations: A Plea for Conceptual Clarity," *IJST* 14, no. 2 (April 2012): 148–60.

Such questions are certainly helpful and necessary, but beneath all of them is an assumption of how language itself functions in relation to reality, and if we do not account for that, then our debates might be misguided and hinder, rather than help, theological progress in our understanding of the deep things of God.

In what follows, I reintroduce Pike's linguistic theory in an attempt to couch the debate on Trinitarian terminology within language theory. Such an attempt, I hope, will refresh the discussion and lead theologians to better account for the place of what Michael Sudduth, and, in reviewing Sudduth's work, K. Scott Oliphint have referred to as a "dogmatic model of natural theology."[3] I first introduce Pike's notion of "conceptualized hypostasis" and then move on to discuss how this fits into an analogical understanding and emic use of language.[4] I end with some implications this has for our discussions in Trinitarian theology.

Conceptualized Hypostasis

Kenneth L. Pike (1912–2000) introduced what he referred to as "conceptualized hypostasis" in 1955, following his understanding of "hypostasis" as laid out by Leonard Bloomfield, his contemporary in the heyday of American descriptive linguistics.[5] For Bloomfield, hypostasis refers to our explicit reference to speech sounds or "the mention of a phonetically normal speech-form, as when we say, 'That is only an *if*,' or 'There is always a *but*," or when we talk about "the word *normalcy*" or "the name *Smith*." . . . Hypostasis is

[3] K. Scott Oliphint, "Is There a Reformed Objection to Natural Theology?," *WTJ* 74 (2012): 171.

[4] On our analogical use of language, see Vern S. Poythress, "Reforming Ontology and Logic in the Light of the Trinity: An Application of Van Til's Idea of Analogy," *WTJ* 57, no. 1 (Spring 1995): 188–95.

[5] It may be confusing to learn here that "hypostasis" in its linguistic usage has almost nothing, as far as I can tell, to do with the Trinitarian use of the same term, though this word choice might be worth investigating.

closely related to *quotation*, the repetition of a speech."[6] In other words, Bloomfield is simply talking about our referral to an element of speech *extracted from a participant context*. The statement, "Mr. Smith went to the park today," is an example of "Smith" used in a participant context. "The name 'Smith' is quite common," would be an example of hypostasis: we focus on a piece of speech in relative independence from its use in a particular context.[7] This, in brief, is where Pike begins when building the notion of what he calls "conceptualized hypostasis."

In his 1955 article, Pike sets out to answer the question, "What is the relationship between the meaning of a word as deduced by the lexicographer, and the meaning of the word which might be reported by a native speaker of that language?"[8] This question, for him, highlights the importance of an *etic* (outsider) and *emic* (insider) approach to meaning.[9] On the one hand, a lexicographer or analyst comes to a community from the outside and observes an utterance in use, extracting from his observations a meaning of that utterance that accords with those observations. That is to say, "the discovery by the analyst of the meaning of such an utterance involves

[6] Leonard Bloomfield, *Language* (Chicago: University of Chicago Press, 1984), 148.

[7] Obviously, we cannot ever talk about a piece of language in *absolute* independence, since we always depend on previous usage and context to understand what it is we are talking about. Suffice it to say that Pike's theory challenges the assumption that we can really discuss terms in isolation, and though this claim may be disturbing or frustrating to some analytical thinkers who want to compartmentalize and rigidly define terms, I believe it is true. This in itself has massive implications for our terminological discussions.

[8] Kenneth L. Pike, "Meaning and Hypostasis," in *Kenneth L. Pike: Selected Writings to Commemorate the 60th Birthday of Kenneth Lee Pike*, ed. Ruth M. Brend (The Hague: Mouton, 1972), 100. This article, as mentioned, was originally published in 1955 in a monograph from the Institute of Language and Linguistics at Georgetown University.

[9] On the etic and emic distinction in Pike's thought, see Pierce Taylor Hibbs, "Where Person Meets Word Part 1: Personalism in the Language Theory of Kenneth L. Pike," *WTJ* 77, no. 2 (Fall 2015): 371–74.

the investigation of its occurrence—or the occurrence of repeated fractions thereof—in various contexts, in order to find in the various contexts the kind of responses which it can be seen to regularly elicit, and which can be predicted for it elsewhere."[10]

On the other hand, for the native speaker, the insider, meaning of an utterance "almost seems to 'reside in' the words, as a mystic entity apart from their phonemic form, apart from the particular contexts in which they happen to occur at the moment, and apart from the regularity of response which he tacitly reacts to while often unaware of the response-elicitation character of meaning."[11] In this sense, native speakers can sometimes be convinced of "the independent existence of mystic meaning units in a particular language *even when he has in fact obtained those meanings by a procedure similar to that of the technician, but with mental compilations of contexts rather than written ones.*"[12]

What we need to take from Pike's explanation is that (1) all meanings of utterances are ultimately derived from participant contexts, and (2) both language analysts and native speakers of the language arrive at meaning by piecing together these specific contexts. This is the case because, for Pike, meaning is always tied to form. Units of language are always "form-meaning composites."[13] We cannot talk purely about form or purely about meaning, and so we must be very careful in how we understand the meanings of terms removed from a specific participant context, and that is where conceptualized hypostasis comes into play.

Here, in essence, is how hypostasis and conceptualized hypostasis work. To start, as was already mentioned, we begin with the

[10] Pike, "Meaning and Hypostasis," 101.

[11] Ibid.

[12] Ibid.; emphasis added.

[13] See Hibbs, "Personalism in the Language Theory of Kenneth L. Pike," 374–77. This concept represents a major contrast of Pike's language theory and those of others in descriptive linguistics. For example critiques, see Pike, *LRUT*, 63, 97, 149, 355, 496, and 536.

meaning of an utterance in a particular participant context. In the context of Trinitarian dialogue, let us say that the following sentence was uttered by Tertullian: "The Father, Son, and Spirit are each divine Persons."[14] Perhaps Tertullian uttered this sentence in conversation with another church father and later recorded it. That conversational context would be a point in a sequence of participant activities—now long passed in history. But what if a contemporary of Tertullian wanted to determine what Tertullian meant by "Person." How would he go about doing this?[15] For Pike, we would practice *hypostasis*.

> Any abstraction of an activity from a normal participant sequence for purposes of viewing it, studying it, mentioning it, analyzing it, listing it, cataloging it, or discussing it as such, we shall call hypostasis of that activity. The mention of a word is an activity of hypostasis. The formation of a dictionary listing is accomplished by the hypostasis of these forms. The practicing of the passing of a football is the hypostasis, and repetition of hypostasis, of the football-passing activity of a normal game, etc.
>
> The native speaker, in quoting a word out of normal context [such as Tertullian's contemporary trying to figure out what he meant by "Person"], is performing an act of hypostasis. If he means the meaning of that word, however, he is doing something further: he is making an abstraction

[14] Tertullian, after all, was the first to use the term *persona* in reference to a "concrete individual." Robert Letham, *The Holy Trinity: In Scripture, History, Theology, and Worship* (Phillipsburg, NJ: P&R Publishing, 2004), 99.

[15] This is the same question we ask ourselves today, though there are two thousand years between our time and the initial use of the word "Person" in its Trinitarian context. This is part of the relational nature of language, which is woven throughout time. Language, Rosenstock-Huessy once wrote, "is obviously not restricted to building up temporal and passing relations. It tries to build up recurrent and remembered relations." Eugen Rosenstock-Huessy, *Speech and Reality* (Norwich, VT: Argo Books, 1970), 120.

> from various contexts of some common phase of the elicitation-response characteristics of those contexts, and is giving to his abstraction a name, or "label." The physical manifestation of the label is a component of the abstracting activity, and, for that activity, fulfills the kind of function which for the non-abstracting activity of normal speech is played by the physical component of that normal speech. Activity units in which a substitute verbalization for hypostasis defining purposes replaces the verbal activity utilized in normal non-abstracting sequences, we may call 'conceptualized hypostasis' to differentiate it from hypostasis which merely repeats, out of context, an item to study it apart from that context.[16]

This may be a fairly dense way to put it, but what Pike is saying essentially is that sometimes we remove a unit of language from its genuine participant context to study it, which is an act of hypostasis. An example would be the word "Person" in the question, "What did Tertullian mean by 'Person'?" Now, if we take one step further back, we might ask, "What does the word 'Person' mean?" Indeed, this question is the one we typically find addressed in introductory texts on the Trinity. In such a question, what we have done with the word "Person" is what Pike would call *conceptualized hypostasis*: we have turned our attention to the *meaning* of a hypostasized unit, and we arrive at that meaning only by gathering meanings (elicited responses) from various participant contexts in which the word "person" occurs, and, based on our understanding of those contexts, created an abstraction. Conceptualized hypostasis, then, is a label that encompasses the mass of specific physical manifestations we have in mind. All of that is behind the deceptively terse question, "What do we mean when we say that the Father, Son, and Spirit are three *Persons*?"

[16] Pike, "Meaning and Hypostasis," 103.

Applying Conceptualized Hypostasis to "Person"

Applying what we have learned thus far to the Trinitarian use of the word "Person" yields some fascinating results. Some theologians, out of adherence to the language and teachings of orthodoxy, have been stalwart in declaring that "Person" in reference to the Godhead is markedly different from "person" in reference to humanity. I certainly agree with them. One cannot ever collapse the Creator-creature distinction without doing serious damage to our understanding of both. But what we often miss, and what Pike's notion of conceptualized hypostasis brings to the fore, is that language itself is built into the fabric of physical reality, so that we cannot pretend that our notion of a divine "Person" is somehow *purely* derived from divine participant contexts (i.e., special revelation).

We might draw this point out a bit more. Imagine Tertullian's contemporary who is trying to understand what he meant by "Person." What are the options at his contemporary's disposal? He must at least *begin* by drawing on specific participant sequences in which the word "person" occurs. "Your father is a kind person." "Mark is a stubborn person." "As a person, I think very highly of her." "Stay away from that person." Such examples each contribute something to the conceptualized hypostasis of "Person." We must, of course, draw on the experiences of others if we are to arrive a well-rounded understanding of "Person," and therein lies the trouble: people do not always arrive at the same conceptualized hypostasis. One scholar's conceptualized hypostasis leads him to say that a "person" is an independent center of consciousness; another leads a different scholar to say that a "person" is merely a relational being, and so on and so forth. Such is the nature of academic dialogue: we all come to the table with our conceptualized hypostases, and the friendly banter (one hopes) of semantics begins.

Now, no doubt, we cannot ever *stop* there, for to do so would in fact ignore the Creator-creature distinction. If we were to merely apply our conceptualized hypostasis to the meaning of the Trinitarian word "Person," then we would be applying all that is creaturely to the Creator. We must, then, let Scripture reform and reshape our understanding, just as Scripture—though we often forget it—is forming and shaping our understanding of participant contexts all along![17]

After forming an initial conceptualized hypostasis and comparing it with those of others, we then go unreservedly to Scripture to see how our conceptualized hypostasis measures up against special revelation.[18] This is particularly difficult with the word "Person," since, as is well known, the term is extra-biblical. But we can certainly observe how the alleged referents of that word (the Father, Son, and Spirit) behave in the Old and New Testaments, allowing what we have observed there to recalibrate our understanding of "Person" when applied to the members of the Godhead, rather than to human creatures.

Analogical "Emic" Language

The point here, however, is that the meaning we assign to words and utterances comes through human language and experience in participant contexts. We access those contexts in order to understand and use language. There is no such thing, in other words, as a "word in itself." Because words are only ever known through what Pike would refer to as an *emic grid*: a unique way of seeing and interpreting the world.[19] In an exhaustive and unfathomable sense, God himself

[17] Here I am referring to what many in the Reformed tradition call a "revelational epistemology." For an introduction to the concept, see G. K. Beale and W. Andrew Hoffecker, "Biblical Epistemology: Revelation," in *Building a Christian World View*, vol. 1, *God, Man, and Knowledge*, ed. W. Andrew Hoffecker and Gary Scott Smith (Phillipsburg, NJ: Presbyterian and Reformed, 1986), 193–216.

[18] I outline a similar approach to our understanding of metaphor. See "In the Beginning Was the Word: John 1:1–5 and a Revelational Theory of Metaphor," *WTJ*, forthcoming.

[19] This goes hand in hand with Pike's rejection of the bifurcation between observer and observed. "A crucial characteristic of tagmemic linguistic theory

dwells in and sees what he has made through his own Trinitarian emic grid. The allusion to the eternal Word in John 1:1 leads us to a God who dwells in his own "emic community," in this case, a heavenly one.[20] Yet, God chose to create humans in their own emic communities in such a way that there could be correspondence between his own eternal emic community and those earthly emic communities of his creatures.[21] This is where our understanding of analogy becomes critical. The analogical correspondence between God's words in revelation and human words in general means that God ordained for us to draw on our emic understanding of participant contexts to begin understanding his message.[22] That is why God revealed himself

---

. . . is its insistence upon a relation between observer and observed; between knower and the item known. Knowledge of autonomous items is denied. Knowledge is seen as a "composite" of an observer component and a component of item as observed. Tagmemics bridges the gap between person and thing by the concept of emic units [units of human behavior with socially-significant contrasts to other units based on their use]. . . . The emic approach . . . leads to a rejection of observer autonomy and a rejection of thing autonomy." Kenneth L. Pike, "The Need for the Rejection of Autonomy in Linguistics," in *The Eleventh LACUS Forum, 1984*, ed. Robert A. Hall (Columbia, SC: Hornbeam Press, 1985), 42–43.

[20] An emic community might be thought of as 'monocultural' because it only perceives internal relations of a person or culture. Pike, "A Stereoscopic Window on the World," *Bib Sac* 114, no. 154 (April 1957): 145. God's emic community must be understood as qualitatively different from human emic communities, since God created and exhaustively knows all other finite emic communities among humanity.

[21] "As part of the result of man's being created in the image of God, the communication system of God and that of man are not disjoint. The implication here is that by creation God has made man's language sufficiently like his own internal communication system, whatever that may be, that man's is a pale reflection of his own and allows talk across the barrier in both directions." Pike, "The Linguist and Axioms Concerning the Language of Scripture," *Journal of the American Scientific Affiliation* 26, no. 2 (June 1974): 48.

[22] On the relation between the eternal Word and God's creational words, see Vern S. Poythress, "God and Language," in *Did God Really Say? Affirming the Truthfulness and Trustworthiness of Scripture*, ed. David B. Garner (Phillipsburg, NJ: P&R Publishing, 2012), 93–106.

> . . . within a particular culture, through a particular culture, by means of events occurring in that particular culture. He made His message concrete by incarnating it in an emic structure, rather than by a series of lectures delivered by messengers aloof from and not a part of the revealing cultural medium.
>
> . . . . The problems of imparting a message across an emic barrier lying between heaven's communication system—whatever that may be—and man's verbal system involved the restructuring of the initial message into the target emic system. The message restructured into human speech had to be cast into the molding limits of noun, verb, lexicon, and sentence structures—in short, into a Hebrew-Greek structural grid—while retaining its conceptual integrity and the faithfulness of its intended impact.[23]

Just as the Word became flesh, so also God's message of special revelation took on the "flesh" of a specific human language that was part of a specific emic community, comprised of people with their own emic grids.[24]

Our understanding of extra-biblical terms such as "Person" is not detached from this. Just as we do in interpreting God's revelation, we must draw on participant contexts in order to begin understanding what a word, phrase, clause, or sentence means. When people say things such as, "I only begin with the Bible," they are not being quite

[23] Pike, "A Stereoscopic Window," 152–53, 154.

[24] "The bearer of the ideal goods of humankind is language, and the *sarx* of language is the written word. In making himself known, God also adapts himself to this reality. To be able fully to enter the life of humankind and for it fully to become its possession, revelation assumes the form and fashion of Scripture. Scripture is the servant form of revelation." Herman Bavinck, *Reformed Dogmatics*, vol. 1, *Prolegomena*, ed. John Bolt, trans. John Vriend (Grand Rapids, MI: Baker Academic, 2003), 380. See also Richard B. Gaffin, Jr., *God's Word in Servant-Form: Abraham Kuyper and Herman Bavinck on the Doctrine of Scripture* (Jackson, MS: Reformed Academic Press, 2008).

accurate. The Bible itself is filled with emically grounded expressions—expressions that are unintelligible apart from the participant contexts we have some knowledge of. *That*, I argue, is part of the incarnational element of language. Immanuel is God *with us*: with our language, with our experience, with our own emic communities.[25]

In this sense, we can say that language is *analogical* (corresponding on a finite scale to the language God himself uses in creation and throughout history) and *emic*.[26] It is always woven into real human history. It is embedded in our experiences, and in the experiences of others in history within their own emic communities. That is what makes language raw, and real, and riveting. Words isolated from human experience, dropped from heaven and disassociated from our communicative contexts, would be utterly unintelligible.

Conclusion and Implications for Trinitarian Theology

At the outset, I mentioned that Pike's notion of conceptualized hypostasis would have implications for our understanding of a "dogmatic model of natural theology." What that means here is that theologians must resist the urge to detach Scripture from the reality of human communication. Language itself demands that we draw on our experience in order to *begin* to understand what is meant by

[25] Oliphint describes this as covenantal condescension. See K. Scott Oliphint, *God with Us: Divine Condescension and the Attributes of God* (Wheaton, IL: Crossway, 2012).

[26] The persons of the Trinity are, as Van Til put it, "exhaustively representational" of one another. Because the persons of the Godhead are exhaustively representational of one another, creatures made in the image of the Trinity are analogically representational of God in all that they do. Cornelius Van Til, *In Defense of the Faith*, vol. 2, *A Survey of Christian Epistemology* (Phillipsburg, NJ: Presbyterian and Reformed, 1969), 78. Language, then, must also be representational. By this we mean that all of our communicative behavior represents on a finite, analogical scale the communicative behavior of the Trinity. In their communicative behavior, the persons of the Trinity exhaustively represent one another; in our communicative behavior, we image the Trinity by analogically representing ourselves.

a particular word, phrase, etc. But it is equally important to remember that we do not end there, for our conceptualized hypostasis is limited, and, if taken in isolation, oftentimes misleading and usually tainted by our corrupted understanding. We need to compare our conceptualized hypostases with those of others, and we then need to allow special revelation to reform our understanding.

When theologians profess to have a revelational epistemology, they cannot then retreat behind Scripture, for Scripture itself is embedded in reality, even if, at times, such embedding looks intimidating or "messy." This has connections to the incarnation of the divine Word. The Word came not in disassociation from humanity, but wrapped in sinew and skin—a breathing, sweating, speaking Godman. If we want the real Christ, we have to take him with his divinity *and* humanity; we must take the blessing with the blood, God's sanitizing grace with the dirt of the cross. We must take the emically embedded Christ.

In terms of our debate over the meaning of "Person" in Trinitarian discussions, we must remember two things: (1) our understanding of that word is based on our conceptualized hypostasis, which needs to be shaped and adjusted in dialogue with others; and (2) we arrive at a sound understanding of the term only in so far as it represents the biblical witness. As Frame writes, "It would be wrong for us to think that a careful historical study of the uses of these terms would yield the essence of the relationships between the one triune God and his three persons. What we know about these relationships (and in this area we often know less than we think we do) comes not from a study of these technical terms, but from the teachings of Scripture. The terms serve merely to label the concepts we derive from the Bible."[27]

Thus, in attempting to define what Tertullian meant by "Person," and what the church should understand about it today, we must delve into the reality of language in history and never assume that

[27] Frame, *Systematic Theology*, 484.

history itself should be thrown by the wayside. What Michael Sudduth has called a "dogmatic approach to natural theology" seems especially relevant in this context. We are surrounded by a linguistically mediated natural world, and we need to appreciate that. At the same time, we need to take a dogmatic (revelational) approach to human experience in order to allow special revelation to reform and inform our conceptualized hypostases. It is my hope that Trinitarian debates will better account for these truths as discussions about technical Trinitarian terms continue.

Appendix 2: Glossary of Terms for Pike's Language Theory

Pike's language theory introduced an array of new terminology to the field, so it is helpful to have a glossary for the most important terms. The definitions below are sometimes explained with my own paraphrase and other times quoted directly from Pike's work or from the work of one of his disciples. Whenever possible, I have listed page ranges in Pike's works that elaborate on the concept.

Acteme. The smallest unit of a manifested behavioreme. An acteme is "a minimum, active, trimodally-structured emic segment or component of human activity . . . . it is characterized by identificational-contrastive components constituted of physical activity" (*LRUT*, 290–91). An acteme is also manifested by particular variants and distributed within larger units of the behavioreme, as well as within a larger physical setting.

Allomorph. An allomorph is a particular variant of a morpheme. Metaphorically, we can say that each day we are a new allomorph of our same self, i.e., we are a unique variant of our contrastive-identificational person (*LRUT*, 176–77).

Behavioreme. A behavioreme is simply a unit of behavior within an emic setting. Pike also provides a more detailed definition for us: "A behavioreme is an emic segment or component of purposive human activity, hierarchically and trimodally structured, having closure signaled by overt objective cultural clues within the verbal or nonverbal behavior of the domestic participants of domestic observers, and occurring through its free or conditioned, simple or complex variants within a behavioral system (or composite of systems) and a physical setting which are also emically, hierarchically and trimodally structured" (*LRUT*, 121).

Class. A class represents one of four components of a tagmeme. It is a "general set of items substitutable appropriately in the slot" (*LC*, 75). A class is simply a collection of linguistic items (e.g., words) that can appropriately fill a functional slot in a behavioreme or uttereme (Waterhouse, *The History and Development of Tagmemics*, 9–10). Pike sees a connection between class and the particle perspective.

Cohesion. Cohesion represents another one of the four components of a tagmeme. In general, cohesion refers to the way in which a linguistic unit is tied to other units in a network of assumptions, beliefs, cultural norms, or trends. Cohesion includes "general background materials from any level of the hierarchy which are controlled by or controlling the item in view" (*LC*, 75).

Conceptualized hypostasis. As indicated below, hypostasis refers to our action of taking an emic unit out of its normal, functional context for the purpose of studying or analyzing it. In this sense, conceptualized hypostasis is another step removed from the normal participant context. When we attempt to give general meaning or purpose to an abstracted (hypostasized) emic unit, we are practicing conceptualized hypostasis; we are drawing on a database of concrete occurrences of that unit and trying to form a more general sense of its meaning or purpose. Thus, conceptualized hypostasis is only possible because we have many concrete manifestations of an emic unit upon which we base our analysis (*LRUT*, 156–57).

Contrast. Contrast is one of the three components of Pike's CVD triad. It refers to the way in which an emic unit is set apart from other emic units. It can also refer to the difference between etic units, but it is important to remember that there can be etic difference and emic sameness simultaneously. For example, there is an etic difference between "Hi" and "Hello"; they differ in their sound and spelling. Yet, emically both units are serving the same function (greeting).

Contrastive-identificational features. For every emic or etic unit, there are features that (a) contrast it with other units and (b) identify that unit even when it is not placed next to similar units. Contrastive-identificational features thus serve to distinguish a unit of human behavior negatively and positively. Negatively, these features tell us what the unit is *not*; positively, these same features help us identify what the unit *is* when we are in a context in which we no longer need to focus on how such a unit is distinct from similar units (*LC*, 42–43).

Distribution. Distribution is another one of the three components of Pike's CVD triad. It is the only component that retained the same terminology throughout Pike's career. Distribution refers to the references that an emic unit has to a "universe of discourse." As such, there are many elements that are involved in distribution, some internal and others external. Internally, an emic unit is a member of one or more subsystems or classes within the grammatical, phonological, and referential hierarchies. For example, English verb tense subsystem is the matrix that lies behind any specific occurrence of a tensed verb. Externally, distribution can include the place of a unit in a larger structure or sequence (*LC*, 60–65).

Distribution mode. Pike's earlier work developed the FMD triad (Feature, Manifestation, and Distribution modes), which would later be replaced by the CVD triad. The use of this "modal" language is likely what led Pike to describe units of human behavior as "trimodally structured." The distribution mode of a unit is "composed of relational components, including its class membership and its function in a slot of a hierarchically-ordered larger construction (its external distribution), and its internal segmentation (its internal distribution), especially in reference to the hierarchy of mechanisms of its physical production" (*LRUT*, 85–86).

Dynamic view. The terms *static*, *dynamic*, and *functional/relational* were synonymous with *particle*, *wave*, and *field*. We take up a dynamic view of language when "the system [of language or behavior] is seen through the units of its manifestation mode and the physical basis of units as they flow into one another in a sequence of fusing, changing segments" (*LRUT*, 511).

Eme. An eme is simply a composite chunk of action within a particular culture. For many people in America, having breakfast is an eme, since it is a contextually relevant chunk of behavior for participants and is yet composed of many smaller behavioremes or utteremes. For instance, having breakfast may include me driving to a diner (a complex behavioreme or acteme), ordering a meal (an uttereme), wiping my hands off after eating (an acteme), etc. (*LRUT*, 128–29).

Emic. Emic is semantically broad and occurs all throughout Pike's theory. Pike first coined the terms *emic* and *etic* by removing the endings of the words *phonemic* and *phonetic*. The former refers to relevant sounds within a system; the latter refers to sounds across languages or, from an analysist's perspective, to sounds that are alien to him. Thus, *emic* was meant to connote a culture-specific viewpoint. "The etic viewpoint studies behavior as from outside of a particular system, and as an essential initial approach to an alien system. The emic viewpoint results from studying behavior as from inside the system" (*LRUT*, 37). When Pike refers to *emic units of behavior*, he is considering units of behavior as understood by the native participants of a given culture. The meaning of such units is found in their eliciting certain participant responses from those inside the culture. As Viola Waterhouse put it, "The etic view has to do with universals, with typology, with observation from outside a system, as well as with the nature of initial field data, and with variant forms of an emic unit. The emic view is concerned with the contrastive, patterned system of a specific language or culture or universe of discourse, with the way a participant in a system sees that system, as well as with distinctions between contrastive units" (Waterhouse, *The History and Development of Tagmemics*, 6).

Emic motif. An emic motif is "a minimum unit of the feature mode [later, Contrast] of the behavioreme" (*LRUT*, 150). Expanding on this simple definition, Pike writes, "An emic motif (or motifeme) is a minimum, active, trimodally structured, emic segment or component of human activity, within the hierarchy of the feature mode of a minimum or included behavioreme or hyper-behavioreme" (150).

Etic. The etic approach to language is the counterpart to the emic approach to language. It is important to remember that the emic and etic are not in opposition; rather, they are complementary. The etic approach "studies behavior as from outside of a particular system, and as an essential initial approach to an alien system" (*LRUT*, 37). For Pike the etic view can treat several languages at a time, relies on criteria for analysis that is external to the language system in focus, approaches a given language with a logical plan (rather than discovering the elements of the language from within the culture), does not require that every unit be viewed as part of a larger whole (while the emic does require this), measures sameness and difference of units systemically (rather than according to participant response), can work with partial information (whereas the emic requires information about the whole system), and is usually preliminary (we begin with the etic and move to the emic) (*LRUT*, 37–38). Both the etic and the emic approaches can be utilized by native participants of the language, each drawing our awareness to elements we might not have otherwise noticed with only one perspective.

Feature mode. Pike's earlier work developed the FMD triad (Feature, Manifestation, and Distribution modes), which would later be replaced by the CVD triad. The use of this "modal" language is likely what led Pike to describe units of human behavior as "trimodally structured." The feature mode of a unit is "composed of simultaneously occurring identificational-contrastive components, with its internal segementation analyzed with special reference to stimulus-response features (including purpose or lexical meaning, where relevant)" (*LRUT*, 85).

Field. The field perspective is one of three perspectives making up the PWF triad. Pike states that "a total set of relationships and of units within these relationships we call a field" (*LC*, 30). A field can exist within the grammatical, phonological, or referential hierarchies. In fact, there is *always* a field present, for without a field—a set of hierarchically arranged relationships—no unit of language or human behavior can be interpreted. For Pike, "the observer interprets data relative to context—within a field. In this sense datum of sensation 'becomes' a 'fact' of human significance when seen relative to its distribution in an environment—relative to a field as structured in the perception of imagination of some person" (*LC*, 30).

Functional view. The terms *static*, *dynamic*, and *functional/relational* were synonymous with *particle*, *wave*, and *field*. We take up a functional view when we approach a system "by way of its distribution mode and the manner in which the units of that mode operate within the matrix of larger units and in relation to the hierarchical structure of the sequences and classes of the system as a whole" (*LRUT*, 511).

Homologous. Two units of language or human behavior are said to be homologous when they are "proportionate in filling the same . . . tagmemic slot" (*LRUT*, 218). In the sentences *John studied Scripture* and *Mark studied Scripture*, *John* and *Mark* are homologous, or homologues.

Homomorph. A homomorph is the behavioral version of a homophone. *Pair* and *pare* are homophones. Homomorphs are behaviors that seem to be identical in form but which are, upon closer inspection, different in meaning (*LRUT*, 105–106). For example, I could chew a piece of gum or I could move my mouth *as if* I were chewing gum, even though I am not. Both behaviors, to an observer, might appear identical. However, in the former, I actually have some sugary, elastic substance in my mouth; in the latter, I am trying to get someone else to *think* that I have something in my mouth. I sometimes do this to my three-year-old to get him to ask me what I have in my mouth. He's puzzled when I open my mouth and he finds nothing inside.

Hyperbehavioreme. A hyperbehavioreme is simply any "behavioreme larger than a minimum one" (*LRUT*, 130). Recall that the minimum unit of the feature mode of a behavioreme is the emic motif. Thus, anything that is more complex than an emic motif is likely a hyperbehavioreme—a larger behavioreme that contains within it more than one smaller behavioreme.

Hypermeaning. Hypermeaning refers to the "meaning of two or more utterances or parts of utterances (1) for which there is culturally-attested conceptualized hypostasis of that meaning by native speakers (that is, the meaning has been talked about in some contexts by the participants in that culture), and (2) for which there is evidence that these participants identify the two verbal expressions as having the same meaning. Where the participants claim that two meanings are the same even though the morpheme sequences involved are different, the common identified meaning is the hypermeaning" (*LRUT*, 612–13). In English, the sentences "I'm sick" and "I'm feeling under the weather" might be identified by native speakers as having the same meaning, i.e., both utterances share a single hypermeaning.

Hypermorpheme. A hypermorpheme is "a multi-morphemic manifestation of an expanded tagmeme, or of a hypertagmeme; i.e., it is any morphemically complex manifested variant of a tagmeme or hypertagmeme, or of an uttereme or hyper-uttereme; it is emically—trimodally—structured" (*LRUT*, 424). The word *bookshelf* could be considered a hypermorpheme, since it is composed of two morphemes: *book* and *shelf*.

Hypertagmeme. A hypertagmeme denotes a composite tagmeme that is at a larger level of the grammatical hierarchy than a simple tagmeme. "Various kinds of structures may be treated as high-level, non-minimum members of the grammatical hierarchy—i.e., as hypertagmemes" (*LRUT*, 432).

Hyper-uttereme. A hyper-uttereme is a larger unit of conversation that contains more than one uttereme (*LRUT*, 133).

Hypostasis. Hypostasis denotes thc phcnomenon that often occurs in linguistic analysis when "any unit of activity is abstracted from the kinds of purposive activity sequence expected by regular participants" (*LRUT*, 107). In other words, when we take an emic unit out of its normal, functional context for the purpose of studying or analyzing it, we are performing an act of hypostasis.

Kineme. A kineme is a non-verbal acteme, i.e., a non-verbal segment of human behavior that belongs to an emic context (*LRUT*, 291).

Manifestation mode. Pike's earlier work developed the FMD triad (Feature, Manifestation, and Distribution modes), which would later be replaced by the CVD triad. The use of this "modal" language is likely what led Pike to describe units of human behavior as "trimodally structured." The manifestation mode of a unit is "composed of nonsimultaneously occurring physical variants (or nonsimultaneous components), with its internal segementation analyzed with special reference to the hierarchy of the mechanisms of its physical production" (*LRUT*, 85).

Margin. Within the wave perspective, an emic unit can be viewed as having margins and a nucleus. The margins are the peripheral elements on either side of the nucleus. In phonology, "the borders, or transitions, from one sound to another can be called the *margins*" (*LC*, 26).

Morpheme. A morpheme is "a verbal emic motif" (*LRUT*, 151). Considered in more general language, a morpheme is the smallest meaningful linguistic unit in a language—whether that unit is free or bound. Thus, "dog" is a morpheme that is free—it stands on its own. The "s" in "dogs" is also a morpheme, marking the noun as plural. For Pike, "A verbal etic motif is a morph" (*LRUT*, 151).

Motifemic-slot-class-correlative. This was Pike's original way of referring to the smallest unit of the distribution mode of a behavioreme. His extended definition is as follows: "A motifemic-slot-class-correlative (or role-eme) is a minimum, active, trimodally-structured emic segment or component of human activity within the pyramided hierarchy of the distribution mode of a minimum or included behavioreme or hyper-behavioreme; it is characterized by an emic slot correlated with a morpheme class (or with a composite class of morphemes plus morpheme sequences); it is manifested by free or conditioned, motifemically-simple of motifemically-complex, fused or clearly-segmented variants through the manifested variants of its manifesting emic motifs or classes of emic motifs, and it occurs within a trimodally- and hierarchically-structured system of motifemic-slot-class-correlatives and within a system of behavioremes, and hence within a structured physical setting" (*LRUT*, 194–95).

Nucleus. Within the wave perspective, an emic unit can be viewed as having margins and a nucleus. The nucleus is the focal point or point of climax for the emic unit. In phonology, "the clearest or steadiest part of a sound during slow pronunciation can be called the *nucleus* of a *wave*" (*LC*, 26). It is important to note here, however, that "if our attention is almost exclusively on the nucleus . . . we may be thinking in terms of particles" (*LC*, 26).

Particle. The particle perspective is one of three perspectives making up the PWF triad. Essentially, the particle perspective views reality as if it were made up of stable units with somewhat discrete borders. He writes, "human nature experiences the world—sometimes—as made up of *particles*, that is, as 'things.'

Houses, trees, and people seem to be obvious physical objects. But often an experience or concept which obviously is not an object is also talked about *as if* it were one, and is perhaps even counted or measured. . . . The normal relaxed attitude of the human being in most of his actions treats life as if it were made of particles" (*LC*, 19).

Phoneme. A phoneme for Pike is a *verbal* acteme (*LRUT*, 291). Phonemes are units of sound within a language system that have contrastive relevance (*LC*, 44). For example, *z* is a phoneme when we are considering the words *zeal* and *seal*. That one sound (*z*) contrasts one referential meaning with another, leading to different participant responses. It is a compliment to say that one has *zeal*; it is nonsensical to say that one has *seal*.

Phonemic shape type. A shape type is a specific sequence of sounds that forms a recognizable pattern (*LRUT*, 175–76).

Predominant focus unit. This phrase was Pike's way of referring to a point "around which the cultural evidence indicates that other included or simultaneous larger units are oriented" (*LRUT*, 106). If a family is taking a day to go watch a college basketball game, we might imagine the game itself as the predominant focus unit, since the whole day (for that family) is structured around (or oriented by) that unit of activity.

Role. A role is another one of the four components of a tagmeme. The role of an emic unit refers to its relevance: Why is it there and how is it functioning? (*LC*, 75).

Slot. A slot is another one of the four components of a tagmeme. It refers to the position of an emic unit within a larger structure or sequence. A slot is a "specific place of part in whole" (*LC*, 75). Pike saw the slot as linked with the wave perspective, since its placement might draw our attention to the margins and nucleus of a larger structure.

Static view. The terms *static*, *dynamic*, and *functional/relational* were synonymous with *particle*, *wave*, and *field*. We take up a static view when we approach "a system of units . . . seen principally through the identificational-contrastive units, or feature mode" (*LRUT*, 511).

Syllabeme. A syllabeme is another name for an emic syllable. It is "further characterized by the fact that most of the manifested members of the system of emic syllables of which it is a part are coterminous with a physical chest pulse, or composed of an etic complex of a strong and a weak etic chest pulse, or composed of part of an etic chest pulse in which each part comprising an emic syllable is identified as such in reference to the stress pattern or potential, the pitch pattern or potential, the quantitative pattern or potential, and the phonemic shape type of the hyperphonemic, morphemic, or hypermorphemic sequences in which it occurs and which it in part comprises" (*LRUT*, 365).

Syntagmeme. A syntagmeme is a sequence of tagmemes, a construction of hypermorphemes (*LRUT*, 451–52).

Tagmeme. In the simplest language, a tagmeme is a "unit in context." There are four components of a tagmeme: *slot*, *class*, *role*, and *cohesion*. "In general, these four components help answer questions well known to everyone: (1) *Where* (in what *slot*) in the *immediate* structural setting does some concrete part occur? (2) *What set* (*class*) of units can be parts of that larger containing unit, in that same place in the unit? (3) *Why* is any member of that set of units *relevant* (*meaningful*) to the sets of units in other slots at that same immediately-in-view structure? (4) *How* does the *generalized frame of reference*, on this or other levels of the hierarchy, *reflect or exercise control* (*give cohesion*) to tie the parts together?" (*LC*, 75). Tagmemes can occur in the grammatical, phonological, and referential hierarchies.

Uttereme. An uttereme is a verbal behavioreme (*LRUT*, 121). "Utteremes constitute a subdivision of behavioremes, such that every uttereme is a behavioreme but not all behavioremes are utteremes" (*LRUT*, 133).

Variation. Variation is one of the three components of Pike's CVD triad. It refers to the way in which a unit of human behavior can change without thereby losing its identity. For Pike, "Normal social behavior requires that we be able to recognize identities in spite of change. Unless we can do so, there can be no human society as we know it. . . . The appropriate observer readily recognizes that certain changes do not affect deeper identities" (*LC*, 52). Variation is evident for a unit of human behavior every time it occurs. No word, for example, is pronounced in *exactly* the same way each time it is spoken, even by the same person. Scientific equipment would show us the minor variations (leading to unique manifestations) with each new pronunciation.

Wave. The wave perspective is one of three perspectives making up the PWF triad. The wave perspective views reality and its constituent components as if it were a dynamic sequence—a fluid movement from sound to sound, event to event, etc. When we focus on one unit within reality, we can think of that unit as a wave having margins and a nucleus. There can be grammatical waves, phonological waves, and referential waves (*LC*, 24–29).

Bibliography

Bahnsen, Greg L. *Van Til's Apologetic: Readings and Analysis*. Phillipsburg, NJ: P&R Publishing, 1998.

Bavinck, Herman. *Our Reasonable Faith*. Translated by Henry Zylstra. Grand Rapids, MI: Wm. B. Eerdmans, 1956.

———. *Reformed Dogmatics*. Vols. 1–2. Edited by John Bolt. Translated by John Vriend. Grand Rapids, MI: Baker Academic, 2003–2004.

———. *The Philosophy of Revelation*. Grand Rapids, MI: Wm. B. Eerdmans, 1953.

Beale, G. K., and W. Andrew Hoffecker. "Biblical Epistemology: Revelation." In *God, Man, and Knowledge*. Vol. 1 of *Building a Christian World View*, edited by W. Andrew Hoffecker and Gary Scott Smith, 193–216. Phillipsburg, NJ: Presbyterian and Reformed, 1986.

Beeke, Joel R., and Mark Jones. *A Puritan Theology: Doctrine for Life*. Grand Rapids, MI: Reformation Heritage Books, 2012.

Berkhof, Louis. *Systematic Theology*. New ed. Grand Rapids, MI: William B. Eerdmans, 1996.

Blackburn, Simon. *The Oxford Dictionary of Philosophy*. New York: Oxford University Press, 1994.

Blocher, Henri. "La Trinité, Une Communauté an-Archique?" *Théologie Évangélique* 1, no. 2 (2002): 3–20.

Bloomfield, Leonard. *Language*. Chicago: University of Chicago Press, 1984.

Bray, Gerald. *God Has Spoken: A History of Christian Theology*. Wheaton, IL: Crossway, 2014.

Brend, Ruth M., ed. *Kenneth L. Pike: Selected Writings to Commemorate the 60th Birthday of Kenneth Lee Pike*. The Hague: Mouton, 1972.

Calvin, John. *Institutes of the Christian Religion: A New Translation of the 1541 Edition*. Translated by Robert White. Carlisle, PA: Banner of Truth, 2014.

Collins, Paul M. *Trinitarian Theology: West and East—Karl Barth, the Cappadocian Fathers, and John Zizioulas*. New York: Oxford, 2001.

Copleston, Frederick. *Greece and Rome: From the Pre-Socratics to Plotinus*. A History of Philosophy 1. New York: Image Books, 1946.

———. *From Wolff to Kant*. A History of Philosophy 6. Westminster, MD: Newman Press, 1964.

Crisp, Oliver D. "Problems with Perichoresis." *Tyndale Bulletin* 56, no. 1 (January 1, 2005): 119–40.

Crowe, Brandon D., and Carl R. Trueman, eds. *The Essential Trinity: New Testament Foundations and Practical Relevance*. London: Apollos, 2016.

Dolezal, James E. "Trinity, Simplicity, and the Status of God's Personal Relations." *International Journal of Systematic Theology* 16, no. 1 (January 2014): 79–98.

Egan, John P. "Toward Trinitarian Perichoresis: Saint Gregory the Theologian, (Oration) 31.41." *Greek Orthodox Theological Review* 39, no. 1–2 (March 1, 1994): 83–93.

Emery, Gilles. *The Trinitarian Theology of Saint Thomas Aquinas*. Translated by Francesca Aran Murphy. Oxford: Oxford University Press, 2007.

———. *The Trinity: An Introduction to the Catholic Doctrine on the Triune God*. Translated by Matthew Levering. Washington, DC: Catholic University of America, 2011.

Frame, John M. *Systematic Theology: An Introduction to Christian Belief*. Phillipsburg, NJ: P&R Publishing, 2013.

———. *A History of Western Philosophy and Theology*. Phillipsburg, NJ: P&R Publishing, 2015.

———. "A Primer on Perspectivalism." The Works of John Frame

and Vern Poythress. Accessed November 9, 2014. http://www.frame-poythress.org/a-primer-on-perspectivalism/.

———. *Cornelius Van Til: An Analysis of His Thought*. Phillipsburg, NJ: P&R Publishing, 1995.

———. *The Doctrine of the Knowledge of God*. Phillipsburg, NJ: P&R Publishing, 1987.

———. *The Doctrine of the Word of God*. Phillipsburg, NJ: P&R Publishing, 2010.

Gaffin, Jr., Richard B. *God's Word in Servant-Form: Abraham Kuyper and Herman Bavinck on the Doctrine of Scripture*. Jackson, MS: Reformed Academic Press, 2008.

Genderen, J. van, and W. H. Velema. *Concise Reformed Dogmatics*. Translated by Gerrit Bilkes and Ed M. van der Maas. Phillipsburg, NJ: P&R Publishing, 2008.

Greshake, Gisbert. "Trinity as 'Communio.'" In *Rethinking Trinitarian Theology: Disputed Questions and Contemporary Issues in Trinitarian Theology*, edited by Giulio Maspero and Robert J. Woźniak, 331–45. New York: T&T Clark, 2012.

Gunton, Colin E. *The Promise of Trinitarian Theology*. 2nd ed. London: T&T Clark, 1997.

Harris, Roy. *Signs of Writing*. New York: Routledge, 1995.

Harrison, Verna E. F. "Perichoresis in the Greek Fathers." *St. Vladimir's Theological Quarterly* 35, no. 1 (January 1, 1991): 53–65.

Hasker, William. *Metaphysics and the Tripersonal God*. Oxford Studies in Analytic Theology. Oxford: Oxford University Press, 2013.

Hibbs, Pierce Taylor. "Closing the Gaps: Perichoresis and the Nature of Language." *Westminster Theological Journal* 78, no. 2 (Fall 2016): 299–322.

———. "Imaging Communion: An Argument for God's Existence Based on Speech." *Westminster Theological Journal* 77, no. 1 (Spring 2015): 35–51.

———. "Where Person Meets Word Part 1: Personalism in the Language Theory of Kenneth L. Pike." *Westminster Theological Journal* 77, no. 2 (Fall 2015): 355–77.

———. "Where Person Meets Word Part 2: The Convergence of Personalism and Scripture in the Language Theory of Kenneth L. Pike." *Westminster Theological Journal* 78, no. 1 (Spring 2016): 117–34.

———. "Words for Communion." *Modern Reformation* 25, no. 4 (August 2016): 5–8.

Hill, Wesley. "Divine Persons and Their 'Reduction' to Relations: A Plea for Conceptual Clarity." *International Journal of Systematic Theology* 14, no. 2 (April 2012): 148–60.

———. *Paul and the Trinity: Persons, Relations, and the Pauline Letters*. Grand Rapids, MI: Eerdmans, 2015.

Hodge, Charles. *Systematic Theology*. Vol. 1. Peabody, MA: Hendrickson, 2013.

Horton, Michael. *The Christian Faith: A Systematic Theology for Pilgrims on the Way*. Grand Rapids, MI: Zondervan, 2011.

Kelly, Douglas. *The God Who Is: The Holy Trinity*. Vol. 1 of *Systematic Theology: Grounded in Holy Scripture and Understood in Light of the Church*. Ross-shire, Scotland: Mentor, 2008.

Kuyper, Abraham. *The Work of the Holy Spirit*. Translated by Henry De Vries. Chattanooga, TN: AMG Publishers, 1995.

Lawler, Michael G. "Perichoresis: New Theological Wine in an Old Theological Wineskin." *Horizons* 22, no. 1 (March 1, 1995): 49–66.

Letham, Robert. *The Holy Trinity: In Scripture, History, Theology, and Worship*. Phillipsburg, NJ: P&R Publishing, 2004.

Levering, Matthew. "The Holy Spirit in the Trinitarian Communion: 'Love' and 'Gift'?" *International Journal of Systematic Theology* 16, no. 2 (2014): 126–42.

Lyons, John. *Semantics*. Vol. 1. New York: Cambridge University Press, 1977.

Marshall, Bruce D. "Christ and the Cultures: The Jewish People and Christian Theology." In *The Cambridge Companion to Christian Doctrine*, edited by Colin E. Gunton, 81–100. New York: Cambridge University Press, 1997.

Martinich, A. P., and David Sosa, eds. *The Philosophy of Language*. 6th ed. New York: Oxford, 2013.

McClean, John. "Perichoresis, Theosis and Union with Christ in the Thought of John Calvin." *Reformed Theological Review* 68, no. 2 (August 1, 2009): 130–41.

Muller, Richard A. *The Triunity of God*. Vol. 4 of *Post-Reformation Reformed Dogmatics: The Rise and Development of Reformed Orthodoxy, Ca. 1520 to Ca. 1725*. Grand Rapids, MI: Baker Academic, 2003.

O'Collins, Gerald. *The Tripersonal God: Understanding and Interpreting the Trinity*. 2nd ed. New York: Paulist Press, 2014.

Oliphint, K. Scott. *Covenantal Apologetics: Principles and Practice in Defense of Our Faith*. Wheaton, IL: Crossway, 2013.

———. *God with Us: Divine Condescension and the Attributes of God*. Wheaton, IL: Crossway, 2012.

———. "Is There a Reformed Objection to Natural Theology?" *Westminster Theological Journal* 74 (2012): 169–203.

———. *Reasons for Faith: Philosophy in the Service of Theology*. Phillipsburg, NJ: P&R Publishing, 2006.

———. "Simplicity, Triunity, and the Incomprehensibility of God." In *One God in Three Persons: Unity of Essence, Distinction of Persons, Implications for Life*, edited by Bruce A. Ware and John Starke, 215–35. Wheaton, IL: Crossway, 2015.

Ong, Walter J. *Orality and Literacy: The Technologizing of the Word*. New York: Routledge, 2002.

Otto, Randall E. "The Use and Abuse of Perichoresis in Recent Theology." *Scottish Journal of Theology* 54 (2001): 366–84.

Pérez, Ángel Cordovilla. "The Trinitarian Concept of Person." In *Rethinking Trinitarian Theology: Disputed Questions and Contemporary Issues in Trinitarian Theology*, edited by Giulio Maspero and Robert J. Woźniak, 105–45. New York: T&T Clark, 2012.

Pike, Eunice V. *Ken Pike: Scholar and Christian*. Dallas, TX: Summer Institute of Linguistics, 1981.

Pike, Kenneth L. "God's Guidance and Your Life Work." *His* 7, no. 1 (1947): 19–28.

———. "Living on Manna." *The Sunday School Times*. May 1, 1948, 3–4.

———. "Language and Life 1: A Stereoscopic Window on the World." *Bibliotheca Sacra* 114, no. 454 (April 1957): 141–56.

———. "Language and Life 2: Slots and Classes in the Hierarchical Structure of Behavior." *Bibliotheca Sacra* 114, no. 455 (July 1957): 255–62.

———. "Prescription for Intellectuals." *Eternity* 8 (August 1957): 11.

———. "Language and Life 3: A Training Device for Translation Theory and Practice." *Bibliotheca Sacra* 114, no. 456 (October 1957): 347–362.

———. "Why I Believe in God." *His* 18, no. 2 (November 1957): 3–7, 32–33.

———. "Language and Life 4: Tristructural Units of Human Behavior." *Bibliotheca Sacra* 115, no. 457 (January 1958): 36–43.

———. "The Sin of Independence." *His* 18, no. 8 (1958): 5–7.

———. "Finishing the Sentence—A Linguistic Parable." *His* 19, no. 6 (1959): 39–40.

———. "Cause and Effect in the Christian Life." *His* 20, no. 1 (1959): 32–34.

———. "Language and Meaning: Strange Dimensions of Truth." *Christianity Today* 5, no. 16, May 8, 1961, 26–28.

———. *With Heart and Mind: A Personal Synthesis of Scholarship and Devotion*. Grand Rapids, MI: William B. Eerdmans, 1962.

———. "A Syntactic Paradigm." *Language* 39, no. 2 (April/June 1963): 216–230.

———. "Man or Robot." *Eternity* 15 (February 1964): 9–11.

———. "A Linguistic Contribution to Composition." *College Composition and Communication* 15 (1964): 82–88.

———. "Language: Where Science and Poetry Meet." In *Language and Literature for Composition: Introductory Readings*, ed. Sanford R. Rader and Susan G. Rader. New York: Crowell, 1973. [Originally published in 1965 in College English 26:283–292]

———. "God in History." *The Church Herald* 23, no. 2 (1966): 4–5, 22.

———. *Language in Relation to a Unified Theory of the Structure of Human Behavior*. 2nd ed. Paris: Mouton, 1967.

———. "Language." In *Christ and the Modern Mind*, ed. Robert W. Smith. Downers Grove, IL: InterVarsity Press, 1972.

———. "Morals and Metaphor." *Interchange* 12 (1972): 228–231.

———. "Language and Self Image." In *The Scientist and Ethical Decision*. Edited by Charles Hatfield, 69–82. Downers Grove, IL: InterVarsity Press, 1973.

———. "The Linguist and Axioms Concerning the Language of Scripture." *Journal of the American Scientific Affiliation* 26, no. 2 (June 1974): 47–51.

———. "Christianity and Culture I. Conscience and Culture." *Journal of the American Scientific Affiliation* 31 (March 1979): 8–12.

———. "Christianity and Culture II. Incarnation in a Culture." *Journal of the American Scientific Affiliation* 31 (June 1979): 92–96.

———. "Christianity and Culture III. Biblical Absolutes and Certain Cultural Relativisms." *Journal of the American Scientific Affiliation* 31 (September 1979): 139–45.

———. "Emotion in God, and Its Image in Us." *The Banner* 114, no. 45 (1979): 4–5.

———. "Intellectual Initiative: The Image of God." *The Banner* 114, no. 46 (1979): 10.

———. "Love God with Mind—and Bless Babylon." *The Gordon Alumnus* 8, no. 4 (1979): 6–7.

———. *Tagmemics, Discourse, and Verbal Art*. Michigan Studies in Humanities 3. Ann Arbor, MI: University of Michigan Press, 1981.

———. *Linguistic Concepts: An Introduction to Tagmemics*. Lincoln, NE: University of Nebraska Press, 1982.

———. "On Understanding People: An Integrative Philosophy." In *The Ninth LACUS Forum*, ed. John Morreall, 129–136. S. Columbia: Hornbeam, 1983.

———. "The Need for the Rejection of Autonomy in Linguistics." In *The Eleventh LACUS Forum*, ed. Robert A. Hall, Jr., 35–53. S. Columbia: Hornbeam, 1985.

———. "Static, Dynamic, and Relational Perspectives Suggested in Words and Phrases." In *Scientific and Humanistic Dimensions of Language*, ed. Kurt R. Jankowsky, 447–452. Amsterdam: John Benjamins, 1985.

———. "The Relation of Language to the World." *International Journal of Dravidian Linguistics* 16, no. 1 (1987): 77–98.

———. *Pike's Perspectives: An Anthology of Thought, Insight, and Moral Purpose*. Langley, British Columbia: Credo Publishing, 1989.

———. "Person beyond Logic, in Language, Life, and Philosophy." In *The Eighteenth LACUS Forum*, ed. Ruth M. Brend, 23–37. Lake Bluff, IL: Linguistic Association of Canada and the United States, 1992.

———. *Talk, Thought, and Thing: The Emic Road Toward Conscious Knowledge*. Dallas, TX: Summer Institute of Linguistics, 1993.

———. "Tagmemics." In *Handbook of Pragmatics*, ed. Jan-Ola Ostman and Jan Blommaert, 533–536. Amsterdam: John Benjamins, 1995.

Poythress, Vern S. "A Framework for Discourse Analysis: The Components of a Discourse, from a Tagmemic Viewpoint." *Semiotica* 38, no. 3/4 (1982): 277–98.

———. "Canon and Speech Act: Limitations in Speech-Act Theory, with Implications for a Putative Theory of Canonical Speech Acts." *Westminster Theological Journal* 70, no. 2 (September 1, 2008): 337–54.

———. "God and Language." In *Did God Really Say? Affirming the Truthfulness and Trustworthiness of Scripture*, edited by David B. Garner. Phillipsburg, NJ: P&R Publishing, 2012.

———. *God-Centered Biblical Interpretation*. Phillipsburg, NJ: P&R Publishing, 1999.

———. "Hierarchy in Discourse Analytics: A Revision of Tagmemics." *Semiotica* 40, no. 1/2 (1982): 107–37.

———. *In the Beginning Was the Word: Language—A God-Centered Approach*. Wheaton, IL: Crossway, 2009.

———. *Philosophy, Science, and the Sovereignty of God*. Phillipsburg, NJ: P&R Publishing, 1976.

———. *Redeeming Philosophy: A God-Centered Approach to the Big Questions*. Wheaton, IL: Crossway, 2014.

———. *Redeeming Sociology: A God-Centered Approach*. Wheaton, IL: Crossway, 2011.

———. "Reforming Ontology and Logic in the Light of the Trinity: An Application of Van Til's Idea of Analogy." *Westminster Theological Journal* 57, no. 1 (March 1, 1995): 187–219.

———. *Symphonic Theology: The Validity of Multiple Perspectives in Theology*. Phillipsburg, NJ: P&R Publishing, 1987.

Rosenstock-Huessy, Eugen. *Speech and Reality*. Norwich, VT: Argo Books, 1970.

Sapir, Edward. *Selected Writings in Language, Culture, and Personality*. London: Forgotten Books, 2012.

Schweitzer, William M. *God Is a Communicative Being: Divine Communicativeness and Harmony in the Theology of Jonathan Edwards*. T&T Clark Studies in Systematic Theology 14. London: T&T Clark, 2012.

Searle, John R. *Mind, Language, and Society: Philosophy in the Real World*. New York: Basic Books, 1998.

Smith, Ralph A. *Trinity and Reality: An Introduction to the Christian Faith*. Moscow, ID: Canon Press, 2004.

Stăniloae, Dumitru. *The Holy Trinity: In the Beginning There Was Love*. Translated by Roland Clark. Brookline, MA: Holy Cross Orthodox Press, 2012.

Stramara, Daniel F., Jr. "Gregory of Nyssa's Terminology for

Trinitarian Perichoresis." *Vigiliae Christianae* 52, no. 3 (August 1, 1998): 257–63.

Tavard, George H. *The Vision of the Trinity*. Washington, DC: University Press of America, 1981.

Tipton, Lane G. "The Function of Perichoresis and the Divine Incomprehensibility." *Westminster Theological Journal* 64 (2002): 289–306.

Torrance, A. J. *Persons in Communion: An Essay on Trinitarian Description and Human Participation*. Edinburgh: T&T Clark, 1996.

Torrance, T. F. *The Christian Doctrine of God, One Being Three Persons*. Edinburgh: T&T Clark, 1996.

Turretin, Francis. *Institues of Elenctic Theology*, Vol. 1, *First through Tenth Topics*. Edited by James T. Dennison, Jr. Translated by George Musgrave Giger. Phillipsburg, NJ: P&R Publishing, 1992.

Van Til, Cornelius. *Christian Apologetics*. Edited by William Edgar. 2nd ed. Phillipsburg, NJ: P&R Publishing, 2003.

———. *Common Grace and the Gospel*. Nutley, NJ: Presbyterian and Reformed, 1977.

———. *In Defense of the Faith*. Vol. 2, *A Survey of Christian Epistemology*. Phillipsburg, NJ: Presbyterian and Reformed, 1969.

———. *Introduction to Systematic Theology: Prolegomena and the Doctrines of Revelation, Scripture, and God*. Edited by William Edgar. 2nd ed. Phillipsburg, NJ: P&R Publishing, 2007.

———. *The Defense of the Faith*. Edited by K. Scott Oliphint. 4th ed. Phillipsburg, NJ: P&R Publishing, 2008.

Vanhoozer, Kevin J. "A Lamp in the Labyrinth: The Hermeneutics of 'Aesthetic' Theology." *Trinity Journal* 8 (1987): 25–56.

———. *Is There a Meaning in This Text? The Bible, the Reader, and the Morality of Literary Knowledge*. Grand Rapids, MI: Zondervan, 1998.

———. *Remythologizing Theology: Divine Action, Passion, and Authorship*. New York: Cambridge University Press, 2010.

Vos, Geerhardus. *Reformed Dogmatics*. Vol. 1, *Theology Proper*. Edited by Richard B. Gaffin, Jr. Translated by Richard B. Gaffin Jr. Bellingham, WA: Lexham Press, 2014.

Warfield, B. B. *Biblical and Theological Studies*. Edited by Samuel G. Craig. Philadelphia: Presbyterian and Reformed, 1968.

———. "Calvin's Doctrine of the Trinity." In *Calvin and Augustine*, edited by Samuel G. Craig, 189–284. Philadelphia: Presbyterian and Reformed Publishing, 1956.

Waterhouse, Viola G. *The History and Development of Tagmemics*. The Hague: Mouton, 1974.

Watson, Francis. "The Triune Divine Identity: Reflections on Pauline God-Language, in Disagreement with J. D. G. Dunn." *Journal for the Study of the New Testament* 80 (2000): 99–124.

Wise, Mary Ruth, Thomas N. Headland, and Ruth M. Brend, eds. *Language and Life: Essays in Memory of Kenneth L. Pike*. Dallas, TX: SIL International, 2003.

Young, Richard E., Alton L. Becker, and Kenneth L. Pike. *Rhetoric: Discovery and Change*. New York: Harcourt, Brace, & World, 1970.

Index of Subjects and Names

Pierce Taylor Hibbs (MAR, ThM) is Associate Director for Theological Curriculum and Instruction in the Theological English Department at Westminster Theological Seminary. He has written several articles on the doctrine of the Trinity and the language theory of Kenneth Pike in the *Westminster Theological Journal* and has written on related topics in the *Journal of Biblical Counseling*, *Themelios*, *VII: Journal of the Marion E. Wade Center*, *Modern Reformation*, and *Perspectives: A Journal of Reformed Thought*. He is also a contributor to Reformed Forum, Place for Truth, and Reformation 21. He, his wife, and their children reside in Quakertown, Pennsylvania.

Available in the Reformed Academic Dissertation Series

◆

It Has Not Yet Appeared What We Shall Be: A Reconsideration of the Imago Dei *in Light of Those with Severe Cognitive Disabilities*,
by George C. Hammond

How Should We Treat Detainees? An Examination of "Enhanced Interrogation Techniques" under the Light of Scripture and the Just War Tradition,
by J. Porter Harlow

Marks of Saving Grace: Theological Method and the Doctrine of Assurance in Jonathan Edwards's A Treatise Concerning Religious Affections,
by Eric J. Lehner

The Doctrine of the Spirituality of the Church in the Ecclesiology of Charles Hodge,
by Alan D. Strange

From Inscrutability to Concursus: Benjamin B. Warfield's Theological Construction of Revelation's Mode from 1880 to 1915,
by Jeffrey A. Stivason

Preaching with Biblical Motivation: How to Incorporate the Motivation Found in the Inspired Preaching of the Apostles into Your Sermons,
by Ray E. Heiple Jr.

The Triune God of Unity in Diversity: An Analysis of Perspectivalism, the Trinitarian Theological Method of John Frame and Vern Poythress,
by Timothy E. Miller

A Development, Not a Departure: The Lacunae in the Debate of the Doctrine of the Trinity and Gender Roles, by Hongyi Yang

The Trinity, Language, and Human Behavior: A Reformed Exposition of the Language Theory of Kenneth L. Pike, by Pierce Taylor Hibbs

Free to Be Sons of God by Geoffrey M. Ziegler

"King of Israel" and "Do Not Fear, Daughter of Zion": The Use of Zephaniah 3 in John 12, by Christopher S. Tachick

Forthcoming

I See Dead People: The Function of the Resurrection of the Saints in Matthew 27:51–54, by Raymond M. Johnson

Do Good to All People as You Have Opportunity: A Biblical Theology of the Good Deeds Mission of the New Covenenat Community, by John Wind

A Strategy for Incorporating Biblical Counseling in North American Church Plants, by Rush Witt

More from P&R on the Trinity

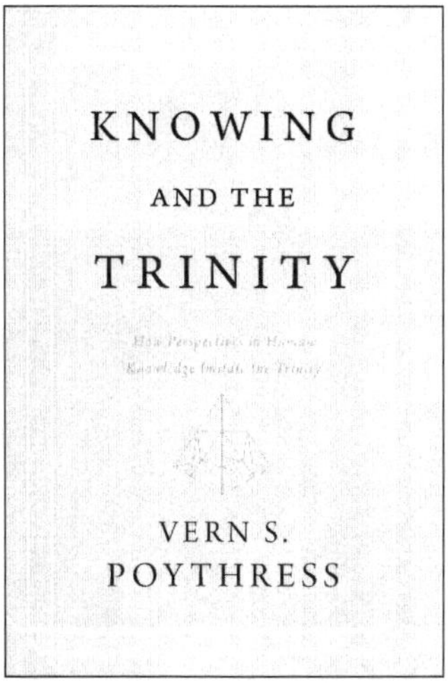

Vern Poythress is one of a growing number of theologians who have developed and used perspectival triads to further our knowledge of God. This book explores the relationship between numerous triads and God's Trinitarian character, and shows that many triads reveal analogies to the Trinity. Understanding these analogies will help readers perceive the fundamental connections between our Trinitarian God, the Bible, and our created world.

"In this fascinating and highly accessible book, Dr. Poythress puts his perspectival method to work in a wide-ranging exploration of Trinitarian theology. Underlying his discussion is the conviction that while this is a mystery surpassing our capacities, God has revealed himself in creation and grace, his triune fingerprints evident wherever we turn. Any discussion of the doctrine of God should take Poythress's important contribution into serious consideration. I know of nothing else quite like it."

—**Robert Letham**, Professor of Systematic and Historical Theology, Union School of Theology (formerly Wales Evangelical School of Theology)

More from P&R on the Trinity

The doctrine of the Trinity is foundational to Christian theology. A careful study of Scripture helps us to better understand and worship the triune God consistently presented in both the Old and New Testaments. Here scholars of the Trinity such as Richard Bauckham, Robert Letham, and Michael Reeves overview Old Testament teaching, provide Trinitarian readings of the entire New Testament corpus, and explore the practical relevance of the doctrine to Christian life.

"Today there are many books on the market dealing with the doctrine of the Trinity. This is my favorite. It is a clear presentation, discussion, and application of the historic doctrine by people who believe it and have studied it deeply. The essays have kept close to their source, the teaching of the Holy Scriptures. . . . I do not agree with every detail of every essay; they do enter into some controversial areas. But the reader will learn even from that controversy to engage the Scriptures with more thought and devotion."
—**John M. Frame**, Professor of Systematic Theology and Philosophy Emeritus, Reformed Theological Seminary, Orlando